Maple Street Press
Guide to New England
Ballparks

Maple Street Press Guide to New England Ballparks

From Maine to Fenway to the Cape ...
and Everything in Between

Tom Mason
with Mark A. Brown
and David Laurila

MAPLE STREET PRESS
Hingham, MA

Maple Street Press LLC is in no way affiliated with Major League Baseball, or any minor league affiliates. The opinions expressed in this book are those of the author and not necessarily those of Maple Street Press.

Jacket design: Garrett Cullen
Interior design: Bryan Davidson
Map design: Jeremy Majewski

Tom Mason with Mark A. Brown and David Laurila. *Maple Street Press Guide to New England Ballparks*
ISBN 978-0-9777-436-4-3

Library of Congress Control Number: 2007930348

All product names and brand names mentioned in this book are trademarks or service marks of their respective companies. Any omission or misuse (of any kind) of service marks or trademarks should not be regarded as intent to infringe upon the property of others. The publisher respects all marks used by companies, manufacturers, and developers as a means to distinguish their products.

Maple Street Press LLC
11 Leavitt Street
Hingham, MA 02043
www.maplestreetpress.com

Printed in the United States of America
07 7 6 5 4 3 2 First Edition

Dear Reader,

Thank you for picking up the inaugural *Maple Street Press Guide to New England Ballparks*. This book is really a testament to the love of the sport of baseball in this area, from Little League all the way up to Fenway Park. If the weather is warm in New England you surely don't have to go too far to hear the crack of a bat or the pounding of a ball into the leather mitt. Like the waves lapping the shores of Cape Cod and the Maine coastline, these are the sounds of summer.

With this book we hope to provide you with the travel guide to all the different baseball utopias our great region has to offer. There are travel tips, things to do, places to go, restaurants to try, bars to hang out at, and of course fun facts and trivia about all the greatest parks, teams, and players to ever grace these six states we call New England. The three authors that wrote the chapters have done a fantastic job with this book, and we are proud to offer it to our fellow baseball-loving New Englanders.

Enjoy the summer,

Jim Walsh
President & Founder
Maple Street Press LLC

I dedicate this book to my wife, daughters, and parents.

– Tom Mason

TABLE OF CONTENTS

Introduction . . . . *xi*

Acknowledgments . . . . *xiii*

About the Authors . . . . *xv*

MASSACHUSETTS

1. Boston—Fenway Park 1

2. Bourne—Upper Cape Regional Technical School 11

3. Brewster—Stony Brook Field 21

4. Brockton—Campanelli Field 29

5. Chatham—Veterans Field 39

6. Cotuit—Elizabeth Lowell Park 47

7. Falmouth—Arnie Allen Diamond at Guv Fuller Field 57

8. Harwich—Whitehouse Field 67

9. Hyannis—McKeon Park 75

10. Lowell—Edward A. LeLacheur Park 83

11. Lynn—Fraser Field 91

12. Orleans—Eldredge Park 101

13. Pittsfield—Wahconah Park 111

14. Wareham—Clem Spillane Field 121

15. Worcester—Hanover Insurance Park at Fitton Field 131

16. Yarmouth—Red Wilson Field 141

RHODE ISLAND

17. Newport—Cardines Field 151

18. Pawtucket—McCoy Stadium 159

CONNECTICUT

19. Bridgeport—The Ballpark at Harbor Yard 171

20. New Britain—New Britain Stadium 179

21. New Haven—Yale Field 187

22. Norwich—Thomas J. Dodd Memorial Stadium 195

VERMONT

23. Burlington—Centennial Field at the University of Vermont 203

24. Montpelier—Mountaineer Recreation Field 213

NEW HAMPSHIRE

25. Manchester—MerchantsAuto.com Stadium 223

26. Nashua—Holman Stadium 231

MAINE

27. Portland—Hadlock Field 239

Bibliography *247*

Index *251*

INTRODUCTION

Somebody had to do it. That's my response to anybody who asks me why I decided to write a guide to New England ballparks. This book literally covers my lifetime.

I don't understand exactly why, but I've always been fascinated with baseball. One of my first memories of the sport is the "Impossible Dream" of the 1967 Red Sox. Fewer and fewer people remember the days when the World Series was mostly played in the afternoons. I do. I can remember my mother ironing while watching the Red Sox and the Cardinals in the World Series. Pretty soon, my father bought my brother and me a glove, a bat, and some baseballs. My uncle later gave me a catcher's mitt for my birthday. We'd play backyard baseball. I can remember standing on my makeshift mound, pretending to be Red Sox pitchers Ray Culp and Sonny Siebert, and throwing strikes against my pitchback.

I was always mystified by how my mother would always know about the latest Red Sox defeat. When I got older, I learned that she'd regularly sneak a peak of televised Red Sox games on Channel 38. I guess I know where I got my interest in the Red Sox.

What turned an interest into a passion was my first transistor radio. I thought it was pretty cool to listen to Ken Coleman and Ned Martin on WHDH. But that wasn't enough. After dark, I would strategically position my transistor to check in on other games and listen to Chuck Thompson on WBAL in Baltimore, Lindsay Nelson and Bob Murphy on WNEW in New York, and Herb Score on WWWE in Cleveland. Adding and subtracting gave me the practical skills necessary to understand box scores. I learned to score baseball games at Fenway Park. And every Sunday, I would buy my weekly package of baseball cards. I quickly discovered some players had more value than others. I had a million Chico Salmon cards, but I would have given them all away for just one Carl Yastrzemski. I still haven't recovered from the time my "friend" tore up a much-cherished Mickey Mantle card. But revenge was sweet. When he traded me his Sandy Koufax for my Bob Tillman, it was the baseball card equivalent of the "Brinks' Job."

Unfortunately, my days on the playing field proved to be a disappointment. Even though I'm a natural right-hander, Dad concluded that after watching his boyhood hero, Ted Williams, if I batted lefty, I would have an advantage. But there was a fly in the ointment: I still couldn't hit. Hope springs eternal. I tried to compensate for my anemic batting by hitting the books. The book *Percentage Baseball* changed my life. Many of the mathematical formulas are still beyond my understanding. But I learned on-base percentage mattered. The book worked like a charm. I applied the strategies of the book. It seemed like I was always in scoring position and our team was winning games. I must have been the first nine-year-old to measure on-base percentage. Why my coaches didn't understand this baseball basic is still mystifying.

At about 12 years old, I finally discovered the reason I couldn't hit. During a game at Fenway Park, I noticed the little white numbers on the Green Monster scoreboard were fuzzy. With glasses, I could finally see the ball. But the time to revive my career in baseball had passed. It was time to focus on academics anyway.

Nevertheless, I still have had lots of fun with the game. At one time, I knew lots of Red Sox trivia (which I've since forgotten). It would drive my geometry teacher crazy that I knew more about the Red Sox than he did. But he had the last laugh, I swear that's one of the reasons I never made the baseball team.

The first minor league team I ever saw was at Lynn's Fraser Field. I can't remember who played for the opposing Bristol Red Sox, but I recall several Lynn Sailors. Even though they were affiliated with the expansion Seattle Mariners, the Sailors were the home team. They were strong up the middle with future Red Sox player Spike Owen at shortstop. The atmosphere was great and the prices were right. I was hooked. Ever since then, I've not been just a Red Sox follower, but a New England baseball fan.

Attending local baseball games has been lots of fun and I have lots of great memories. The way Carl Yastrzemski, Fred Lynn, and Dwight Evans would play outfield. Seeing a slimmed-down Mo Vaughn bat cleanup for Pawtucket. Cold beer on hot afternoons in Fenway's center-field bleachers. Taking my family to Brockton Rox games. David Ortiz's walk-off home runs. Pedro. Roger. Going to a sparsely attended Cape Cod League game between Bourne and Hyannis with my friend Johnny V. and seeing a young left-hander for Hyannis pitch a no-hitter. The time I went out and had a few beers with former PawSox/Brockton Rox skipper Ed Nottle, though, is a bit cloudy.

Anyway, my story has a happy ending. The days I've spent following baseball finally have amounted to something. This book is more than about sports. This is about things that make our area unique. New England is my home. I am very fortunate to live here. There are plenty of interesting things to do in our region. Not everything is in this book, but at least it's a good place to start. Have fun reading this book. Enjoy good times with your family and friends. I hope your trips to New England ballparks have a happy ending too.

Tom Mason
March 2007

ACKNOWLEDGMENTS

My wife Anne, daughters Julie and Laura, and mother Sally have been patient. I couldn't have gotten the chapters about Lynn, Nashua, and Manchester without Dad. Thanks Dad! Many years ago, my father was part of a group that almost bought the Eastern League Manchester Yankees. In those days, the price to buy a professional baseball team was next to nothing. Believe it or not, the group could have bought the team with practically no money down. Times have changed. Now professional teams are worth millions. Who would've thought it?

Thanks to Carol Costa-Crowell, Sue Pawlak-Seaman, and Anne Humphrey who gave me the opportunity to write for the *New Bedford Standard-Times*. Dave Echols and Tom Whaley of the Goldklang Group. They hired me to write for the first Brockton Rox yearbook. The owners and operators of the Brockton Rox are remarkable. I am grateful for the staff of the Pawtucket Red Sox, particularly Bill Wanless, for giving me the opportunity to contribute to their yearbook. Many thanks for the patience, intelligence, and professionalism of publisher Jim Walsh. My thanks to Mark Brown and David Laurila, and the other contributors to this book. Thanks to Rick, Paul, Greg, and Joe for being great pals. Friday afternoon rules!

ABOUT THE AUTHORS

Mark A. Brown lives in Falmouth on Cape Cod, where he reports for the *Falmouth Enterprise* newspaper. A member of the Sons of Sam Horn message board, Mark also writes for *Summer Stars*, a summer weekly covering the Cape Cod Baseball League. He contributed the Falmouth, Bourne, Cotuit, Hyannis, and Yarmouth-Dennis chapters in the Massachusetts section and both the Montpelier and Burlington chapters in the Vermont section.

David Laurila is a lifelong Red Sox fan who grew up in Michigan's Upper Peninsula and now writes about baseball from his home in Cambridge, Massachusetts. A weekly contributor to *Baseball Prospectus*, his work also appears in *Baseball America*, *Boston Sports Review*, and *Red Sox Magazine*. David contributed the Lowell, Boston, and Portland chapters.

Tom Mason is an environmental lawyer and a freelance writer with more than a hundred articles to his credit. He has written about sports and other topics for a number of New England magazines and newspapers, including several articles for area minor league baseball teams. A member of the Society for American Baseball Research, he lives in Lakeville, Massachusetts. Tom contributed all other chapters in the book, as well as some photos.

BOSTON, MA

FENWAY PARK

Address: 4 Yawkey Way, Boston, MA 02215-3409

Web Site: *www.redsox.com*

First Game: April 20, 1912

Dimensions: 310 left field; 379 feet left center field; 390 feet center field; 420 feet deep center field; 380 feet deep right field; 302 feet down the right field line.

Directions and Parking: The best way to get to Fenway Park is via the subway. The Kenmore Square and Fenway stops on the Green Line are both within easy walking distance of the ballpark. There is also access via commuter rail train, with the Yawkey Station stop within easy walking distance of the park. Bus service is also available from locations around the city.

If you have to drive, be aware that Fenway Park is in a bustling neighborhood and parking is at a premium. If you're driving into Fenway via I-90 (the Massachusetts Turnpike): from the Cambridge tolls, proceed toward Cambridge and turn right (east) onto Storrow Drive before crossing the Charles River. Continue east on Storrow Drive until the Fenway exit. Take the Fenway exit off Storrow Drive. Turn right onto Boylston Street and there is a public parking venue immediately on your right. For driving directions from other locations in and around Boston, visit *www.redsox.com*.

Home of the Boston Red Sox of the American League

Claim to Fame

Fenway Park's claim to fame is Fenway Park. It is the oldest baseball park still in use in the major leagues, and is arguably the most famous and beloved. While modern ballparks have replaced historic ones all over the country, Fenway has remained a constant, evoking memories of bygone eras and the all-time greats who once played there. In a city steeped in history, should it be any other way?

Strange but True

Moe Berg, who played for the Red Sox from 1935 to 1939, spoke several languages and was a spy for the United States government. Two books have been written about his life: *Moe Berg: Athlete Scholar Spy*, and *The Catcher Was a Spy*.

Buck O'Brien, who won 20 games for the 1912 World Series championship team, spent the winter after the championship touring as part of a vaudeville act called the "Red Sox Quartette." The group sang novelty tunes such as "Buck O'Brien, the Spit-Ball Artist." O'Brien reported to camp out of shape in 1913, went 4-11, and never pitched in the big leagues again.

In 1932, while attending a sendoff party before spring training, Red Sox pitcher Ed Morris was stabbed to death by a jealous husband.

In 1974 Willie Horton of the Detroit Tigers hit a foul ball that struck a low-flying pigeon over Fenway Park. The pigeon fell from the sky and landed in front of home plate.

Eddie Jurak, a reserve infielder for the Red Sox in the 1980s, once caught a rat that had wandered onto the field during a game. He scooped it up in his glove and dumped it into a trash can, earning a loud ovation from the Fenway Faithful. The glove reportedly suffered bite marks.

The initials of former owners Tom and Jean Yawkey (T.A.Y. and J.R.Y.) appear in strips of Morse code on the left-field scoreboard.

Who's Who in Boston

Baseball has been played at Fenway Park since 1912, and the list of legends who have performed there is longer than a Babe Ruth home run. The Babe is one of 30 players who have worn a Red Sox uniform and been inducted to the Hall of Fame. Among those who played a significant portion of their career in Boston are: Wade Boggs, Jimmy Collins, Joe Cronin, Bobby Doerr, Dennis Eckersley, Carlton Fisk, Jimmie Foxx, Lefty Grove, Harry Hooper, Tris Speaker, Ted Williams, Carl Yastrzemski, and Cy Young.

In the eyes of many fans and historians, there are a number of Red Sox players not in the Hall of Fame who are worthy of induction. They include Dominic DiMaggio, Dwight Evans, Jim Rice, and Luis Tiant.

Several current and recent members of the Red Sox are among the best of their generation. Former Red Sox pitchers Roger Clemens and Pedro Martinez are future Hall of Famers. Outfielder Manny Ramirez and pitcher Curt Schilling are two current Boston favorites that are future candidates for Cooperstown. The reputation and fame of David Ortiz continues to grow.

No mention of Boston's baseball history is complete without bringing up Johnny Pesky. Dubbed "Mr. Red Sox," Pesky signed with the team in 1940 and remains with the organization to this day.

About Boston

Boston is the capital of the Commonwealth of Massachusetts and the largest city in New England. The city has a population of approximately 600,000. The Greater Boston metropolitan area is home to approximately 4.4 million people.

Boston was founded in 1630, making it one of the oldest cities in the United States. Established by English colonists, it is the birthplace of the American Revolution, the Boston Massacre, the Boston Tea Party, and numerous other events recorded in textbooks. The United States' first public school (Boston Latin, opened in 1635) and first college (Harvard

College, opened in 1636) were both founded in Boston, the city that Oliver Wendell Holmes once referred to as "the Hub of the Universe."

With more than 100 colleges and universities in Greater Boston, the city has been called "The Athens of America." Some of the world's most prestigious institutes of higher learning can be found in the area, including Harvard University, the Massachusetts Institute of Technology (MIT), Tufts University, Boston University, Northeastern University, and Boston College.

Boston is the cultural center of New England. The city's theatres include the Wang Center for the Performing Arts, the Majestic Theatre, the Boston Opera House, and the Schubert Theater. Performing arts groups include the Boston Symphony Orchestra, the Boston Ballet, the Boston Pops, the Boston Lyric Opera Company, and the Handel and Haydn Society.

The city is home to a number of leading biotechnology and pharmaceutical companies, and to some of the country's most highly respected hospitals and research facilities. They include Harvard Medical School, Massachusetts General Hospital, Brigham and Women's Hospital, Beth Israel Deaconess Medical Center, Children's Hospital, and the Dana-Farber Cancer Institute. The Jimmy Fund, which is dedicated to battling children's cancer and is part of the Dana-Farber Cancer Institute, is one of the Red Sox' primary charities.

The area's most prominent newspaper is the *Boston Globe*. Other dailies include the *Boston Herald* and the *Met-*ro. The *Phoenix* is a weekly known for its arts and entertainment coverage.

The best way to get around Boston is on foot or via the nation's oldest subway system. Boston is a relatively small city, with many of its desirable sites within walking distance of each other. The subway, known as the MBTA or simply "the T," extends throughout the metro area and is both safe and relatively efficient. The subway system is made up of the Red, Green, Blue, and Orange lines, with Park Street station being the primary connecting point. Fenway Park is located on the Green Line, while service to Logan Airport is via the Blue Line. Bus service, available throughout the city, is also part of the MBTA network. If you enjoy navigating streets that don't follow logical patterns, and don't mind finding your way without adequate signage, driving in Boston is for you.

Census data shows Boston's racial makeup is 54.47 percent White, 25.33 percent African American, and 14.44 percent Hispanic or Latino. People of Irish descent count for 15.8 percent of Boston's population, making it the city's largest ethnic group.

A Baseball Backgrounder

Originally known as the "Americans," Boston's baseball team was a charter member of the American League in 1901. In the team's inaugural season, the hitting star was Buck Freeman, who finished second in the league in both home runs (12) and RBIs (114). The pitching star that same year was Cy Young, who posted a record of 33-10 with a league-best 1.62 ERA.

An aerial view of Kenmore Square in Boston, MA.

Led by player/manager Jimmy Collins, the Americans won the first ever World Series, defeating Pittsburgh in 1903. One of baseball's best teams through the Deadball Era, they would go on to win five more World Series championships through the 1918 season. The team was renamed as the Red Sox in 1908.

From 1919 until 1935 the Red Sox failed to have a winning season. The two most important events in that period were the sale of Babe Ruth to the Yankees in 1920, and the purchase of the team by Tom Yawkey in 1933. Ruth would go on to be, well, Babe Ruth. The Yawkey family would own the team for 40 years.

In 1946, the Red Sox won their first pennant since 1918. Led by Ted Williams, Bobby Doerr, and Johnny Pesky, the Sox went 104-50 but lost the World Series to the St. Louis Cardinals in seven games. In both 1948 and 1949, they tragically lost the pennant on the final day of the season.

The 1967 season revitalized baseball in the city of Boston. Following eight consecutive seasons where they finished in the bottom half of the American League, the "Impossible Dream" Red Sox had a Cinderella season for the ages. Led by Carl Yastrzemski, who won the Triple Crown, the team exceeded all expectations and captured their first pennant since 1946. However, just like the 1946 team, they lost the World Series in seven games to the Cardinals.

The 1970s and 1980s brought more heartbreak for Red Sox fans. The 1975 team, led by Fred Lynn and Jim Rice, won the pennant and went on to play in what many consider the greatest World Series ever played. However, despite Carlton Fisk's dramatic game-winning home run in Game 6, the Red Sox lost another Game 7, this time to the Cincinnati Reds. The 1978 team would also lose in tragic fashion, falling to the Yankees in a one-game playoff that forever made the name "Bucky Dent" an expletive in much of New England. The bad luck, or what some inaccurately called a curse, continued. The 1986 team was one pitch away from a World Series title when the Mets rallied. The name "Bill Buckner" has been an expletive in much of New England ever since.

In 2002, a new ownership group led by John Henry, Tom Werner, and Larry Lucchino took over the team. Theo Epstein was named general manager a year later.

In 2003, the Red Sox were two innings away from an American League championship when the Yankees rallied, which forever made the name "Grady Little" an expletive in much of New England.

In 2004, life as we know it changed. The Red Sox, behind the heroics of Curt Schilling, David Ortiz, and many more, won their first World Series championship in 86 years. In the words of Red Sox play-by-play announcer Joe Castiglione, "Can you believe it?!"

Take Me Out to the Ballgame

Getting tickets to a game is easier said than done. Tickets sell out as quickly as they are put on sale, and are the priciest in Major League Baseball. If you can't find tickets on the team's Web site, *www.redsox.com*, your best bet is to get in line early for the limited number of "day of game" tickets that are made available at the ballpark, or go to the "scalp-free zone" on Ipswich Street that is next to the statue of Ted Williams.

Historic Fenway Park, opened in 1912, remains one of the best parks to catch a game. Many improvements have been made to the park in recent years, from new seating to wider concourses to expanded fan services. The team's new ownership is committed to making the fan experience at "America's Most Beloved Ballpark" even more enjoyable.

The "Green Monster" is probably baseball's best-known landmark. Constructed in 1912, the 37-feet, 2-inches wall stretches from the corner of left field to center field and features a manual scoreboard that is still in use. Only 310 feet from home plate (some claim it is closer to 305 feet), it has long been an inviting target for hitters.

Atop the Green Monster are the "Monster Seats," which are among the most sought after, and most difficult to obtain, tickets in Fenway Park. Prior to the 2003 season, the team's management replaced a 23-foot net that prevents balls hit over the wall from landing on Landsdowne Street.

The second most famous feature of Fenway Park is the right-field foul pole, which is known as "Pesky's Pole." Only 302 feet from home plate, former Red Sox shortstop Johnny Pesky hit more than one of his six career home runs toward the pole. Pitcher Mel Parnell, a teammate of Pesky's, is credited with coining the term in the 1950s.

The longest home run ever hit at Fenway Park is commemorated with a red seat deep in the right-field bleachers. On

June 9, 1946, Ted Williams hit a ball that landed on the straw hat of an unsuspecting fan named Joseph Boucher, who was seated in Section 42, Row 37. The "Red Seat" has been measured at 502 feet from home plate.

Displayed on the right field façade at Fenway Park are the numbers 1, 4, 8, 9, and 27, which honor the players who have had their number retired by the Red Sox. The numbers were worn by Bobby Doerr, Joe Cronin, Carl Yastrzemski, Ted Williams, and Carlton Fisk. Also displayed is the number 42, which Major League Baseball has retired in honor of Jackie Robinson.

"Take Me Out to the Ballgame" isn't the only refrain heard at Fenway Park. The song "Sweet Caroline," a Top-10 hit for Neil Diamond in 1969, is played at every game after the top of the eighth inning, and most fans sing along. If the Red Sox win, the song "Dirty Water" is played after the game, followed by "Tessie." "Dirty Water," which features the refrain "Boston, you're my home," was recorded by the Standells in the 1960s. "Tessie" is a remake of a show tune that was sung by a group of Boston fans known as the "Royal Rooters" in the early 1900s. The song was later recorded by a Boston-based Irish punk band called the Dropkick Murphys.

Best Game (When You Think About It, How Does Someone Decide Which Game Was the Best?)

Since we're looking for a game that was played at Fenway Park, eliminated are Game 7 of the 2004 American League Championship Series and Game 4 of the World Series. That leaves as good candidates Game 4 and Game 5 of the American League Championship Series, which *were* played at Fenway.

But in the minds of most fans, the best game played at Fenway Park was Game 6 of the 1975 World Series. Featuring Carlton Fisk's 12th inning home run off the left-field foul pole, complete with body English, it is considered by many to be the greatest World Series game ever played. They might be right.

By Game 6, Boston trailed in the Series three to two. The Red Sox were eager to settle the score with the game, which was postponed for three consecutive days due to rainouts. When Game 6 was finally played on October 21, Luis Tiant was on the hill for the Red Sox against Cincinnati's Gary Nolan. It took more than four hours of drama—the game ended after midnight—for the Sox to draw even.

After taking a 3-0 lead in the first inning, the Red Sox saw the "Big Red Machine" storm back and by the bottom of the eighth they trailed 6-3 with their chances looking as dreary as the previous week's weather. Then, with two on and two out, lightning struck when pinch-hitter Bernie Carbo drove a two-strike pitch into the center-field bleachers and the game was tied. (The ball was reportedly caught by future Mets pitcher Ron Darling in the bleachers.)

After the Reds were retired in order in the top of the ninth, the Red Sox loaded the bases with none out in the bottom half. But they didn't score. It was on to extra innings, and one of the great clutch defensive plays in Series history.

Anne Haggerty Photography

Nothing beats an afternoon at Fenway especially if the Sox are winning.

With a man on at the top of the 11th, Cincinnati's Joe Morgan hit a line drive into deep right field. The ball appeared to be headed over the short three-foot wall, which would have given the Reds the lead. However, in spectacular fashion, Dwight Evans raced back and snared the ball at the last moment, robbing Morgan and saving Boston's season.

In the bottom of the 12th inning, at 12:34 A.M., Fisk hit what has become a historic home run that won the game for the Red Sox. At 12:35 A.M., Fenway Park organist John Kiley played the "Hallelujah Chorus."

Greatest Team (Not the '27 Yankees, but Who Is?)

Fifteen years before the 1927 Yankees, there were the 1912 Red Sox. Posting a record of 105-47, which remains the best in team history, the Red Sox rolled through the American League with a win total unsurpassed until New York's historic 1927 season.

Playing their first season at Fenway Park, the 1912 Red Sox certainly *did not* play like the Bronx Bombers. In the midst of the Dead Ball Era, Boston hit a total of only 29 home runs. Hall of Fame outfielder Tris Speaker, who along with Harry Hooper and Duffy Lewis formed Boston's famous "Million Dollar Outfield," led the way with a league-leading 10 round trippers to go with a batting average of .383.

The Red Sox pitching staff was led by right-hander "Smoky Joe" Wood, who went 34-5 with an ERA of 1.91. In an era when pitchers finished what they started, Wood threw 344 innings and had 35 complete games. The team had two other 20-game winners, with

When the Red Sox and Yankees match up in Fenway it captures the attention of the entire New England region.

Hugh Bedient going 20-9 and Buck O'Brien going 20-13.

The 1912 World Series, which the Red Sox won in eight games (Game 2 was called because of darkness and ended in a tie), was a classic. After the New York Giants scored in the top half of the 10th inning to take a 2-1 lead, Boston rallied with two in the bottom half. Larry Gardner drove in the winning run with a sacrifice fly off of Christy Mathewson to give Boston the title.

Best Player . . . in My Opinion

Ted Williams played for the Red Sox from 1939 to 1960, and finished with a career batting average of .344 and the highest on-base percentage in the history of the game (.482). A 17-time All-Star, Williams hit 521 home runs.

Williams' home run record is a considerable feat by any means, but the accomplishment seems all the more spectacular when you consider that he lost four seasons of his prime while serving his country in two wars. He has been called "The Greatest Hitter Who Ever Lived." As the legendary leader of the Royal Rooters, Michael "Nuf-Ced" McGreevy, used to say, "Nuf Said!"

Round Tripper (Some Suggestions for Sightseers)

Boston is home to some of the country's best museums. The Museum of Fine Arts (MFA), which was founded in 1870, has the second-largest permanent collection in the United States and regularly features world-class special exhibits. The MFA is located on Huntington Avenue, not far from Fenway Park.

Nearby is the Isabella Stewart Gardner Museum, which was established in 1903. It is much smaller than the MFA, but is world-reknowned for both its collection and garden courtyard. Once the home of Isabella Stewart Gardner, it has gone relatively unchanged since her death in 1924.

Other prominent museums in the city are the Museum of Science, the Boston Children's Museum, and the Institute of Contemporary Art. The New England Aquarium, on the city's waterfront, is another popular destination.

The Boston Common is the oldest public park in the United States. The Boston Public Garden, adjacent to the Common, features swan boat rides. The Franklin Park Zoo offers another option for those looking for outdoor activities.

If you can't get enough baseball, the Red Sox have minor league affiliates in Lowell (Massachusetts) and Pawtucket (Rhode Island). Commuter rail train service from downtown Boston can get you to either city in just under an hour.

Places to Eat . . . If You Want More Than Cracker Jack

There are a number of eating and drinking establishments near Fenway Park. Many of them have at least one large-screen TV, and you can expect them all to be crowded on game day.

The Cask 'n Flagon on Brookline Avenue, literally across the street from Fenway Park, has been in business for more than 30 years and is a game-day standard. The historic Red Sox photos adorning the walls add to the charm of the place. If you haven't visited in a few years, "the Cask" has been renovated and is larger than it used to be.

Another old standard that has been renovated—actually, it has been moved—is The Baseball Tavern. A small, unassuming gathering place for Red Sox fans for more than 40 years, it is now located in a larger and more modern setting just down the street from its old location on Boylston Street. No longer "your father's Baseball Tavern," it is a great place to stop before or after a game, and the new roof deck is a nice way to spend a summer afternoon after watching a Red Sox win.

Right down the street from the Cask 'n Flagon is Boston Beer Works, which has more than 15 microbrews on tap.

Around the corner on Ipswich Street, near the bleacher entrance, is Jillian's. Featuring more than 30 billiard tables and 16 bowling lanes, Jillian's is on three levels. They also have a dress code after 8 P.M., so be prepared to be asked to take off your baseball cap.

Two other options, a few doors away from each other on Brookline Avenue, are the Boston Billiard Club and Copperfield's—the latter features cheaper beer prices and less of a line than most Fenway area taverns.

In the Kenmore Square area, a little hidden on Commonwealth Avenue, is Cornwall's, a small English pub with a good selection of beer on tap that serves great hand-packed burgers and fresh-cut fries.

If you are looking for a quick bite to eat on your way to the park, the sausage vendors are always alluring, and what they sell is usually quite tasty.

Sources:

Grossman, Leigh. *The Red Sox Fan Handbook*. Cambridge, Massachusetts: Rounder
    Books, 2005.
Nowlin and Tan. *The 50 Greatest Red Sox Games*. New York: Wiley, 2006.

www.baseball-reference.com
www.boston.com/ae
http://en.wikipedia.org/wiki/Boston%2C_Massachusetts
http://redsox.com/
www.retrosheet.org/

2

Address: 200 Sandwich Road, Bourne, MA 02532

Web Site: *www.bournebraves.org*

First Game: June 30, 2006

Dimensions: LF 325 CF 390 RF 325

Directions: Sandwich Road runs along the south side of the Cape Cod Canal between the Bourne and Sagamore bridges. Those heading south on Route 3 should exit onto Route 6 west (Scenic Highway), and follow it along the north side of the canal to the Buzzards Bay rotary. Just keep to the right, and follow the signs for the Bourne Bridge. Those heading south on I-495 or east on I-195 will exit onto Route 25 south, which also leads to the Bourne Bridge. Once across the bridge, follow the rotary three-quarters around and bear right onto Sandwich Road. The school is ahead on the right.

BOURNE, MA

UPPER CAPE REGIONAL TECHNICAL SCHOOL

Home of the Bourne Braves of the Cape Cod Baseball League

Strange but True

President Grover Cleveland, Bourne's most famous summer resident, is the only U.S. president to serve two non-consecutive terms. In 1891, following his first term, President Cleveland bought a waterfront estate with several acres on Monument Neck and named the property Gray Gables.

That home served as a backdrop for one of the most elaborate ruses ever pulled off by an American politician. In June 1893, Cleveland learned a rough spot on his palate was cancer, which had spread into his upper jaw bone. Refusing to allow the press—and the country—to learn of his malady, he clandestinely set sail on June 30 from New York aboard a yacht along with several doctors. The team removed two teeth, his left upper jaw, and part of his palate.

They remained at sail for three days, until the President could walk. After dropping off the doctors, the yacht took President Cleveland to Gray Gables, where he recuperated for several days under the guise of a visit to his pregnant wife (two of his five children were born at the estate). Three weeks later he delivered a critical address to Congress without anyone learning of his surgery. The secret was not revealed until months afterward.

President Cleveland's "Summer White House" was destroyed by a fire in 1973, and the intersecting roads near where it stood have been re-named Presidents Road and Cleve-land Circle.

Who's Who in Bourne

Brian Anderson, Joe Blanton, John Caniera, Chris Capuano, Mark De-Rosa, John Dockery, Jeremy Giambi, Jerry Hairston Jr., Bobby Higginson, J.P. Howell, Tim Hummel, Brandon Inge, Conor Jackson, Mark John-son, Mark Kotsay, Noel Kinski, Brad Lincoln, John McDonald, Mark Mc-Lemore, Lou Merloni, Bill Mueller, Mark Mulder, Micah Owings, Tony Plansky, Justin Pope, Chris Ray, Greg Reynolds, Jack Sanford, Bob Schaefer, Tello Tontini, Ron Villone, and Kevin Youkilis.

About Bourne

Bourne was originally part of Sand-wich, the Cape's oldest town, which was established in 1637. Ten years ear-lier, Pilgrim settlers opened a trading post along the Manomet River (which was eventually joined with the Scusset River to form the Cape Cod Canal) to barter with Native Americans and the New Amsterdam Dutch.

Throughout the 1800s, residents of present-day Bourne developed com-mercial industries such as fish piers, factories, iron foundries, and shipyards. Farming and cranberry cultivation also played key roles in Bourne's growth.

Factions split from Sandwich in 1884, citing disproportionate taxation. The new town took its name from vil-lage native Jonathan Bourne, a whal-ing magnate and philanthropist.

The building of the canal involved the taking of land, which was then ex-cavated and flooded. Many businesses were displaced by the taking of land for the canal. Among the victims was the Keith Car Works in Sagamore, at one time the largest employer on the Cape and one of the largest in New England with 1,400 workers. The firm produced railroad boxcars for about 75 years.

Few towns in New England are as fragmented as Bourne, which has a year-round population of about 19,000. Besides being bisected by the canal, two major divided highways (Route 25/28 and Route 3/6) traverse its limits. In addition, about 15 square miles of the town are part of Massa-chusetts Military Reservation.

With those highways whisking drivers through the town, Bourne is no longer a tourist center. When pas-senger trains made several daily excur-sions to the village of Buzzards Bay, the area was a destination. But with-out the ease of train travel, the area has suffered. While neighboring Wareham has a busy commercial district, retail development in Bourne has been lim-ited by regulation to small strip malls and a string of car dealerships.

Many mainstay businesses have closed up shop. When the Buzzards Bay Theater closed a few years ago, the last movie shown was, ironically, *Sum-*

mer Catch, the plot of which centered on the Cape League.

Bourne is relatively free of urban sprawl, but its economy is dependent on year-round residents and ownership of summer homes.

Bourne and its seven distinct villages have a lot to offer, with great beaches, boating, shellfishing, biking trails, kayak-friendly coves, and a rich history. Civic leaders recognize this, and are in the midst of efforts to revitalize Buzzards Bay to attract more visitors. Plans are in the works for a waterfront park along the canal, an extension of the MBTA commuter rail service from Middleboro, and the creation of the Greenbelt Pathway—a walking tour connecting points of interest within the village.

A Baseball Backgrounder

Bourne's baseball history is not as deep as those of other Cape towns, and it certainly lacks continuity. In the years leading up to and during World War II, organized baseball in Bourne had a sporadic presence. Bourne fielded a town team from the 1920s until 1939. Sagamore's club, the Clouters, was formed in 1946 and ruled the Cape League for most of the 1950s.

During the 1960s the town intermittently fielded three separate teams: the Clouters, the Bourne Canalmen, and the Otis Air Force Base Minutemen. The Canalmen began play in 1961, sharing Keith Memorial Field with Sagamore. The Minutemen played six seasons between 1955 and 1964. During that final year for Otis, all three teams briefly coexisted.

Sagamore and Bourne then merged their squads as the town slashed its baseball budget. The consolidation of talent made for a powerful 1965 team that won the Cape Cod Baseball League championship. The success was short-lived, however, and the Canalmen finished no higher than fourth the rest of the decade.

The downward trend in the late 1960s was a harbinger of things to come. The team struggled financially while playing before sparse crowds. In 1970 Bourne did not field a team, and from 1973 to 1987 it was without a team altogether.

The league returned in 1988 with the formation of the Braves, who played home games at Hendy Field on the campus of the Massachusetts Maratime Academy (MMA). The setting, just yards from the Cape Cod Canal and in the shadows of the railroad bridge, was idyllic.

The MMA Buccaneers have a rich history of their own and actually played in the Cape League's Upper Cape division in 1957 and 1958. Pitcher Larry Butler made the Cape Cod Baseball League's All-Star team both seasons, and was the game's Most Valuable Player in 1957. Current head coach Bob Corradi has won 449 games over 32 seasons at the academy. The Bucs, who play at the NCAA Division III level, won the Eastern College Athletic Conference championship in 1982.

A major proponent of the Braves was the MMA's president, Rear Admiral Jack Aylmer, a former state senator. Twice he tried to obtain funding for lights for Hendy Field. In each case the academy presented honorary

SportPix photo by Bill Vaughn

The thick woods in the distance, part of Massachusetts Military Reservation, serve as the backdrop to the Braves' new field.

degrees: first to broadcasting magnate and yachtsman Ted Turner, and then to shipping tycoon and New York Yankees owner George Steinbrenner. Both made contributions to the academy, but not for the lighting.

In 1997 the Braves moved south across the canal to Coady School in Bourne, now the Waldorf School of Cape Cod. It remained their home for the next nine years. The field proved somewhat troublesome as a venue. Parking was limited, and children would scamper across busy Trowbridge Road to chase down foul balls. Home plate was a target for the setting sun, and the early-evening glare routinely forced umpires to delay games.

In 2004 the team broke ground on its newest field, which opened in June 2006.

Bourne's ball clubs have seen some terrific players and figures come and go. One of the early greats for the town team was Tony Plansky, a star running back for football's New York Giants in 1928–29. He played baseball in Bourne during the summer of 1929, and then for the Philadelphia Phillies' minor league system in 1931.

Plansky was with Bourne from 1933 to 1939, winning two batting titles and making the Cape League All-Star team six times. A legendary decathlete at Georgetown University and a long-time track coach at Williams College, *Sports Illustrated* named Plansky one of the top 50 Massachusetts sports figures of the twentieth century.

Dante "Pat" Sorenti, who managed Sagamore from 1946 to 1949, spent 50 years with the league and is the namesake of the Cape Cod Baseball Leagues' Most Valuable Player award.

The great Sagamore teams of the 1950s won four Cape League championships. The Clouters featured All-Star pitchers George Karras, Bill Powers, and dominant southpaw Jack Sanford. The lineups included first baseman Don Cunningham, shortstop Tullo Tonini, outfielders Fred Dunbury and John Jenkins, and catcher Manny Pena.

Karras also managed the team to titles in 1951 and 1954, while Pena guided Sagamore to the 1956 and 1959 crowns. Both are Cape League Hall of Famers.

Sanford, also a Hall of Fame inductee, posted a 14-1 record in 1951, and followed that up with an 11-1 mark in 1952. He was named the league's outstanding pitcher both seasons, which led to his signing with the Boston Braves in 1953. The 14 wins set a single-season league record that stood for 20 years, and his 60 career wins remain the most in the history of the Cape Cod League.

Noel Kinski, a star hurler for Providence College, pitched for Bourne in 1964 and joined the town's combined team the following season. That 1965 campaign was stellar as he went 10-1 with 11 complete games, and a 1.91 ERA while compiling 85 strikeouts and just 31 walks. His final win that year came at Harwich as he whiffed a season-high 12 hitters. The squad went on to win the Cape Cod Baseball League championship, the most recent title won by any Bourne team.

The return of the Braves in 1987 ushered in a new era for Bourne. The team sent numerous players to the major leagues including future Red Sox Lou Merloni, Jeremy Giambi, Bill Mueller, and Kevin Youkilis.

In 2006, ex-Braves right-handers Greg Reynolds and Brad Lincoln were the second and fourth players taken in the June amateur draft, selected by the Colorado Rockies and Pittsburgh Pirates respectively.

Take Me Out to the Ballgame

About 80 percent of the work on the new field was done by students, which might make it the most intriguing show-and-tell project in the history of American education. The tasks included grading the field, laying the sod, and constructing the clubhouse, press box, concession stand, and backstop.

Former school superintendent Barry Motta first got the idea to involve students in building a ball field in 1990. That vision was realized 16 years later, thanks in part to a grant from the Yawkey Foundation that helped cover the cost of materials and professional contractors.

The field, tucked safely behind the school, eliminates the problems posed by the former Coady School field. Batters now face due east, eliminating any issues with sun glare. Parking is also no longer an issue and the school has parking space for more than 200 cars. The increased space at the field allows children to safely scamper after foul balls.

The field's backstop consists of thin black netting, which is nearly invisible to the eye. The netting is mounted on poles atop a three-foot-high brick wall, which evokes an old-time ballpark feel that is similar to Camden Yards.

As with all Cape League venues there is bleacher seating available, but fans are always welcome to bring their own folding chairs if desired. The best place to watch is from the third-base line, between the concession stand and the Braves' dugout, but good views are also found behind the brick wall, where many scouts sit.

To satisfy hunger pangs, burgers and dogs come hot off the grill, and fans can also enjoy nachos and surprisingly good pizza. There are nine picnic tables down the left-field line, which allow families to dine and take in the action.

For now all home games begin at 5 P.M. There are no home games on Tuesday nights; that's when the local classic car club holds its rallies at the school.

The best feature of the park is yet to come: new field lighting. Installation is scheduled for spring 2007.

Best Game (When You Think About It, How Does Someone Decide Which Game Was the Best?)

While the old Sagamore club won its share of titles, a championship has thus far eluded the grasp of the present-day Bourne Braves. In 2005 they came close in the final series against Orleans. The Braves dropped the opener, a heartbreaker of a pitcher's duel between Bourne's Greg Reynolds and the Cardinals' Andy Graham. Orleans broke the ice in the ninth when Emmanuel Burris tagged up and scored from third on a bases-loaded foul pop

fly to short right field as the Cardinals escaped 1-0.

But the Braves stormed back in Game 2, as Brett Bartles, Robbie Widlansky, Josh Stinson, Beau Mills, and Mike Hernandez combined to go 13-for-18 with eight runs scored and eight runs batted in. Bourne starter J.R. Crowel held the Cardinals to just one run and three hits over six and a third innings, while Nick Manganaro and Andrew Carnigan provided shutout relief to close out the 11-1 Braves victory.

Though Orleans turned the tables in Game 3, taking the championship with a 13-1 pummeling, Bourne's win in Game 2 set a modern franchise record for wins in a season with 26.

Greatest Team (Not the '27 Yankees, but Who Is?)

The 1951 Cape League champion Sagamore Clouters, featuring Jack Sanders and Tullo Tontini, get the nod. Though subsequent Sagamore teams were strong in their own right, none were as dominant.

No Braves team has won a title, but the 1989 squad went 24-17-3 and claimed the West Division crown.

Best Player . . . in My Opinion

Tullo Tontini, a lifelong Bourne resident, played all nine positions for the Sagamore Clouters from 1946 to 1952, including the 1951 championship squad. Primarily a shortstop, he was named to the Cape League's All-Star team in each of his seasons in the league. Tontini, who compiled a .390 career batting average over seven years, won batting titles in 1950 (.403) and 1952 (.413).

He was also named MVP in 1949 and 1951. In the 1951 All-Star game, he slugged three homers to lead the Upper Cape squad to victory over the Lower Cape. Tontini was inducted into the Cape League Hall of Fame in 2004.

Round Tripper (Some Suggestions for Sightseers)

Heritage Museum & Gardens in Sandwich has been home to the Cape Cod Baseball Leagues's Hall of Fame exhibit since 2000. That arrangement will expire in 2008, when the collection will move to the John F. Kennedy museum in Hyannis. Even without baseball memorabilia, the 76 acres at the museum are worth a visit. Along

with the blooms and blossoms, the grounds feature a collection of antique cars, a Shaker round barn, and a working 1912 carousel.

Sandwich also features historical sites that can be taken in within a few hours. They include the Sandwich Glass Museum, Dexter's Grist Mill, the Thornton W. Burgess Museum, and the Ella Hoxie House.

Most of Bourne's attractions center on the canal, which for nearly the entire length of the waterway features paved bicycle paths. If you're a fisherman, bring your surf rod and cast for striped bass and feisty bluefish from the rocky banks.

Hy-Line offers canal cruises, which depart from Onset Town Pier in Wareham. The best deal is the two-hour 4 P.M. cruise, where adults save $2 and kids ride free. After returning to shore,

SportPix photo by Bill Vaughn

Players mill around the first base dugout just behind Upper Cape Regional Technical School.

take time to explore Onset Village and its quaint shops.

At the east end of the canal in Sandwich, the Army Corps of Engineers maintains a visitor's center. Films and exhibits detail the canal's history, current operations, and marine life. Try your hand at piloting an oil tanker from the virtual bridge. The center also offers a variety of summer outdoor and interpretive programs.

At the other end of the canal sits the Massachusetts Maritime Academy in Buzzards Bay. The Cape's only four-year college was established in 1891. Several tugboats that ply the canal tie up here, along with the academy's training ship, the 540-foot *Enterprise*. Two small memorial parks pay homage to merchant marine and naval sailors who perished at sea.

Also in Buzzards Bay is the National Marine Life Center, which rehabilitates rescued turtles and seals. It is undergoing a major expansion that will include a pool large enough to treat pilot whales. A visitors' center is open daily in the summer.

The Bourne Scallop Festival, held in September in Buzzards Bay, comes about a month after the end of the Cape Cod Baseball League season. It attracts about 40,000 visitors and features rides, arts and crafts, and entertainment along with endless plates of juicy scallops.

Beneath the Sagamore Bridge on Sandwich Road sits Keith Memorial Field, former home of the Sagamore Clouters. Local youth leagues now use the venue.

Aptuxcet Trading Post Museum in Bourne Village is a replica of the seventeenth-century bartering post built atop the post's original foundation. Run by the Bourne Historical Society, the grounds also include a replica salt works, flower and herb gardens, and archaeological artifacts unearthed at the site by scientists.

The personal train station of President Grover Cleveland, which once stood mere yards from his Gray Gables home, has been moved to the museum site. Also there is a Dutch-style windmill that once stood on the estate of actor Joseph Jefferson, the president's neighbor and fishing buddy.

Cataumet, with its winding, wooded roads, is home to many hidden estates, especially along the coast, and serves as an enclave for many artists. Among its residents is baseball writer and Cape League aficionado Peter Gammons, who owns a summer home on Scraggy Neck.

Places to Eat ... If You Want More Than Cracker Jack

The Beachmoor, next to MMA, offers a great dinner menu including Beachmoor stew and seafood triology, its house specialties. It's open for dinner and Sunday brunch.

The décor of Mezza Luna in Buzzards Bay may be dated, but it's the best authentic Italian food for miles around, including an unforgettable seafood fra diavolo. The service is fast and friendly, and portions are huge. The bar attracts a smiling crowd of regulars.

For upscale dining, the Chart Room, overlooking Red Brook Harbor in Cataumet, sets the standard. Celebrity sightings are common, as its location off the beaten path makes it an ideal hideout for the rich and famous.

The pricy Sunset Grille, off MacArthur Boulevard in Pocasset, sits atop the town's newest golf course, The Brookside Club. Views from the restaurant and the first tee extend to Buzzards Bay in the distance.

Locals flock to Leo's Restaurant in Buzzards Bay for the best breakfasts in town. Other nice spots for a morning bite are Hollyberry's on Shore Road in Monument Beach, and The Corner Café on Barlow's Landing Road in Pocasset. To relax with coffee and a book or laptop, head to Daily Brew Coffee Bar on Route 28A in Cataumet, which offers wireless Internet access.

Trowbridge Tavern & Ale House, inside the Best Western south of the canal, is a popular watering hole with locals. Further to the west, past Gray Gables, is the lively Mashnee Island Grill and Beach Bar.

Bourne is home to many former Boston Bruins hockey players including Jay Miller, who owns the Courtyard Restaurant and Bar at the intersection of Route 28A and County Road in Cataumet.

In neighboring Sandwich, the British Beer Company, Bobby Byrne's Pub, the Dan'l Webster Inn, and Aquagrille are all worth checking out. A unique ambience is found at the Belfry Inn and Bistro, a renovated Catholic church.

To the west of town in Onset Village, relax and soak in the tunes at Onset Bay Blues Café.

For seafood, head to the Lobster Trap on Shore Road in Cataumet, which serves the best clam chowder and stuffed quahogs in town. Another reliable spot is Seafood Sam's in Sandwich, across from the canal visitors' center.

For pizza, Effie's, Nick's, and Buzzards Bay House of Pizza, all in Buzzards Bay, offer traditional New England pies and grinders in nondescript surroundings.

For an ice cream fix, hit Somerset Creamery or Cataumet Scoops, both on Route 28A in Cataumet.

Sources:

Falmouth Enterprise newsprint archives (*www.capenews.net*).

Price, Christopher. *Baseball by the Beach—A History of America's National Pastime on Cape Cod*. Yarmouthport, Massachusetts: On Cape Publications, 1998.

www.bournebraves.org
www.capecodbaseball.org
www.mma.mass.edu
www.townofbourne.com

3

Address: 384 Underpass Rd., Brewster, MA 02631

Web Site: *www.brewsterwhitecaps.com*

First Game: 2006

Dimensions: LF 325 CF 375 RF 325

Directions: Take Route 6 to Exit 11 (Rt.137). Turn right at top of the ramp, proceed 2.8 miles on Rt.137, turn right on Underpass Road. Stony Brook School is on the left, the field is located behind the school buildings.

BREWSTER, MA

STONY BROOK FIELD

Home of the
Brewster Whitecaps of the
Cape Cod Baseball League

Claim to Fame

The Bayside skippers, a local team of third through tenth graders, recently won the nation's skip-roping team championship. Brewster has long been associated with the sea and is famous for its many pristine old sea captain mansions.

Strange but True

Brewster Whitecap alumnus Tim Maloney can drive a golf ball more than 400 yards with a club speed of more than 150 MPH. In 2004, Maloney finished third in golf's RE/MAX World Long Drive Championship. But he's best remembered in Brewster for leading his team in home runs, doubles, triples, and RBIs. He also won the Cape Cod League's Ty Brown award for sportsmanship, attitude, and hustle.

Who's Who in Brewster

Kip Wells, Billy Wagner, Todd Walker, Aaron Rowand, Eduardo Perez, Mike Myers, Bobby Kielty, Matt Herges, Brandon Duckworth, Brian Buchanan,

SportPix photo by Matthew Scott

A view from the press box at Stony Brook Field.

Geoff Blum, Jason Grilli, Adam Melhuse, Chad Mottola, Lyle Mouton, Craig Paquette, Mark Thompson Brewster, and Chase Utley.

About Brewster

The seaside community of Brewster, named after one of Plymouth's original pilgrims, is one of our nation's first settlements. The town is located along the shores of Cape Cod Bay, and can trace its history back to 1656. For more than a century, Brewster was the North Parish section of Harwich. From its founding, the Town of Brewster was known for its many sea captains. It was once said that more sea captains lived in Brewster than in any other town in the country. Many other seaside communities, like New Bedford, debated this claim.

From the time you enter Brewster, you've got to be impressed with its sea-

faring history. Along the town's main drag, Route 6A, there's plenty of evidence of the community's past. There aren't many old sea captains left and the only remaining local whalers go out to watch whales, not kill them. But there are many well-preserved examples of their pre-Victorian residences around town. The town's skyline, if you could call it that, boasts towering widow walks where families waited for loved ones to return home from long ocean voyages. Today the mansions that once belonged to sea captains are restaurants, bed and breakfasts, and private homes.

Brewster's natural beauty has never changed. The Cape Cod Natural Museum offers a number of innovative programs to better appreciate nature. "Mudflat Mania" is one of the museum's most popular exhibitions. Sometimes, particularly in off-season, tourists think Brewster is just a sparsely populated seaside community. But there's a whole other world in town. There are countless varieties of crustaceans, mollusks, fish, frogs, turtles, birds, and snakes. Just miles away from the shoreline, the heavily wooded 1,900-acre Nickerson State Park has five kettle ponds, numerous campsites, and countless trails for walking, running, and biking.

Another favorite outdoor activity is golf. The Captain's Golf Club, owned and operated by the town, is one of the finest public courses in the Northeast. There are no large hotels or motels besides Ocean Edge Resort. The lodgings are, for the most part, small inns or bed and breakfasts. There are no fast-food restaurants, except in the summer. There are also several cozy, comfortable gourmet restaurants nearby.

Brewster's not the liveliest place, but it does have culture. Within the small town, there's a great library, a nice little bookstore, and a summertime theater. Brewster's greatest assets are its history and accessibility to nature.

A Baseball Backgrounder

The Cape Cod League has had its ups and downs. But by the mid 1980s, the Cape was on a roll. Six veterans of the Cape League were taken in the first round of the 1985 major league baseball draft, a record-setting accomplishment. With top-notch competition, professionally run amateur teams, and great community support, the time was ripe for expansion. Many communities, all the way north to Plymouth, applied for admission into the eight-team league. The board of directors chose Bourne as the ninth but needed a 10th to balance out the league. The clear choice was Brewster.

In 1988, the Brewster Whitecaps took the field. Its first manager was Harvard coach Joe Walsh. Like any other first-year team, the team had a few kinks to work out, finishing in the cellar of the Eastern Division with a 15-25 record. But, by the second year, the Whitecaps had their sea legs. New Brewster skipper Rolando Casanova's team tied the Chatham A's for second place. The Whitecaps won a one-game play-in to make its first appearance in the playoffs.

For its first 18 years in existence, the Brewster franchise never played a home game. Until 2006, the Whitecaps' ballpark was at Cape Cod Regional Technical School in Harwich. For many years, Harwich was a two-team town. The Harwich Mariners' ballpark was about a five-minute ride from Brewster's.

From the beginning, the Whitecaps' management promised to move back to Brewster. But nothing seemed to work out. At one time, plans were on the drawing board to move the team to old Brewster Elementary School on Route 6A. Cape Cod Tech made the Whitecaps feel very much at home. After almost a two-decade stay, the Whitecaps left the nest and finally moved to Brewster. Their brand new ballpark is located at the Stony Brook School on Underpass Road, a stone's throw away from their old digs in Harwich. Trophies of the Whitecaps glorious past are proudly displayed in the children's room of the local library.

The theme of Brewster's 2006 year could have been "Go East, Young Man." The Whitecaps' opening day roster had 14 players from west of the Mississippi. Represented on Brewster's roster were UCLA, USC, Cal State Fullerton, the University of San Francisco, Arizona State, and the University of Arizona. The team's infield made it strong. On paper, it may have been one of the greatest infields assembled in amateur ranks. Matt Cusick of USC was at third, Andrew Romine of Arizona State was at shortstop, and speedy second baseman Jamine Weeks of the University of Miami were originally scheduled to be the starters. Romine is the son of former Red Sox outfielder Kevin Romine and Weeks' big brother Rickie plays for the Milwaukee Brewers.

Brewster's franchise has had more than its share of good hitters. Current Philadelphia All-Star second baseman Chase Utley spent a summer with the Whitecaps. Brewster's J.C. Holt won the team's third league batting title in six years (he was preceded by Bobby Kielty in 1998 [.384] and Steve Stanley in 2000 [.329]). His .388 average is a team record. Aaron Bates (.333, three home runs, 16 RBIs) was crowned the champion of the Baseball Factory Home Run Hitting Contest at the 2005 All-Star Game.

Red Sox draftee Matt LaPorta, one of the most powerful hitters in baseball, set Florida's all-time high school record by hitting 26 home runs. Red Sox brass came to Brewster to check out the powerful first baseman.

"Hang one too many curveballs and you end up selling raffle tickets," it says in the team's programs. For the most part, the Whitecaps have played winning baseball in their 19 years of existence. Over the years, the team has had five first-place finishes. The Whitecaps won their first and only league championship in 2000. As of May 2006, 25 White Cap alumni were in the majors.

Take Me Out to the Ballgame

It's been a long wait. But the Brewster Whitecaps finally have a place they can call home. For the last 18 years, the home of the Brewster Whitecaps was actually in Harwich. Ever since first pitch, the Whitecaps have played their home games at Cape Cod Technical School.

Recently the Whitecaps' board of directors finally decided to make a great leap. In January 2002, team president Gene L'Etoile was authorized to explore the feasibility of bringing the Whitecaps home to Brewster. After more a year and a half of meetings, consultations, and cajoling, in August of 2003 the Whitecaps signed an agreement to provide, at no cost to the Town of Brewster, a new, NCAA-regulation baseball field that would be located at the Stony Brook School on Underpass Road.

Even when they played in Harwich, the Whitecaps were always the pride of Brewster. The children's room of the Brewster Ladies Public Library has an impressive display of Whitecaps pictures, awards, and memorabilia. The team's "autograph" day is great family fun. Having a hometown team has allowed the organization to step it up a notch and get more community involvement. Team volunteers have

SportPix photo by Matthew Scott

Players pitch in with all aspects in the Cape League—including lining the field.

open grass for lawn chairs and beach blankets on the first-base side, but there are a few blind spots. It makes sense to arrive early for the games to get a good parking space and the right seating location. The school parking lot fills up on game night.

Sea captains' mansions, quaint Cape Cod charm, widow's walks, and Nickerson State Park are now within bike riding distance of Brewster's new ballpark. The Cape Cod Bike Trail runs next to the ballpark. All games are played in daylight. Many spectators may prefer night baseball, but lights are expensive. It will be quite a while until night baseball comes to Brewster.

worked diligently to bring local clubs and church groups out to the park. The Men's Club from Our Lady of the Cape had their own night. The Bayside Skippers, the town's world championship jump-roping team, operates the concessions booth by the third base at every home game. Team members, it is said, jump through hoops to raise money for its trips and local charities.

The new playing field is immaculate. The new scoreboard in left center field is one of the best. Nevertheless, the new ballpark has a few quirks. The playground, located behind home plate, can be dangerous. The equipment is covered with netting. Anyone who ventures outside of the protected area during play needs to be alert for stray balls. There's a berm behind home plate where fans sit. There's plenty of

Best Game (When You Think About It, How Does Someone Decide Which Game Was the Best?)

Many observers say the 2000 Cape League All-Star Game at the White-caps' old home, Cape Cod Regional Tech, was one of Brewster's most memorable games. While most Cape League games feature speed and defense, the 2000 game was about raw power. The daylong festivities began with a memorable home run hitting contest. Falmouth's Doc Brooks, who won the previous year's contest, looked like he was going to win another one. Falmouth star Jason Cooper, a freshman from Stanford University, hit six to win it.

The game looked like a pitching duel at first, but was a humdinger. In the fourth inning, Harwich Mariner and East Division Most Valuable Player Ryan Stegall hit a long home run off Cotuit Kettleer righty Ryan Combs to give the East Division a 1-0 lead.

Hyannis Mets and Notre Dame star Brian Stavisky responded with a three-run home run. Going into the ninth inning, the West had a four-run lead. But the East still had some fight left. Orleans Cardinal and Georgia Tech catcher Bryan Prince hit a three-run double to tie the game up with two outs. Minnesota Twin/Harwich Mariner shortstop Jason Bartlett drew a game-winning, bases-loaded walk to lead the East to a dramatic 7-6 win.

Greatest Team (Not the '27 Yankees, but Who Is?)

It's pretty difficult to argue with results. The year 2000 was a watershed one for the Cape League's newest team. After hosting one of the greatest All-Star games in league history, Brewster capped off the year by winning its first championship. The Whitecaps have a tradition of great hitting. Brewster was the best batting team in the regular season. The hits continued straight through the playoffs, leading to a two-game sweep of the West Division winning Hyannis Mets to win it all.

The clincher was a rout. Current Braves farmhand and pitcher Matt Coenen lasted just four innings against the Whitecaps. Brewster made a strong start against the Mets

ace, building a 5-0 lead against Bourne. Some of Brewster's best players were, as usual, from the West Coast. Brewster middle reliever George Carralejo (Cal State Fullerton) did a great job in middle relief. Brewster southpaw Ryan Olson (University of Nevada at Las Vegas) outpitched Stanford ace Jeff Brucksh for eight innings to win game one. The Most Valuable Player of the playoffs was Santa Clara alum Jack Headley, who had a .312 average. The closer was Mike Sollie of North Carolina State.

Best Player . . . in My Opinion

Mo Vaughn and Frank Thomas were distinguished members of the Cape Cod League's class of 1983. Perhaps the best first baseman for that summer, though, was Dave Staton of the Brewster Whitecaps. In Brewster's very first game in the Cape Cod League, Staton hit two home runs. His 16 homers and 46 RBIs led the league. Only former Cleveland Indian Cory Snyder hit more round-trippers in a summer. But Staton's record may be more impressive. All of his records, unlike Snyder's, were set with wooden bats. Staton still owns Cape Cod League records for home runs, RBIs, and total bases using a wooden bat. It's hardly a surprise that Staton was named the league's Most Valuable Player. His .772 slugging percentage was the Cape's third-best mark of all time. After graduating from Orange Coast Community College, Staton was drafted, signed, and played with the San Diego Padres.

While not the best in team history, another notable is pitcher Shaun Seibert who was named the Cape's 2006 Pitcher of the Year. As a freshman at the University of Arkansas, Seibert battled an injured elbow that caused him to miss three weeks of his season, but he was still able to prove himself with a 3.60 ERA and a 5-3 record. In 2006, it was predicted that Seibert would be one of the top pitchers in rotation in the Cape Cod Baseball League. He had a "pitcher perfect" year. Seibert had a 6-0 record, leading the league in wins, ERA, and starting the All-Star game. Allowing just 26 hits in 46 innings pitched, Seibert displayed incredible command. Siebert had a miniscule 0.39 ERA, the third lowest in Cape history. His game of the year may have been Game 1 of the Eastern Division. Seibert defeated Co-Pitcher of the Year, Terry Doyle, a duel of the two best pitchers on the Cape. New York Mets star closer Billy Wagner won the Cape League All-Star game Most Valuable Player.

Round Tripper (Some Suggestions for Sightseers)

Few state parks compare to Nickerson State Park located off Route 6A. Just a stone's throw away from Cape Cod Bay, the piney 1,900-acre preserve features eight fully stocked trout ponds. There are plenty of opportunities to swim, canoe, bike, walk, or simply enjoy the beauties of nature. One of the most difficult challenges on the Cape is getting a reservation for a campsite. Normally reservations must be made six months in advance. Campsites can be reserved at ReserveAmerica.com or at *www.mass.gov/dcr*. Trails around Cliff, Flax, and Little ponds are great for walking. During the season, maps are available at the park entrance on Route 6A and during the off season they are available at the administration building off season. For more information contact Nickerson State Park, 3488 Main Street, Brewster, MA 02631-1521, or call 508-896-3491. The Cape Cod Rail Trail runs through the park.

Since 1954, the Cape Cod Museum of Natural History has offered a wide range of fun, educational programs for all ages. It's a great little museum. In the basement, a small interactive aquarium, with fresh and saltwater tanks, is always a popular attraction. Outside of the museum, there are several short yet invigorating hikes through woodlands and marsh. The longest path, about a mile and a half long, ends at Wing Island along Cape Cod Bay. Guided programs are offered year round. Trail guides are available at the museum.

The Captains Golf Course is one of the East Coast's premier public courses. Captains has not one, but two, championship courses—Port and Starboard. A benefit of living in Brewster is access to the golf course. It's just $600 for an annual resident's pass. What a deal! For more information, check out *www.captainsgolfcourse.com*.

For culture, check out some of the local art galleries. There are many little antique shops and artist's galleries in the area. The Cape Playhouse and Repertory Theater is also located along Route 6A.

Places to Eat . . . If You Want More Than Cracker Jack

The best way to describe Brewster's dining is plain and fancy. It's one of the few communities to have more fine, gourmet-style establishments than fast-food restaurants. During the summertime, there are a few New England–style fried food take outs. JT's Seafood Restaurant, Cobie's, and Kate's offer ice cream, burgers, hot dogs, and fried seafood.

For something more fancy, the menus offered at Bramble Inn & Restaurant, Captain Freeman Inn, and Chillingsworth's satisfy the most discriminating palette. The Bramble Inn recently received a top rating by the influential *Zagat's* guide to the region. Chillingsworth's, located on a large old estate, specializes in French cuisine. The Bramble Inn is located in a Civil War–period farmhouse; the property is on the National Register of Historic Places. This isn't a comprehensive list, but is a good reflection of what's offered. Brewster is a bed-and-breakfast type of place. Practically all of the town's restaurants and attractions are located on Route 6A.

Sources:

The Baseball Almanac, 1995–2007.
Boston Globe, 1900–2007.
Brewster Whitecaps Media Guide, 2005–2007.
Cape Cod Times, 1990–2007.
Glassman-Jaffe, Marcia. *Fun with the Family in Massachusetts: Third Edition*. Guilford, Connecticut: The Globe Pequot Press, 2002.
Price, Christopher. *Baseball by the Beach—A History of America's National Pastime on Cape Cod*. Yarmouthport, Massachusetts: On Cape Publications, 1998.

www.all-baseball.com
www.ballparkdigest.com
www.ballparkreviews.com
www.baseballalmanac.com
www.baseballamericaonline.com
www.brewsterwhitecaps.com
www.capecodbaseball.org
www.capecodcommission.org/pathways/trailguide.htm#orleans
www.patmaloneygolf.com/bio.html
www.ccmnh.org
www.chillingsworth.com
www.explorenewengland.com/travel?article=massachusetts/articles/2005/
    05/01/fine_dining_and_a_comfortable_stay_at_a_family_run_inn
www.sabr.org
http://wikitravel.org/en/Brewster_(Massachusetts)

4

CAMPANELLI FIELD

Address: One Lexington Avenue, Brockton, MA 02301

Web Site: www.brocktonrox.com

First Game: 2002

Dimensions: LF 300 CF 400 RF 330

Directions: From the north, take I-93/Route 1 South to Route 24 South toward Brockton. Take Exit 17A to Route 123 East (Belmont Street). Follow Belmont Street for approximately one mile. Bear right onto West Street. Turn right onto Lexington Avenue. Campanelli Stadium will be on the right, adjacent to Brockton High School.

From the west, take I-290 East to I-495 South to I-95 North to Exit 7A to Route 140 South to Route 106 East to Route 24 North toward Brockton. Take Exit 17A to Route 123 East (Belmont Street). Follow Belmont Street for approximately one mile. Bear right onto West Street. Turn right onto Lexington Avenue. Campanelli Stadium will be on the right, adjacent to Brockton High School.

From the east, take Route 6 West to Route 25 West to I-495 North to Route 24 North toward Brockton. Take Exit 17A to Route 123 East (Belmont Street). Follow Belmont Street for approximately one mile. Bear right onto West Street. Turn right onto Lexington Avenue. Campanelli Stadium will be on the right, adjacent to Brockton High School.

From the south, take Route 24 North toward Brockton. Take Exit 17A to Route 123 East (Belmont Street). Follow Belmont Street for approximately one mile. Bear right onto West Street. Turn right onto Lexington Avenue. Campanelli Stadium will be on the right, adjacent to Brockton High School.

Home of the Brockton Rox of the Canadian-American League

Claim to Fame

Brockton is called the "City of Champions." Rocky Marciano and "Marvelous" Marvin Hagler were longtime residents of the city.

Strange but True

Former *Saturday Night Live* star Bill Murray was one of the owners of the Brockton Rox.

Who's Who in Brockton

Former Red Sox star "Oil Can" Boyd played for the Rox. Former Patriots player Greg McMurtry, Steve Balboni, Hall of Famer Mickey Cochrane, Bill McGunnigle (inventor of the catcher's mitt), former Red Sox star Buck O'Brien, and Oakland Raiders Al Davis were once Brockton natives.

About Brockton

Brockton's fortunes reflect the rise and fall of the American shoe industry. A Salem cobbler, Thomas Beard, is credited as the inventor of mass-produced footwear. Soon, local cities, like Haverhill, Lynn, and Lowell discovered innovative manufacturing techniques. The cost to make shoes was cut. Highly skilled cobblers struggled to earn a living. Low-wage immigrants found work at local shoe factories. For many years, Massachusetts was the world leader in shoe making.

In Brockton, thousands of workers made millions of shoes. At the turn of the twentieth century, the city had more than 100 hundred factories. While Chicago was the "city with broad shoulders," Brockton was the city with big feet. Several Massachusetts cities called themselves the "Shoe City," but Brockton may have had the strongest claim.

Since the Civil War, thousands of boots made in Brockton have been worn by our troops. Some historians believe more than half of the Union Army wore Brockton-made boots.

Between 1900 and 1920, the city was the world's leading shoe manufacturer. The city's workshops made local merchants wealthy, and the city's merchants brought many innovations to Brockton. Thomas Edison, the "Father of the Electric Light," flipped the switch on an electrical system that was the first of its kind. The city had the first all-electric theater as well as the first electric-powered fire station. Local engineers and workers perfected an electric-powered street railway. The city also boasts the first inland sewage disposal system. The first department-store Santa was James Edgar of Edgar's Department Store in Brockton. Right before the Great Depression, for more than 30,000

workers, there was no business like the shoe business.

Unfortunately, many other cities made the same discovery. Sweetheart deals, tax breaks, and lower labor costs sent local companies south. After 1920, 10 major manufacturers moved and another 58 closed. Old-line companies, like Douglas Shoe, went to the Midwest. Sales of sneakers took another big bite out of the shoe business. Brockton's industry tried to develop niches and become more specialized. Pioneers developed specialized golf and men's footwear. But no matter what was tried, nothing could stop the decline. It was too little, too late. Competition caught up with Brockton. Today, there's only one sole surviving shoemaker, Foot Joy.

Brockton still has a strong claim for its other title—the "City of Champions." The community has always been sports crazy. The football team is a perennial Massachusetts power. Three of boxing's greatest champions lived in Brockton, including John L. Sullivan. Residents still love former middleweight champion "Marvelous" Marvin Hagler. But the pride of the community is the former heavyweight champion of the world, Rocky Marciano. Born and brought up in Brockton, Rocky never let fame go to his head. Even when he became famous, the undefeated champ never forgot where he came from.

Brockton has been down but has gotten off the canvass and is coming back. The team's independent baseball team, the Brockton Rox, have been an important part of the city's revitalization. The influential magazine *Inc.*

Tom Mason

Fans on the field for a promotion during a break in Rox action.

recently gave the city high grades for being business friendly. A recently released study by Carnegie Mellon rated the city second in the nation for growth potential over the next 10 years.

A Baseball Backgrounder

Brockton is known as the "City of Champions." And at the top of its honor roll of champions are heavyweight champion Rocky Marciano and middleweight champion Marvin Hagler. Coach Armand Columbo led Brockton High's football team to more victories than any other coach in Massachusetts history. The most famous event in Brockton sports was when Rocky Mar-

ciano took Jersey Joe Walcott's best shot—a hard left hook to the chin— and pulled himself off the floor to win the heavyweight championship.

There have been plenty of other champions in many different sports. Boxing? Remember the Petronellis (Goody, Pat, and Tony)? Oakland Raiders owner Al Davis was Brockton born. Greg McMurtry was drafted by the Red Sox and played wide receiver for the Patriots. Fred Frame won the 1932 Indianapolis 500.

Many local champions have worn Brockton High's black and red. The Boxers, both boys and girls, have state championships in baseball, basketball, football, track and field, softball, and a number of other sports. No history of Massachusetts sports can he written without mentioning Brockton and its surrounding communities.

Brockton has an important place in baseball history. In 1874, the first Brockton Agricultural Fair featured a baseball game. Since before the Civil War, local neighborhoods, employers, schools, churches, and clubs all over the city have organized teams to play America's pastime.

The area has an important place in baseball history. One of the greatest catchers in history, Mickey Cochrane, is from Bridgewater. Irish immigrant Bill McGunnigle was one the first professional ballplayers to come from the Shoe City. "Mac" either captained or managed eight championship teams. He skippered the Brooklyn Dodgers to two pennants, including its first National League pennant. Bill McGunnigle is best known as the inventor of the catcher's mitt. Some historians say that McGunnigle invented the mitt to protect his sore hand after enduring innings of abuse as his team's catcher. His hands were so sore that he couldn't bat or catch any more balls.

Years ago, many professional teams called Brockton home and Brockton has played in the New England, Colonial, and Eastern leagues. But Brockton has always been in Red Sox country. For many years, the biggest local event on the sports calendar was the Red Sox' annual game. The games were played at Keith Field off West Elm Street, just a few blocks away from downtown Brockton. The Red Sox played against a team of the area's best amateurs.

Brockton was well represented at Fenway Park's first game. After learning to pitch on local sandlots and playing with Brockton's New England League team, the "Shoemakers," Buck O'Brien was signed by the Red Sox. In 1912 he threw the first pitch in a regular season game at Fenway. He also started two games against the New York Giants in the 1912 World Series.

The city has produced more than its fair share of professional ballplayers. One of Brockton's more famous players is first baseman Steve "Bye-Bye" Balboni who hit tape measure home runs for the Kansas City Royals and New York Yankees. Pitcher Jim Mann is the last Brockton player to play in the majors. The right-hander played for the New York Mets and Houston Astros.

Brockton's greatest baseball enthusiast may have been the great Rocky Marciano. He learned about the game on the city's playgrounds. Before he was a boxer, the "Rock" was a ballplayer. By most accounts, he was an excellent power hitter but as slow as molasses. For hours, Rocky would make his pals pitch to him. Father Minnehan, Rocky's coach at St. Patrick's, would chide Rocky for not letting anyone else have a turn at the plate.

Rocky tried out for Kingsport in the Appalachian League, but didn't make it. One year after his unsuccessful baseball tryout, Rocky decided to give boxing a try. Everything worked out for the best for the Brockton blockbuster. After years without a professional team Rocky's favorite sport returned to Brockton in 2002, thanks to the independent Northern

League, right by where Brockton's baseball history started—next to the Brockton Fairgrounds.

Take Me Out to the Ballgame

Campanelli Stadium's design was inspired by the oldest working ballpark in the United States, Cardines Field in nearby Newport, Rhode Island. Van Schley, the team's owner, and John Curran, the stadium architect, wanted to build a stadium that reflected the community's values. Old-time ballparks may have lacked modern amenities, but provided intimacy.

Before starting the project, the team organized working sessions with various members of the community. The exterior siding boards that overhang over the first level, the colors on the exterior, and balconies outside of the ballpark create a nineteenth-century feel. Cardines Field is considered to be a close cousin to ballparks like Ebbets Field and Fenway Park.

The stadium's place right next to the Brockton Fair is important. If you think about it, the area around the ballpark is quite an area for recreation and sports. There is a football stadium, a swimming pool, a racetrack, and athletic fields nearby. The area is one of the largest, most diverse concentrations of sports complexes in New England. And of course, it has the flair of the fair.

Campanelli Stadium was just the beginning of Brockton's reemergence on the sports scene. The city is just getting started. In 2003, the ribbon was cut on a state-of-the-art conference center, Shaw's Center, a 14,000-square-foot-facility that's flexible enough to suit every need. Businesses can catch a great Rox game right after a business conference. Once a week, the team hosts "Fat Tuesday"—a massive belly-busting buffet right outside of the Shaw's Center.

It's a great way for anybody, even if you don't have much money, to have a good night out. In the summer, the concourse is the city's main meeting place for people from the age of 6 to 60. Because of the new additions, more fans are making a whole day of visiting Brockton. From the grandstand, everyone can see where champions have competed at the Brockton Fair and Brockton High School. The fairgrounds are reminded that sports should be fun. And that fun is good. The franchise's name, the "Rox" is reminiscent of the Red Sox, but is pure Brockton, reflecting the accomplishments and spirit of the city as well as its greatest athlete, Rocky Marciano.

Fans have already seen plenty of unique promotions, surprises, and fun. The Rox bring the Brockton Fair, as well as the tradition of great competition, to baseball fans all summer. Metro South may be Red Sox country, but from this day forward, Brockton rocks.

Best Game (When You Think About It, How Does Someone Decide Which Game Was the Best?)

Bringing professional baseball back to Brockton was both a marathon and a sprint. For decades, the very idea of having a professional team in the city was just a pipe dream. Many years ago,

Tom Mason

The entrance to Campanelli Stadium in Brockton, MA.

Brockton, like many other cities, had its own minor-league baseball team. The Great Depression affected every aspect of our country. Brockton's team went out of business. Minor league baseball boomed after World War II, but soon went bust. The growth of televised baseball sent the minors into a tailspin. Major leagues also limited competition. The National Association of Baseball Leagues, the governing body of American baseball, passed regulations to limit competition.

At one time, many teams were unaffiliated and functioned independently from the majors. Independent teams would generate revenue by buying and selling player contracts. St. Louis general manager Branch Rickey was tired of paying high transfer fees to club owners and decided to cut out the middleman. He created the baseball's farm system and put the independents out of business.

But a couple of innovators didn't forget about the independents. Van Schley purchased a team in Salt Lake City but couldn't find a suitable major league affiliate. He wasn't going to have his team roster held hostage by the whims of a major league team. He decided to strike out on his own. Van Schley shocked the world. His homegrown scouting operation beat the big boys at their own game. His team, the Salt Lake City Trappers, won an all-time record 29 consecutive games. Mike Veeck, too, wanted to be part of professional baseball but was tired of being under the thumb of the majors. As owner of the Miami Miracle in the Florida State League and the St. Paul

Saints of the American Association, Veeck proved that there was still life for independent baseball.

The Brockton Rox are the brainchild of Schley, the team owner, and Veeck. By any measure, opening night was the team's greatest moment. Brockton was considered to be too close to Boston and Pawtucket. The city was too poor to have its own ballpark. It would take too much time to build a new ballpark. And where would new owners find the players to field a competitive team? But the Rox did it—with only a couple of hours to spare.

Just days before the Rox' opening night, May 31, 2002, workers were rushing to put the finishing touches on the new ballpark, Campanelli Field. With less than a week before the first game, the construction crew was finishing the dugout's floors, pouring sidewalks, testing generators, and individually testing each of the 4,750 stadium seats.

The effort paid off. The Rox, led by a former Pawtucket manager, were ready to take the field as planned. Opening night was one of the greatest nights in Brockton history. Mayor John T. Yunits threw out the ballpark's ceremonial first pitch to motion picture superstar and team owner Bill Murray. There was only one thing that could put a damper on the city's great celebration—the rain.

After a two-hour rain delay, the game was called. The Brockton Rox and Elmira Pioneers waited another 24 hours to finally play ball. Despite the inclement weather, the night was good fun. It was the greatest night in Brockton baseball history.

Greatest Team (Not the '27 Yankees, but Who Is?)

Back in the early days of baseball, Brockton had many great teams. Adopted son and local legend Bill McGunnigle managed and led a local franchise to the old New England league championship. But that was more than a century ago. In their first year, just fielding a team was a challenge for the Brockton Rox. After successfully surviving the growing pains of being an expansion independent team, management went all out and made a commitment to win a Northern League championship. Heading into the 2003 season, the Rox were, on paper, a very strong team. The team was very strong up the middle. Finding a good catcher and shortstop is always a challenge, but the Rox had a couple of good ones. Catcher Mel Rosario played for Oakland Athletics and shortstop Saul Bustos was in the Chicago Cub farm system.

The Rox started the season hot, winning 9 of their first 10 games. However, the Rox' pitching fell apart and caused the team to slump. Management was fast on its feet. The roster was completely changed during the season. Hitting safely in 31 of 36 games played, former major leaguer Francisco Matos was added in late July. Perennial independent All-Star Darren Blakely was acquired. Former Pawtucket manager Ed Nottle was able to work wonders to rebuild the pitching staff. Plymouth native Conor Brooks was on the mound when Brockton defeated New Jersey.

Best Player . . . in My Opinion

Brockton's greatest ballplayer really didn't really live there. He grew up in neighboring Bridgewater, and that's close enough. Hall of Fame catcher Mickey Cochrane was one of the greatest athletes to ever grow up in the area. A member of the Bridgewater High School Class of 1920, Cochrane was a star in five different sports at Boston University and is considered to be one of Connie Mack's greatest discoveries. In his first year with the Philadelphia Athletics, Cochrane made an immediate impact. He was fast enough to lead off, hit well enough to bat third, and played outstanding defense. By the late 1920s, Cochrane and the Athletics were ready to win. They were able to finally overtake Babe Ruth and the New York Yankees to win the 1929 World Championship. Many historians believe that the 1929 A's were better than the 1927 Yankees. Nicknamed "Black Mike," the left-hand-hitting catcher had a terrible temper. As player-manager of the Detroit Tigers, Cochrane led the Tigers to the 1934 and 1935 World Championships. Cochrane's career suddenly ended at 34 years old. Like Tony Conigliaro, Cochrane was hit in the head with an errant fastball. He survived, but his playing days were over. He retired with a lifetime batting average of .320, best among all retired major league players.

Former Brooklyn Dodger manager Billy McGunnigle is also a local legend. McGunnigle started on local sandlots, but quickly moved up through the ranks to the majors. He pitched, played outfield, and was a catcher for Buffalo Bisons, Worcester Ruby Legs, and Cleveland Blues. What made McGunnigle's reputation was his intelligence. After his days as a major-league player were over, he was a player-manager for Brockton's New England League champions. While McGunnigle achieved great fame as a player, he received much more acclaim as a manager. He managed Buffalo, Brooklyn, Pittsburgh, and Louisville. He brought two championships to Brooklyn—in 1889 and 1890. During 1891, McGunnigle managed the Providence team in the first organized baseball game ever played in New England, at Rocky Point in Warwick, Rhode Island. But his real claim to fame is being the inventor of the catcher's mitt. Some local sources indicate that McGunnigle once wore a pair of bricklayer's gloves in a game against Harvard in 1875, becoming the first catcher to wear a glove in a baseball game.

As a manager, McGunnigle employed a tin whistle to signal his players. Among those who managed at least one full season, McGunnigle has the best winning percentage in the history of the Dodgers franchise.

Round Tripper (Some Suggestions for Sightseers)

Brockton no longer leads the competition toward world footwear dominance. It has vivid memories of days gone by. At the Brockton

Tom Mason

Players limber up and balloons are set to be released before a Rox game.

Historical Museum, there's a great exhibit about the history of shoes. At the Brockton Museum "The Rise and Fall of the American Shoe Industry" is a walk through the history of American shoemaking. Practically everything you want to know about shoes and were afraid to ask—unless you are Imelda Marcos. You don't even need to bring foot powder. All shoes are fully fumigated. There are Native American moccasins and slave shoes. The celebrity footwear exhibit includes shoes worn by Ted Williams, Arthur Fiedler, and Rocky Marciano. The White House section is highlighted by donations from Mamie Eisenhower, President Ford, and President Clinton. The curator has been beating the bushes for

Paris Hilton's footwear. There are also exhibits devoted to fire fighting, Thomas Edison, and, of course, Rocky Marciano.

Who'd ever think that the pride of Brockton would be a museum? Well, it is. The Fuller Museum is one of the most unique and respected museums in the country. At one time, the museum focused on art, but the board of trustees recently made a momentous decision—to create the finest collection of American crafts in the country. The decision was wise. The burgeoning museum has grown by leaps and bounds. It's a great addition to the area's cultural life.

One of the great things about Brockton is its convenience. It's close to Boston and Providence. Don't forget it's also a short drive away from the Mayflower and all of the attractions in Plymouth. Particularly in the summertime, the city is a great place to start for trips around New England.

Places to Eat ... If You Want More Than Cracker Jack

Like most other cities, you can find practically any kind of food you want in Brockton. If the choices aren't suitable, nearby towns like Stoughton and Easton offer plenty of alternatives. However, for real local cuisine, there are two obvious choices for sampling some real hometown cooking. Both offer tasty filling dishes at moderate prices. No wonder both places have served generations of Brockton diners.

Christo's, at 782 Crescent Street, is the world-famous home of Greek salads. Time after time, the famous restaurant lives up to its acclaim. The menu offers a wide variety of entrees. The fish is usually especially fresh. The service is excellent. Christo and his family take pride in offering delicious, affordable meals.

Another great choice is George's Café at 228 Belmont Street. George's is a tavern offering hardy fare for working men and women. The restaurant specializes in Italian food. The key to Italian dining is the sauce. George's homemade sauce is consistently delicious. Sports lovers appreciate the tavern's décor. There's nowhere else that has such a fine collection of Rocky Marciano and Marvin Hagler pictures. George's is just up the street from Campanelli Field—a great place to go before or after a Rox game. Former Brockton Rox manager Ed Nottle loved to eat at George's and has given it his personal stamp of approval.

Sources:

The Baseball Almanac, 1995–2007.
Boston Globe, 1900–2007.
Brockton Enterprise, 1990–2007.
Glassman-Jaffe, Marcia. *Fun with the Family in Massachusetts: Third Edition.* Guilford,
    Connecticut, The Globe Pequot Press, 2002.

www.all-baseball.com
www.ballparkdigest.com
www.ballparkreviews.com
www.baseballalmanac.com
www.baseballamericaonline.com
www.brockton.ma.us
www.brocktonrox.com
www.canamleague.com
www.nefan.com
www.sabr.org
www.thomasedison.com/brockton.htm

5

Address: Route 28, Chatham Center, MA 02633

Web Site: *www.chathamas.com*

First Game: 1920

Dimensions: LF 340 CF 385 RF 314

Directions: Take Route 6 to Exit 11 (Route 137, Chatham). Turn left at the end of the exit ramp on to Route 137. Follow Route 137 until it intersects with Route 28. Take the left onto Route 28 towards Chatham Center. Follow Route 28 for several miles. Veterans Field is behind the old Chatham Elementary School on the left. The field is to the left of school and up a small hill.

CHATHAM, MA
VETERANS FIELD

Home of the Chatham A's of the Cape Cod Baseball League

Claim to Fame

Shipwrecks, the Chatham Light, and spectacular scenery along the Atlantic shore.

Strange but True

In 1935, a carpenter, a dry-goods importer, two housewives, and a lobsterman made a strange report to local authorities. They claimed to have seen a six-foot long floating metal "orb." After hovering over a local church, the orb drifted out to the sea. Two months later, all five were missing, never to be seen again. Bob Staake, a local writer, recently wrote a book about it. What's most strange is that the "Orb of Chatham" is most likely fact not fiction.

Who's Who in Chatham

Jeff Bagwell, Jason Bay, Eric Byrnes, David DeJesus, Seth Etherton, Brad Halsey, Rich Hill, Mike Lowell, Mike MacDougal and Kevin Mench, Andrew Miller, Greg Norton, Brian Roberts, Scott Schoeneweis, Kyle Snyder,

Mark Sweeney, Scott Williamson, Chris Young, Thurman Munson, Albert Belle, Charlie Hough, and Walt Terrell.

About Chatham

Chatham's history is older than the Plymouth Rock. French Explorer Samuel de Champlain wrote about sailing around present-day Harding's Beach and Stage Harbor in October 1606, 14 years before the pilgrims found their way to the New World. Champlain said: "Along this coast we observed smoke which the Indians were making; and this made us decide to go and visit them. Here there is much cleared land and many little hills, whereon the Indians cultivate corn and other grains on which they live. Here are likewise very fine vines, plenty of nut-trees, oaks, cypresses, and a few pines. This would prove a very good site for laying and constructing the foundations of a state, if the harbour were a little deeper and the entrance safer than it is."

Champlain was prophetic, but he never lived to see his prediction fulfilled. France never settled Cape Cod. The founder of Chatham was an Englishman, William Nickerson. The price he paid for it was a local sachem, a shallop, 10 coats, 6 kettles, 12 axes, 12 hoes, 12 knives, 40 shillings in wampum, a hat and 12 shillings for land that's now Chatham. Nickerson thought he made the deal of a lifetime. However, buying the land wasn't as easy as it looked. There was a catch to the deal. It took 16 years of wrangling in Plymouth County courts for the Nickerson to gain control of the property. The lawyers probably made the most money in this transaction.

Nickerson's first move as Chatham's proprietor was to ask Massachusetts' colonial governor to incorporate the tiny town. However, there weren't enough residents to meet legal requirements. Therefore, Nickerson took matters into his own hands. He and the missus had five sons, three daughters, and many decedents. Eventually, there were enough Nickersons and non-Nickersons to organize a town. The Nickerson Family Genealogical Research Center has a trove of information about the Nickersons as well as the area's first families.

The town is no stranger to war, unfortunately. Peace between the first French explorers and Native Americans lasted just two weeks. Three Frenchmen and many Monomoyick were killed. Champlain quickly decided that discretion was the better part of valor and decided to abandon his plans to settle Chatham.

Chatham men and women have served bravely, and with distinction, in every military engagement. During the Revolutionary War, local militia served at Bunker Hill. Local sailors were crewmembers on American privateers. The town held its ground when a British ship raided Chatham harbor. One man's pirate is another man's privateer. Chatham men returned the favor to the British as some of America's first privateers. In the Civil War, many local boys died at Cold Harbor, Spotsylvania, Petersburg, and at the infamous Andersonville prison. It's only fitting

SportPix photo by Matthew Scott

A view from the third base line at Veterans Field.

that a Chatham villager, 16-year old James Freeman Clark, witnessed the first modern submarine battle, between the *Monitor* and the *Merrimac*.

Even though Chatham may be named after an English seaport, its first cash crop was actually corn. At the time, Chatham's second-busiest enterprise was fending off pesky blackbirds and crows. The birds loved Chatham corn. Residents didn't want someone eating their corn without paying for it. Crows and blackbirds had a bounty on their head. In the early 1700s, selectmen passed an ordinance required all homeowners to do their part to stop the pests. Each resident was required to kill their yearly quota of 12 blackbirds or three crows per year

Selectmen wouldn't just accept the word of residents about the birds' demise. They demanded proof. Each resident had to personally deliver dead bird heads

to local leaders or be fined six shillings. By 1800, Chatham had more fisherman than farmers. Stage Harbor was a major Eastern seaport. The shipping route around the Cape was one of the world's busiest. Many Chatham boys dreamed about buying their own fishing boat. A good catch was a priority. Otherwise, everyone in town would be stuck eating corn meal mush, a typical local breakfast. Strong Atlantic currents off the coast can be dangerous. The salvage industry was also a big business. In the dead of the night, "mooncussers" would walk along the beach searching for bits and pieces of old wrecks. When he was president, Thomas Jefferson appointed Samuel Nye to serve as keeper of the town's two wooden lighthouses. Today, the Chatham Light is one of the town's most famous landmarks and, incidentally, a great place to surf.

The town's main trade is now tourism. The expansion of railroad changed Chatham forever. Wealthy families purchased summer homes. Entrepreneurs started motels, restaurants, souvenir shops, and other businesses. Chatham is a small town of approximately 10,000, but in the summer, that number swells to 40,000.

A Baseball Backgrounder

Chatham is one the Cape's first franchises. The A's trace their lineage all the way back to 1923, when they played in a four-team Cape Cod Baseball League. Three of the four—Barnstable, Sandwich, and Osterville—are now gone. Chatham is the last team standing. And it's still going strong, just as it's been for more than eight decades.

Almost right from the start, Chatham has been a league powerhouse. The original team, the Townies, was one of the Cape's first baseball dynasties. During the 1930s, Chatham won seven consecutive championships. League historians consider 1963 to be the beginning of the league's modern era. The 1960s were Chatham's second great era. The Chatham Red Sox, wearing old major league uniforms.

Times change, and so did the franchise's name. In the 1970s, Chatham became the A's. The organizers weren't nearly as flamboyant as Oakland owner Charley Finley or outfielder Reggie Jackson. The idea of orange baseballs and designated pinch-runners was out of the question. Gold and green are now the official team colors.

A's manager Ed Lyons once held the record for most wins, 331, by any manager in Cape League history. Under current manager John Schiffner, Chatham has won three championships, in 1992, 1996, and 1998. With 27 post-season appearances in the last 47 years, the A's always seem to be in contention.

Chatham is very nostalgic about its past. A couple of years ago, the team had its first old-timers game. More than 30 of the A's greatest players came home to celebrate their days on the Cape. It gave the fans an opportunity to reminisce about the team's great accomplishments. In 1963, Ken Voges hit an incredible .505 all-time best batting average. Pitcher Steve Duda threw a no-hitter and led the team to the Cape League championship. Jon Palmieri was an All-Star first baseman for the 1998 championship team.

Of course, many of the A's greatest players had a good reason for not attending. The great reunion happened during the professional baseball season, and many alumni were understandably busy. The team's home, Veterans Field, is considered to be a pitcher's ballpark. Yet some of baseball's greatest hitters have played here. In 1967, Hall of Famer Thurman Munson hit .420. Former Houston Astros star first baseman Glenn Davis set the team record for runs and runs batted in. Former Cleveland Indians outfield Albert Belle is remembered for more than his temper. Belle's 12 home runs set the team's all-time record. Red Sox star Mike Lowell is an alumnus. Future Hall of Famer Jeff Bagwell played two seasons for Chatham.

For many years, John Schiffner has skippered the A's. As the league's active leader in wins, Schiffner has a reputation for being a "player's manager." In 2005, eight Chatham players were named to the Cape League All-Star Team. In 2006, two alumni were among the top six players drafted by Major League Baseball. Tampa Bay picked Long Beach Evan Longoria from Long Beach State. Detroit drafted North Carolina left-hander Andrew Miller from North Carolina. The San Diego Padres selected six Chatham A's in the 2003 draft. With all of the big name talent, it must be challenging to keep talented players focused. Throughout the years, Schiffner has effectively kept his players' heads in the game.

Take Me Out to the Ballgame

The home of the Chatham A's is widely considered to be one of the Cape's best ballparks. What's not to like about Veterans Field?

Located just off of Route 28, Veterans Field is just a short walk or drive from downtown Chatham. It's easy for tourists to grab a bite, do some shopping, and catch a great evening of baseball. The bowl-shaped field is a jewel. Impeccably groomed, there's seating in the old-fashioned clapboard stands that run from first to third base. The grassy berms in center and right field are perfect for beach blankets. The tree-lined outfield landscape includes a couple of Cape Cod–style buildings. The sunsets behind left center field can be spectacular. There's a playground along the right-field foul line.

The playing field itself has some unusual dimensions. Right-handed pull hitters have a slight disadvantage. It's

a long shot down the 340- field line. Jeff Bagwell only hit .2 his first year at Chatham. Hitters wh learn to go the opposite way have been extremely successful. Paradoxically, the A's best major-league players have been right-handed hitters. Since right field is a more manageable 320 feet, team management likes left-handed hitters. Rivals, Harwich and Orleans, are wise to load up on lefty pitching.

Summer nights in Chatham can be cool. So it's usually a good idea to bring along a sweatshirt. The most unique aspect of the park is the fog. The damp air can drive hitters to distraction, turning sure home runs into fly balls. Several years ago, Chatham had its first few games of the year fogged out. Generally, the thick-as-pea-soup atmosphere works to Chatham's advantage. But not always. In 2005, one of Chatham's greatest teams was on its way to another championship before the fog enveloped Veterans Field. The deciding playoff game against Orleans was suspended. When the teams resumed play, all of the A's momentum was lost. Orleans came back with a vengeance. The fog giveth and the fog taketh away.

Best Game (When You Think About It, How Does Someone Decide Which Game Was the Best?)

In 1984, the Chatham A's played the United States Olympic baseball team to a standstill. What makes it amazing is that the Olympians were, maybe, the greatest amateur team ever assembled. They were practically "Who's Who" of our nation's greatest young ballplay-

Photo courtesy of the Chatham A's

Checking out the action from behind home plate at Veterans Field in Chatham.

ers. Coached by legendary Southern California coach Ron Dedeaux, 17 Olympic players on the 20-man roster were first-round major-league draft picks. The U.S. National Team had not one, not two, but three potential Hall of Famers—Mark McGwire, Barry Larkin, and Will Clark. Former Brewers player B.J. Surhoff, ex-Indian Cory Snyder, former Twin outfielder Shane Mack, former Red Sox catcher John Marzano, and Tony Gwynn's Dodger brother Chris played in the field. The pitching staff featured Canton's Bobby Witt, University of Maine's Bobby Swift, and southpaw Scott Bankhead.

Chatham was on the verge of an upset, holding onto a tenuous one run lead into bottom of the ninth. But Team USA rallied. Texas Ranger Oddibe McDowell had a walkoff game-winning RBI, a ground-rule double to right. The Olympians eventually won the silver medal at the Los Angeles games.

Greatest Team (Not the '27 Yankees, but Who Is?)

The best players don't necessarily make the best teams. The 2005 team had eight All-Stars; the Cape's best pitcher, Andrew Miller; the best pro prospect, Evan Longoria; and the best reliever, Derrick Lutz. Yet it couldn't win a championship. The 1992 championship team had very few big names. But it had plenty of grit and pitching. The leader of the staff was Pepperdine graduate Steve Duda, who also led his team into the College World Series. For two years, Duda baffled Cape Cod hitters. In 1991, he threw a no hitter against the Yarmouth-Dennis Red Sox. In 1992, he had 6-1 record with a 0.90 ERA. The righty finished his final season with a flourish. As the playoff's Most Valuable Player, he won both of his starts to lead his team to the Cape Cod Baseball League championship. A bunting, base-stealing scrappy bunch, the 1992 team proved that you don't always need big names to win. Duda never made it in the majors but was recently inducted into the league's Hall of Fame.

The 1998 team should also be mentioned. It was one of the best balanced teams in Cape League history. The staff was led by right-handed Red Sox pitcher Kyle Snyder, who was the first player picked in the major draft. Reliever Mike MacDougal and second baseman Brian Roberts have both been major league All-Stars. Longtime Texas Rangers player Kevin Mench has had a great professional career.

Best Player . . . in My Opinion

Thurman Munson, the great Yankees catcher, is one of the Cape's unforgettable players. Many historians believe the Cape Cod League's modern era began in 1963—when the league was primarily for collegiate ballplayers. Munson was maybe the Cape's first great player. In many ways, today's players follow Thurman Munson's path. A great college player, he wanted to further develop his skills and catch the eye of major-league scouts. He was sensational. Leading the league with a .420 batting average, Munson was the heart of Chatham's 1967 team, which won the championship. One summer after the Cape, he was the first round pick of the New York Yankees. Two years later, Munson was the Yankees' starting catcher. The Thurman Munson Award is given to the Cape's batting champion.

Round Tripper (Some Suggestions for Sightseers)

One of Cape Cod's best beaches is just minutes away from downtown Chatham. Lighthouse Beach on Shoreline Road is an alluring but unpredictable natural beauty. There are no snack bars or bathrooms, and parking is very limited. While most of Chatham has warm water, the Caribbean gulf stream doesn't pass by here. This is the town's only cold-water beach. The bluff overlooking the shore offers a breathtaking view of chilly Atlantic waters. It's ideal for sunbathing and long walks. Surfers love the waves and the wind. So do the seals. But swimmers need to watch out for the strong undertow.

Chatham isn't just known for its shipwrecks. The great Chatham Light has safely guided thousands of ships past the Cape's rocky coastline. Seeing the light itself is spectacular, particularly at night. On a clear day, the light has an amazing 70-mile range. Getting a chance to go inside the building to see how a lighthouse operates is a rare treat. The Chatham Light is a working Coast Guard station; volunteers of the US Coast Guard auxiliary occasionally give guided tours of the facility.

Generations of tourists have visited the Chatham Railroad Museum, at a Victorian-style former train depot. The railroad officially discontinued its service in 1937, but the town never forgot its history. The museum has been chugging along since 1960. Chatham's center is a bustling and busy commercial area. There are many small quirky shops within a concentrated area. Weekly concerts by various bands are a traditional favorite.

Places to Eat . . . If You Want More Than Cracker Jack

There are more than 20 different eateries in Chatham. Chatham is one of the first places discovered by European explorers yet one of the last places that's still untouched by fast-food chains. The last McDonald's and Burger King on the Cape are miles away from Chatham's town center.

One of the area's best known restaurants is the Chatham Bar's Inn, located just a stone's throw away from Lighthouse Beach. One of the Cape's first resorts, the main building is an architectural masterpiece—a grand hotel with a sweeping staircase, a wood paneled library, and a large veranda that has a spectacular view of the Atlantic Ocean. There are many good reasons why the Cape's annual winter baseball meeting is held at the Chatham Bar's Inn. If having an extended stay at the hotel is a budget breaker, why not visit for breakfast? The daily breakfast buffet isn't too pricey.

For lovers of fried fish, a good bet is the Kreme 'N Kone on Route 28, which serves very fresh fish, lots of variety, and superior onion rings. It's a good place to stop after a day at the beach. There are many different restaurants within walking distance of the town center. The Wayside Inn, Red Nun Bar & Grill, the Captain's House Inn, and Queen Anne Inn offer fine dining in eighteenth- and nineteenth-century settings. When walking around town, don't get trampled by the New Yorkers. Many New Yorkers love to spend their summer vacations in Chatham.

Sources:

The Baseball Almanac, 1995–2007.
Boston Globe, 1900–2007.
Cape Cod Times, 1990–2007.
Chatham A's Program, 2007.
Glassman-Jaffe, Marcia. Fun with the Family in Massachusetts: Third Edition. Guilford, Connecticut: The Globe Pequot Press, 2002.
Price, Christopher. Baseball by the Beach—A History of America's National Pastime on Cape Cod. Yarmouthport, Massachusetts: On Cape Publications, 1998.

www.all-baseball.com
www.ballparkdigest.com
www.ballparkreviews.com
www.baseballalmanac.com
www.baseballamericaonline.com
www.bootsnall.com/travelstories/na/dec03chat.shtml
www.capecodbaseball.org
www.capecodcommission.org/pathways/trailguide.htm#orleans
www.chathambarsinn.com
www.cranberryinn.com/attractions.ccml
www.sabr.org

Address: 10 Lowell Road, Cotuit, MA 02635

Web Site: *www.kettleers.org*

First Game: 1947

Dimensions: LF 320 CF 399 RF 320

Directions: Take US Route 6 to Exit 2 and follow Route 130 South. Follow it to the end, and take a left on Route 28. Take an immediate right at the sign toward Cotuit Center, and follow Main Street for 1.2 miles. Turn left onto Lowell Avenue. The ballpark is on the left.

COTUIT, MA

ELIZABETH LOWELL PARK

Home of the Cotuit Kettleers of the Cape Cod Baseball League

Claim to Fame

Cotuit Skiffs, standardized 14-foot racing sailboats, have plied the waters of Cotuit Bay since the early twentieth century. Also known as Cotuit Mosquitos, the boats are based on the flat-bottomed skiffs used in the 1800s for oyster and clam harvesting. With a centerboard, a large gaff-rigged mainsail, and no jib, the small boats are considered challenging to control without capsizing.

Strange but True

Kurt Vonnegut, who penned the acclaimed *Slaughterhouse Five* in 1968, moved to the neighboring village of West Barnstable in 1951. It was there that he wrote and published his first novels, *Player Piano* and *The Sirens of Titan*, in 1952 and 1959 respectively. Vonnegut's 1968 book *Welcome to the Monkey House* makes frequent mention of his adopted hometown.

In between books, Vonnegut worked a variety of jobs and even opened the nation's second Saab auto dealership,

Friendly faces and inviting aromas greet visitors to Lowell Park in Cotuit.

Saab Cape Cod, on Route 6A. But sales of the Swedish cars never took off and the business flopped. In 2005 Vonnegut published *A Man Without a Country*, in which he wrote, "I believe my failure as a dealer so long ago explains what would otherwise remain a deep mystery: why the Swedes have never given me a Nobel Prize for literature."

Who's Who in Cotuit

Jermaine Allensworth, Garrett Atkins, Jeff Austin, Howie Bearse, Mark Bellhorn, Darren Bragg, Eric Bruntlett, Mike Buddie, Nate Bump, Cal Burlingame, Bobby Butkus, Will Clark, Doug Creek, Jack Cressend, Ron Darling, Scott Erickson, John Franco, Joe Girardi, George Greer, Aaron Harang, Jeff Kent, Bernie Kilroy, Braden Looper, Mike Matheny, Jack McCarthy, David McCarty, Dallas McPherson, Arnold Mycock, Tim Naehring, Josh Paul, Jim Perkins, Kyle Peterson, Robb Quinlan, Omar Quintanilla, Jeff Reardon, Bill Richardson, Kirk Saarloos, Tim Salmon, Ed Sprague Jr., Terry Steinbach, Tim Teufel, Eric Valent, Greg Vaughn, Chris Widger, and Dan Wilson.

About Cotuit

One of eight villages that make up the Town of Barnstable, Cotuit is situated at its southwest corner. The village covers only about 6.5 square miles and is bordered by the Town of Mashpee to the west, the villages of Marstons Mills and Osterville to the north and east, and Vineyard Sound to the south. About 5,000 people make their year-round homes in Cotuit.

The village, which took its name from a Wampanoag word meaning "place of council," was established by members of the Crocker family in the mid-1700s. The protective shelter of Cotuit and Popponessett bays eventually gave rise to busy harbors and docks, and Cotuit became home to prosperous merchants and sea captains. Schooners carrying supplies to Martha's Vineyard and Nantucket often staged in Cotuit.

In the late nineteenth and early twentieth centuries, Cotuit became a popular spot for educators and administrators at Harvard University, many of whom built second homes there. At one point, residents reputedly considered renaming the village "Little Harvard." Large waterfront estates, built along Main Street and Ocean View Drive, have been passed down through families and have remained largely unchanged over the generations.

Shellfishing became an important commercial venture for the village in the 1850s. Demand exploded for oysters plucked from Cotuit's shallow, fertile beds, which were shipped to hotels and restaurants across the nation.

The oyster trade has seen a series of setbacks over the past seven decades. The military had a major presence on Cape Cod during World War II, and Cotuit was no exception. The U.S. Army established a training ground just above the narrows in North Bay, where landing craft trained for the D-Day invasion against German forces at Normandy, France. The activity stirred the fragile bottom, churned silt and sediments, and devastated shellfish grounds.

A hurricane bashed the coast in 1944, which further disrupted beds for oysters and other shellfish. More recently, development has seen nitrogen-rich septic runoff feed algae blooms, which deplete oxygen, inhibit eelgrass growth, and rob oysters and shellfish of their habitat.

Towns, including Barnstable, have become more attentive to the plight and measures to abate the pollution of coastal waters are ongoing. Private firms, such as the 150-year-old Cotuit Oyster Company, are finding renewed success raising shellfish in offshore upwellers.

Cotuit retains its quiet character, and has spurned development along Route 28, the busy road between Falmouth and Hyannis that bisects the village. It is served by a fire station, small public library, fire station, general store, post office, bait and tackle shop, an ice cream parlor, antique shops, and a few restaurants. You'll find no subdivisions or strip malls in Cotuit, and the only traffic jams of note take place following Kettleers home games.

A Baseball Backgrounder

Accounts of baseball in Cotuit date back as early as 1883, when the *Barnstable Patriot* published an account of a game against neighboring Osterville, won 25-7 by Cotuit. Over the following decades, the game was played on meadows and lots around town, including Crocker's Field off Old King's Road, which eventually became a golf course.

During World War II, when the Cape League ceased operations, Cotuit fielded a team in the Barnstable Recreation Commission Twilight League. The village officially became host to a Cape League franchise in 1947.

The franchise's name stems from a local legend that closely resembles the reputed origins of Hyannis. Pilgrim settler Myles Standish allegedly purchased land from Cotocheset, a Native American sachem. Cotuit and nearby Osterville were later established on the land. The price? A brass kettle and a garden hoe.

Among the early Cotuit players was Barnstable football legend Howie Bearse, who manned center field from the team's inception until 1952. He played his first four seasons while still a student at Barnstable High School, and his brother, Eddie, also played for the Kettleers. Howie, who batted left, had a knack for setting the table as speedy leadoff hitter, and showed outstanding range in the field. He later signed a pro contract with the Milwaukee Braves, and spent a year in their minor league system.

On opening day, May 15, 1949, slugger Jim Perkins achieved a feat that garnered national acclaim in *Ripley's Believe It Or Not*. Perkins crushed two home runs in the same inning and knocked in 11 runs total as the Kettleers defeated Sandwich 21-6. In another standout performance, he went 7-for-8 with two home runs, including a grand slam, in a 31-9 clubbing of Hyannis. On the season, Perkins hit .432 with 12 homers.

Cotuit would soon benefit from the misfortune of neighboring franchises. When Sandwich folded after the 1949 season, most of the remaining half-dozen players joined the Cotuit squad. History repeated in 1954 when Mashpee's team ceased operations, and many of its stars, such as pitcher Donald Hicks, began playing for the tiny village team.

General Manager Arnold Mycock oversaw the additions of college stars and locally grown talent in the 1950s and 1960s. They included pitcher/outfielder Cal Burlingame, a Cotuit native, and Holy Cross catcher Jack McCarthy, who hit .318 and made the All-Star team in 1964. Soon the Kettleers were the dominant franchise in the Cape Cod Baseball League (CCBL), with four straight championships from 1961 to 1964 under manager Jim Hubbard.

Cotuit finished no higher than third place the rest of the decade. In 1968, a fresh-faced Tufts University hurler named Bill Richardson pitched as a reliever for the Kettleers, striking out 20 in 17 1/3 innings with a 1.04 ERA. Richardson went on to a career in politics, serving as energy secretary in President Bill Clinton's administration. He became governor of New Mexico in 2003, and launched his own presidential candidacy in January 2007.

McCarthy, the former catcher, succeeded Hubbard as manager in 1970. His tenure heralded another period of Kettleers dominance as they won five championships in six years from 1972 to 1977. Those teams featured several future major leaguers including pitcher Joe Beckwith, catcher Sal Butera, and closer Jeff Reardon, who was inducted with the CCBL's first Hall of Fame class in 2000. Boston College third baseman Paul O'Neill won the league's Most Valuable Player award for the champion Kettleers in 1975.

The 1980s brought another string of success for Cotuit. Under manager

George Greer, the team won championships in 1981, 1984, and 1985 and lost in the title round in 1983 and 1986. Right-handers Ron Darling and Jeff Innis, first basemen Terry Steinbach, Will Clark and Greg Vaughn, and center fielder Greg Lotzar all excelled for the Kettleers. All but Lotzar made the major leagues, but Lotzar later joined Steinbach and Clark, who hit .367 for the Kettleers in 1983, as inductees to the Cape League Hall of Fame.

Two more titles came to Cotuit in 1995 and 1999 under manager Mike Coutts. The 1996 team featured eventual big-league catcher Josh Paul, also a CCBL Hall of Famer. The 1999 club included third baseman Garrett Atkins, pitcher Kirk Saarloos, and catcher Dane Sardinha, all of whom made the majors.

Since 2004 the Kettleers have been managed by Mike Roberts, who coached 22 years at the University of North Carolina. He is also the father of Orioles second baseman Brian Roberts, a former Cape Leaguer himself.

Take Me Out to the Ballgame

Elizabeth Lowell Park is named for the wife of former Harvard University President Abbott Lawrence Lowell. The couple, among the first Harvard affiliates to summer regularly in Cotuit, donated land to the town for a new high school in 1906. The school, which stood on the parcel until 1926, was built about 200 yards west of the third baseline.

When the Kettleers joined the Cape League, the land where they hosted home games was a field only in the sense that it had been cleared. The terrain was irregular and unkempt, and in 1952 it underwent a major overhaul. The playing surface was brought to level grade, and grass was planted in the infield. Dugouts, bleachers, and an outfield fence were added. The scraggy, sandy field was transformed into a ballpark.

The layout and aesthetics of the park have remained largely unchanged over the past 55 years, but modern accoutrements such as rest rooms, a sprinkler system, a press box, and an electronic scoreboard are among the improvements made.

Lowell Park is a true treasure of the game that oozes history and tradition. Here fans come to enjoy baseball in its purest and most intimate form. Aside from the parking lot behind home plate, the field is entirely surrounded by thick, lush woods, insulating the park from the noisy intrusions of emergency sirens and passing traffic (which are rare in Cotuit to begin with).

The landscaping at Lowell Park is immaculate, and the field is groomed to perfection. The structures surrounding the diamond are either faced in red brick or painted a fresh coat of rich hunter green. Even the chain link fences are coated with dark green vinyl.

Behind home plate, a walkway with numerous engraved bricks pays homage to people past and present. The display represents one of the more creative fundraising efforts in the Cape League. Depending on size and location, engraved bricks can be purchased for $175 to $345. Some are used to advertise businesses, while a few even honor departed pets.

The snack bar, the Kettleer Kitchen, has been run since 2005 by Joe and John Contalessa, who own The Original Gourmet Brunch on Main Street in Hyannis. Fans can sample their renowned New England clam chowder and hearty chili, as well as hot dogs, sausages, pizza, nachos, and doughy pretzels.

At the souvenir stand, myriad items from beach balls to Frisbees to license plate frames can be had. Hats, jerseys, jackets, t-shirts, and sweatshirts are also available in the Kettleers' maroon and white colors.

There are simply no bad spots to watch a game at Lowell Park. Cotuit's dugout is on the third-base side, and the team's bullpen is in an enclosed area beyond the left-field fence. Large sets of bleachers flank both baselines, and chairs and blankets are often spread out toward right and left field.

The area immediately behind the backstop is usually roped off except for pro scouts, but on days where there's space available it's a fantastic vantage point.

There are no lights at Lowell Park, and it's doubtful such an idea would ever gain support from the community, especially those who live close to the field. It's a good thing, because the simple flavor of the park would be lost.

Since all home games start at 5 P.M., fans are well-advised to head for the park as early as possible—not only to get a prime parking spot, but to avoid the rush-hour traffic congestion on Routes 28 and 130, and for the opportunity to soak up the ambience while taking in batting practice.

Like other CCBL venues, parking can be a problem. Once the lot behind home plate fills up, drivers jockey for spots along Vineyard Road, Main Street, and Peppercorn Lane.

Cape League games are free of charge, though a donation of $2 per person at each game is encouraged.

Best Game (When You Think About It, How Does Someone Decide Which Game Was the Best?)

There have been many magical moments at Lowell Park over the past six decades, and the success of the Kettleers might suggest that their "Best Game" might come from one of their fabled championship runs. But on June 29, 2003, with Cotuit on its way to a 20-21-2 record, the Kettleers staged the unlikeliest of comebacks. The Brewster Whitecaps tattooed Cotuit starter Taylor Cobb for seven runs in two-thirds of an inning. Cotuit got one back in the second, but the Whitecaps answered back in the bottom half to make it 8-1.

Joe Little, who had relieved Cobb, was masterful as he held Brewster scoreless for 7 2/3 innings. The Kettleer batters hung tough and finally got to Whitecaps starter Ricky Bauer, striking for five runs in the fourth inning. In the last of the sixth, Cotuit took advantage of a throwing error by Bauer and added a towering two-run homer by Jeff Baisley to take a 9-8 lead.

After tacking on an insurance run in the seventh, Cotuit looked to seal the 10-8 win in the top of the ninth. A walk and a single put

Brewster runners on first and second with one out, when Ben Crabtree laced a double to right. Cotuit right fielder Jeff Fiorentino tracked it down but bobbled it briefly before uncorking a cannon shot toward home plate. One run had scored easily and the tying runner was chugging around third. As Ryan Patterson slid, catcher Clint Sammons blocked the plate and applied the tag as the umpire gave an emphatic "out" sign on a close play.

The Brewster dugout erupted in protest and stormed the field, but the verdict was in. The remaining Kettleer faithful, who didn't leave when hope seemed lost, went home with smiles.

Cotuit's team logo on the grass behind home plate.

SportPix photo by Matthew Scott

Greatest Team (Not the '27 Yankees, but Who Is?)

The 1964 Kettleers won the last of Cotuit's four straight league titles while compiling a 31-3 mark. The team was led by pitcher/outfielder Ken Huebner, the league's Most Valuable Player; Bowdoin College lefty Bob Butkus, a five-time CCBL All-Star who posted a perfect 9-0 mark and went 32-8 over his career; and Boston College hurler Bernie Kilroy, who also went undefeated on the mound at 8-0.

The club reeled off 18 straight wins at one point. They also played 17 games against teams outside the league, going 15-2. Seven players from the 1964 Cotuit squad went on to play professionally.

Best Player ... in My Opinion

In 1982 Terry Steinbach had a season for the ages, hitting .431 while leading the league in hits (75), total bases (129), and RBIs (54). All those are still team records, along with the 18 doubles he collected. They will likely remain unbroken, as the league's 1985 decision to use wood bats exclusively has substantially deflated offensive numbers. Steinbach went on to enjoy a 14-year major league career as a catcher, including a World Series ring with the 1989 Oakland A's.

Round Tripper (Some Suggestions for Sightseers)

Since 1992, Tom and Christine Bednark have been crafting custom-made wooden baseball bats in a barn behind their home. The Barnstable Bat Company began supplying bats to Cape League players, and many of them stayed on as loyal customers after they reached the majors.

Their illustrious list of clients includes Chase Utley, Darin Erstad, Nomar Garciaparra, Jason Varitek, Jeff Bagwell, Albert Belle, Frank Thomas, and Chuck Knoblauch. The company's showroom is on Pleasant Pines Avenue in Barnstable, less than a mile south of Route 6 and just off Route 132. There are more than 500 regulation bats on display, along with a selection of decorative mini-bats, and personalized embossing is done on-site. Tom and Chrtistine are more than happy to show visitors around their factory, where computer-guided lathes turn maple, ash, and birch stock into works of art.

The Historical Society of Cotuit & Santuit maintains a trio of museums on Main Street, including the Samuel B. Dottridge Homestead, the William Morse Fire Museum, and the Historical Society Museum.

Loop Beach and Rope Beach in Cotuit are beautiful spots, but parking nearby is reserved for residents only. Biking is always an option. In neighboring Mashpee, South Cape Beach State Park is a popular spot on Great Oak Road. It's part of the Waquoit Bay National Estuarine Research Reserve, which has hiking trails and an informative visitor's center on Route 28 in Waquoit, a village of Falmouth, about 3.5 miles southwest of the Mashpee Rotary.

If you've got kids in tow, head to the Cape Cod Children's Museum in Mashpee, which has a vast array of interactive displays and apparatus to keep children occupied both physically and mentally. It sure beats video games and DVDs. You'll find it on Great Neck Road South, about two miles south of the Mashpee rotary.

The Cotuit Oyster Company on Little River Road raises shellfish in stacked underwater cages, or upwellers, spread out over 34 acres off the village shoreline. Learn how oysters grow to marketable proportions from about the size of a grain of sand.

The Cotuit Center for the Arts on Route 28 features an exhibition gallery, and also hosts performing arts events. The Cahoon Museum of American Art, also on Route 28, is where the late Ralph and Martha Cahoon lived and worked. They maintained a studio and gallery in the 1775 Georgian Colonial, which has been restored. Several noted works by Ralph Cahoon focused on the Kettleers.

Golfers may want to try out one

of the two courses at The Country Club at New Seabury. The Dunes course was recently lengthened and redesigned to challenging standards by Marvin Armstrong. The Ocean Course, designed by William Mitchell in 1962, is one of the most picturesque links venues anywhere in the country. Sweeping views of both Nantucket and Vineyard sounds have led golfers to proclaim the layout as "The Pebble Beach of the East."

At the Mashpee Rotary sits the 90-store Mashpee Commons, an attempt to create a village-style shopping complex. It falls short of the scale for ambience, and includes ho-hum national chains such as The Gap, Banana Republic, and Pottery Barn. There are, however, some shops that offer a genuine local flavor such as Kensington's, Rosie Cheeks II, Cape Cod Toys, Ghelfi's Candies, and the independent Market Street Bookshop.

Places to Eat . . . If You Want More Than Cracker Jack

There aren't many food options in Cotuit, but for a first-rate dining experience Regatta of Cotuit on Route 28 is hard to beat. Chef Heather Allen melds traditional and esoteric selections with flare and fashion, such as the Seared Filet of North Dakota Buffalo Tenderloin.

For something more laid-back, the locals hang out at the Kettle-Ho Tavern on School Street. Afterward, cool off with a cone from Chad's Ice Cream on Route 28.

At New Seabury, The Raw Bar on Shore Drive serves what it claims is the largest lobster roll in New England. While that contention is up for debate, there's no doubt that you'll get a heaping helping of sweet, juicy lobster chunks unspoiled by excessive mayo. Also on site are the upscale Popponessett Inn and Bob's Seafood Café & Wine Bar.

In Osterville, there are some great eating spots on Main Street. Wimpy's is the most notable, with generous portions, reasonable prices, and incredible seafood bisque. They also run a seafood market on site, so you're eating fresh. Other choices include Sweet Tomato's Pizza, Five Bays Bistro, and La Petite Maison. Grab a cup of java at Breaking Grounds, or venture to nearby Wianno Avenue for some ice cream at Osterville Sundae News.

In Mashpee, seek out The Flume on Lake Avenue off Route 130. It's right on Mashpee-Wakeby pond, which is a nice spot for an after-dinner stroll. At Mashpee Commons you'll find Bleu and Siena, which offer terrific menus but so-so service during busy summer evenings. Bobby Byrne's Pub is a nice spot to savor a poured pint.

There aren't many sports bars on Cape Cod, but Dino's on Route 151 in Mashpee will satisfy that video fix. With plenty of TVs, the burgers and personal pizzas are hot and fresh. Just north of the rotary on Great Neck Road North is the Ninety-Nine, always a reliable spot. Persey's Place (Route 28) and The Picnic Box (right on the rotary) offer quick breakfasts on the

Sources:

Crowley, Dan. *Baseball on Cape Cod*. Mount Pleasant, South Carolina: Arcadia Publishing, 2004.

Price, Christopher. *Baseball by the Beach—A History of America's National Pastime on Cape Cod*. Yarmouthport, Massachusetts: On Cape Publications, 1998.

Vonnegut, Kurt. *A Man Without a Country*. New York: Seven Stories Press, 2005.

www.barnstablebat.com
www.barnstablepatriot.com
www.capecodbaseball.org
www.capecodonline.com
www.insidecapecod.com
www.kettleers.org
www.town.barnstable.ma.us

Address: 780 Main Street, Falmouth, MA 02540

Web Site: *www.falcommodores.org*

First Game: 1952

Dimensions: LF 320 CF 385 RF 320

Directions: From points north, take Route 28 South, continue through Falmouth Center along Main Street. Guv Fuller Field is on the left behind the Falmouth Police station and Gus Canty Recreation Center. From Hyannis and points east, take Route 28 west toward Falmouth. After passing Falmouth Plaza on the left, Guv Fuller Field will be on the right.

FALMOUTH, MA
ARNIE ALLEN DIAMOND AT GUV FULLER FIELD

Home of the Falmouth Commodores of the Cape Cod Baseball League

Claim to Fame

In 1859 Katharine Lee Bates was born in a small colonial home just west of the village green on Falmouth's Main Street. In 1893, while teaching English at Colorado College, she took a trip to Pike's Peak. That visit inspired her to write a poem that would later become the song "America the Beautiful."

Strange but True

On July 19, 1939, the Falmouth club played Barnstable in the Cape Cod Baseball League's first regular season night game. Playing under rented lights not much taller than the nearby roof-tops, the poor visibility caused many fielders to lose sight of batted balls.

Who's Who in Falmouth

David Aardsma, Steve Balboni, Sid Bream, Daniel Carte, Jacoby Ellsbury, Darin Erstad, Mike Flanagan, Tony Fossas, Khalil Greene, Adam Kennedy, Mike Kinkade, Javier A. Lopez, Mark Loretta, Val Majewski, Tino Martinez, Jim Mecir, Eric Milton, Luke

SportPix photo by Mike Tureski

Commodores players doff their caps for the pre-game playing of the National Anthem.

Scott, Brett Sinkbeil, Scott Strickland, Kevin Tapani, Mike Trombley, Jeff Weaver, Turk Wendell, Kris Wilson, and Scott Winchester.

About Falmouth

Settled in 1660, Falmouth, like many Cape Cod towns, has a lineage enriched by the sea. Fishing, whaling, shipbuilding, and salt works were the primary trades that led to the economic growth of the town. Bordered on the west by Buzzards Bay and to the south by Vineyard Sound, Falmouth has more miles of coastline (68) than any other town in the state. The population of about 33,000 year-round residents swells to around 60,000 in summer. It is also the primary embarkation point for visitors to the island of Martha's Vineyard.

Since the mid-1800s, the village of Woods Hole, at the confluence of Buzzards Bay and Vineyard Sound, has been the nation's leading center for ocean research. The Woods Hole Oceanographic Institution, Marine Biological Laboratory, National Marine Fisheries Service, and U.S. Geological Survey employ more than 1,300 people year-round, while about 2,500 students and visiting researchers spend summers there.

Falmouth also has a deep farming tradition. For the better part of the twentieth century, the town's strawberry crop was revered by hoteliers and restaurateurs in Boston. In the early 1900s, Falmouth was the leading strawberry-producing community east of the Mississippi River. Cranberries also remain a key crop, with about 43 acres of town-owned bogs still in production.

Military history has long been woven into the town's fabric. British warships pummeled waterfront buildings with cannon fire during the war of 1812. During World War II, U.S. sailors and marines preparing for amphibious invasions, such as the attack on German forces at Normandy, drilled for those beach assaults at Washburn Island in Waquoit Bay.

The town is culturally diverse for its size. Many Portuguese and Cape Verdeans settled in Falmouth over the past two centuries, drawn by the sea's bountiful harvests. Today, a steady influx of Brazilian newcomers, along with summer workers from Jamaica, Ireland, and Eastern Europe, continue to enrich the town's ethnic character.

With 818 acres of freshwater ponds and about 2,200 acres of saltwater bays and harbors, recreational opportunities in Falmouth's waters are abundant for boaters, swimmers, boardsurfers, and fishermen alike. There are also nearly 5,000 acres of protected conservation land with walking, hiking, and biking trails scattered throughout the town. The popular six-mile Shining Sea Bikeway, which runs between Woods Hole and Falmouth Center, is slated to undergo a seven-mile extension to North Falmouth by summer of 2008.

A Baseball Backgrounder

Baseball's history in Falmouth co-incides with the development of the sport in other parts of New England. The Cape Cod Baseball League has officially held the line that it formed in 1885, though some historians dispute that date. Regardless, the popularity of baseball took hold on the sandy peninsula.

In the early 1900s, the more prominent and popular games were played at Falmouth Heights Ball Park, which may have provided the most scenic coastal setting in the history of the sport. From the first baseline, one could walk less than 100 yards across Grand Avenue to dip their toes in the light surf of Vineyard Sound. Observ-ers often sat right in front of their cars, which were parked facing left field, or would congregate on a hillside to the west of the third baseline, which provided a great view of the action and of the vast expanse of beaches and blue water in the distance.

The old Falmouth Heights field still exists, and is the site of youth league games as well as softball contests. Its more prominent role in sports these days is as the terminus of one of the most famous 10-kilometer running events in the world, the Falmouth Road Race.

By 1920, the Cape's town-based baseball teams were taking on semi-pro teams from other southeastern Massachusetts towns such as Bridgewater, Brockton, Middleboro, New Bedford, Taunton, and Weymouth. Some hotels in Falmouth and on the Cape, hoping to offer an interesting amenity to attract guests, also sponsored teams.

Each fall, the Barnstable County Agricultural Society sponsored a tournament involving teams from on and off the Cape. The event drew huge crowds, but the excessive travel costs of bringing some teams to the tournament eventually prompted organizers to limit participation to Cape teams only. Falmouth's team won the inaugural Cape-only tournament in 1921.

Some baseball historians, pointing to a July 9, 1923, article in the *Hyannis Patriot*, trumpet June 27 of that year as the true birth date of the Cape Cod Baseball League. The article announced the formation of "a brand new base league" with college and prep school ballplayers comprising teams from Falmouth, Hyannis, Osterville, and Chatham.

Harry Albro, a town resident and the league's secretary, organized the Falmouth squad. Falmouth dominated the 1923 regular season, but lost in the semifinals at the county fair. In 1925, Danny MacFayden of North Truro, perhaps the best baseball player born on Cape Cod, pitched for Falmouth, coming within one out of a no-hitter against Hyannis. Two years later he made his major league debut with the Boston Red Sox. In 1929, Falmouth played the Boston Braves in an exhibition contest, losing by just one run, 8-7.

Falmouth dominated league play for a decade, winning championships in 1929, 1931, 1932, 1935, 1938, and 1939. Following the 1939 season, the Falmouth team, which was funded in part through the town budget, dropped out of the league when the town failed to vote more funding. The Town of Bourne soon followed suit. As America was drawn into World War II, the league suspended operations.

Falmouth's team returned to the league in the early 1950s, playing at the town field on Main Street shared by the Lawrence High School football team. Attendance at Cape League games remained lackluster throughout that decade, however. A realignment of the league in 1962 ushered in a new era, which saw 10 teams separated into Upper Cape and Lower Cape divisions. Falmouth native John DeMello was named deputy commissioner of the league in 1963, with oversight of the Upper Cape division.

The Commodores, managed by the effervescent Bill Livesey, finished

atop their division in 1970 and 1971, winning the league championship in the latter season. They won another division title in 1975, but lost in the title game.

Since then the Commodores have won just two division crowns, in 1994 and 2004. Following the 2006 season, general manager Chuck Sturtevant announced his retirement after 20 years with the team. He will be replaced by his son-in-law Dan Dunn, who has been assistant general manager the past several years.

Take Me Out to the Ballgame

Guv Fuller Field is at the center of many town recreational activities, serving as home turf for Falmouth High School's football and track and field teams. But the park is at its best when baseball is played. It was named for longtime Lawrence High School football coach Elmer "Guv" Fuller in 1952 after he retired as the school's athletic director. Mr. Fuller remained active in sports all his life, playing tennis until the months preceding his death in 1981 at age 93.

The diamond itself was named for another longtime Falmouth sports figure. Arnie Allen, a special needs child with a learning disability, became a batboy for the team in 1957. He remained with the Commodores for the next 46 years, and was named equipment manager by Sturtevant in 1987.

After he was diagnosed with esophageal cancer in 2002, Arnie continued to don his uniform and attend games the following summer, despite being weakened by treatments and medi-

SportPix photo by Shannon Taylor

Homer, the Commodores' mascot, coaxes grins and giggles from children at Guv Fuller Field.

His framed jersey is on display inside the field house in the neighboring Gus Canty Community Center.

One visit to Falmouth is all it takes to see what Arnie loved. The field attracts more than 1,000 people a game on average, many of whom fill the large bleacher seats behind the Commodores' first-base dugout. Others spread blankets and set up lawn chairs on the adjacent hillside. A smaller set of bleachers is behind the visitors' dugout.

A fan-friendly experience is a given in Falmouth, especially for families. Cape League games are ideal for gaining an appreciation of the game. Youngsters will often scramble into nearby woods in search of foul balls, which Commodores players are always happy to sign.

Homer, the team's baseball-headed mascot, entertains children and even does his trademark dance atop the Falmouth dugout. He also gathers kids on the field between innings, leading them in a rendition of "Take Me Out to the Ball Game."

Music fills the air between innings, and as Commodore hitters stroll to the plate to the beat of their personal theme songs.

Behind home plate, a small two-story building houses a concession stand as well as the press box. Ron Braga, a fixture in Falmouth sports, mans the grills cooking up juicy burgers, hot dogs, and spicy Italian sausages. Just up the hill next to the bleachers is Stewart's Sports Shack, a

cations. He was honored that winter at the Cape Cod Baseball League's (CCBL) Hall of Fame dinner, receiving a standing ovation and glowing words of praise from noted baseball writer Peter Gammons. Former Commodores Darin Erstad and Adam Kennedy, playing that fall with the World Champion Anaheim Angels, sent along autographed memorabilia for Arnie.

Following his death in October 2003, the Commodores retired number 30, which he had always worn, and dedicated the diamond, along with a new electronic scoreboard, in his honor. The teary-eyed ceremony was held on June 18, 2004—opening night.

souvenir stand where caps, shirts, and other Commodores and CCBL items are available.

In the narrow space between the backstop and the concession stand, major league scouts take positions with notepads and Juggs guns at the ready. Their vantage point is about 20 feet away from home plate. If you want to see what a 95-MPH fastball looks like to hitters, it's the perfect spot.

Guv Fuller Field is one of six Cape League venues with lights, allowing home games to start at 7 P.M. The Commodores, with a grant from the Yawkey Foundation and funding from the Community Preservation Act voted by the town, hope to install eight new energy-efficient light towers around Arnie Allen Diamond in 2007.

Cape League games are free of charge, though a donation of $2 per person at each game is encouraged. That's a bargain price to catch the country's top collegiate players and future major league stars playing in a humble environment.

Best Game (When You Think About It, How Does Someone Decide Which Game Was the Best?)

Some fans cite as greatest game the fifth and deciding contest of the 1971 CCBL championship series against the Orleans Cardinals. Orleans pitcher Tom White, who had shut out Falmouth in game one, had again registered six scoreless innings. His opponent, Tom Lukas of the Commodores, had done the same. In the

bottom of the seventh inning, Dave Creighton walked and stole second base. He was singled home by Ray O'Brien and narrowly beat the tag at the plate. It was the third 1-0 final score of the series, and it still stands as the Commodores' most recent league championship.

But the greatest game played in Falmouth regardless of outcome has to be the 2004 championship loss to Yarmouth-Dennis. Needing a win to stay alive in the series, the Commodores had taken a 4-2 lead in the fourth inning on solo home runs by first baseman Mark Hamilton and shortstop Chris Lewis. The Red Sox tied it up in the top of the ninth after the first three batters walked and Frank Curreri swatted a seeing-eye single up the middle to plate a pair.

Falmouth appeared poised to win it in the last of the 10th as they loaded the bases with two outs, but a diving catch by Y-D right fielder Jim Rapaport of Danny Perales' blooper ended the Commodores rally. The Red Sox then scored four in the top of the 11th to put the game out of reach and clinch the league title.

Greatest Team (Not the '27 Yankees, but Who Is?)

The 2004 team was loaded with CCBL Player of the Year Daniel Carte (.308, 11 HR, 38 RBI), infielder Cliff Pennington (.289, 20 RBI, 21 SB) and third baseman Matt Antonelli (.280) all earning all-league honors. Other studs included first baseman Mark Hamilton (.254, 7 HR, 29 RBI) and defensive standout Jacoby Ellsbury in center field. The pitching staff was anchored by Dalls Buck (4-1, 0.77 ERA) and Jensen Lewis (4-0, 1.73 ERA), who combined for 118 strikeouts and just 35 walks in 110 innings.

Best Player . . . in My Opinion

The best player ever to wear a Falmouth uniform was arguably Pie Traynor, who later became a Hall of Fame third baseman with the Pittsburgh Pirates. Traynor played shortstop and batted cleanup for the Falmouth town team in 1919.

Among former Commodores, the nod must go to pitcher Mike Flanagan, a member of the first class inducted into the CCBL Hall of Fame in 2000. Flanagan pitched for Falmouth in the summer of 1972, going 7-1 with a 2.18 ERA. He also played 28 games in the outfield, batting .286 with seven home runs. Flanagan went on to play 18 years with the Baltimore Orioles and Toronto Blue Jays. He won the 1979 American League Cy Young award, going 23-9 with 190 strikeouts and a 3.08 ERA.

Round Tripper (Some Suggestions for Sightseers)

Come for the baseball, stay for the beaches. Facing west on Buzzards Bay, Chapoquoit and Woodneck beaches offer 70-degree water temperatures in the heat of the summer. Woodneck has a gently flowing tidal lagoon that's ideal for small children. Bristol, Surf Drive, Menauhant, and Falmouth Heights are four south-facing public beaches on Vineyard Sound, where the

winds are more robust, the surf a bit rougher, and the waters a little chillier.

For a great short hike, The Knob is a must-see. Donated for conservation by the late Cornelia Carey, this tiny spit juts into Buzzards Bay just north of picturesque Quissett Harbor. A series of trails join up at an isthmus, and a set of granite stairs leads visitors to a bluff with panoramic views.

Many of the historic buildings around Falmouth's village green are open to visitors, including Museums on the Green and the birthplace of Katharine Lee Bates. In the steeple of the First Congregational Church hangs a bell cast by Paul Revere.

Nobska Light is the crown jewel of Falmouth's coastal roads. Now automated by the U.S. Coast Guard, the 40-foot lighthouse was erected atop a rocky bluff in 1828 and rebuilt in 1876.

Bring your kids to the Woods Hole Science Aquarium, where they can handle horseshoe crabs, snails, and other sea creatures in a touch tank. An outdoor pool houses a pair of harbor seals, which are fed by aquarium staff daily at 11 A.M. and 4 P.M.

The start of the CCBL season in mid-June coincides with peak strawberry harvests in Falmouth. Head to Tony Andrews Farm on Andrews Road to pick a pint of the sweetest berries you'll ever taste.

Other local historical and environmental treasures include Ashumet Holly and Wildlife Sanctuary, Beebe Woods, Bourne Farm, Coonamessett Farm, Highfield Hall, Peterson Farm, Spohr Gardens, and Waquoit Bay National Estuarine Research Reserve.

Places to Eat . . . If You Want More Than Cracker Jack

Falmouth has a walkable village center, with many great dining spots along Main Street. They include Liam Maguire's Irish Pub, The Quarterdeck, Firefly Woodfire Grill, and Café Villagio. While a bit pricy, Roo Bar might be the best restaurant in town, combining a hip ambience with outstanding menu selections. All of these are close to the village green and the Falmouth Public Library. Other upscale spots include the Coonamessett Inn and the Flying Bridge, the latter of which overlooks Falmouth Inner Harbor.

On East Main Street, great New England grub can be found at Betsy's Diner. Across the road is Peking Palace, offering Asian cuisine. Friendly's, Ninety-Nine, D'Angelo's Sandwich Shop, Box Lunch, Mary Ellen's Portuguese Bakery, and Dairy Queen are all just a short walk from the ball field.

If it's pizza you want, Steve's Pizzeria and More offers a great variety of grinders and Greek-style pies. Other fine spots include Pi Pizza Bistro, Paul's Seafood and Pizza, and Papa Gino's. For a fried seafood fix, Paul's, McMenenamy's, and The Clam Shack turn out tender, juicy clams and scallops.

Away from the town center, you'll find the British Beer Company in Falmouth Heights. It's right next to that venerable old field where baseball really developed in Falmouth a century ago. One of the newest dining spots, Casino FX, opened in January 2007 across from the old field.

The Nimrod restaurant, on Dillingham Avenue, is housed in a building that took the brunt of cannon fire during the War of 1812. It was moved from the shore to its present site, and features live jazz in the evenings to accompany the superb menu from owner Jim Murray. Crabapple's, on Palmer Avenue just north of the town center, serves the best breakfasts in town.

In Woods Hole, belly up to the bar for a drink at the Captain Kidd, which also offers fine outdoor dining overlooking the placid waters of Eel Pond. The Landfall is another classic spot in the village, with large picture windows providing views of the Steamship Authority docks in Great Harbor. Fishmonger's and Shucker's are other good seafood joints, and great takeout sandwiches can be had at Woods Hole Market.

Ay! Caramba serves authentic Mexican fare at the Falmouth Mall. Further off the beaten path, great dining can be found at Chapoquoit Grill in West Falmouth, Silver Lounge in North Falmouth, and Emporio Brazilian Cuisine in East Falmouth.

To relax with a cup of java, there's no better place than Coffee Obsession, with locations in Woods Hole and on Palmer Avenue in Falmouth. Both offer free wireless Internet access for customers, so bring your laptop and catch up on box scores. Pie in the Sky in Woods Hole offers tasty baked goods, sandwiches, and homemade soups.

Sources:

Falmouth Enterprise newsprint archives (*www.capenews.net*).
Price, Christopher. *Baseball by the Beach—A History of America's National Pastime on Cape Cod*. Yarmouthport, Massachusetts: On Cape Publications, 1998.

www.capecodbaseball.org
www.falcommodores.org
www.town.falmouth.ma.us

8

Address: 105 Oak Street, Harwich, MA 02645

Web Site: *www.harwichmariners.org*

First Game: 1969

Dimensions: LF 330 CF 395 RF 330

Directions: Take Route 6 East to Exit 10 (Route 124). Make a right at the end of the ramp. Take your first left at the flashing light (Queen Anne Road). After 0.3 miles, make a right onto Oak Street. Follow Oak Street for 0.8 mile, and make a left turn just before Harwich High School. Look for the Harwich Mariners Sign at the parking lot's entrance. Whitehouse Field is on the left at the back of the parking lot.

HARWICH, MA

WHITEHOUSE FIELD

Home of the Harwich Mariners of the Cape Cod Baseball League

Claim to Fame

The first commercially produced cranberries were grown in Harwich. Some of the first cranberry bogs, beside Pleasant Lake and Hinckley Pond, are still being harvested.

Strange but True

Residents of Harwich were once called Hairleggers. Historians speculate the name emerged because the town's baseball team didn't wear socks. Boston has the Red Sox, and Harwich had the Hairleggers. No wonder the team was renamed the "Mariners."

Who's Who in Harwich

Jason Bartlett, Dewon Brazelton, Scott Downs, Craig Hansen, Kevin Jarvis, Mitch Maier, Shaun Marcum, Adam Melhuse, Kevin Millar, John Nelson, Carlos Pena, Joe Saunders, Kelly Shoppach, Matt Smith, Adam Stern, Joe Magrane, Scott Kameniecki, Cory Snyder, Craig Hanson, and Pat Pacillo.

About Harwich

Harwich is more than a town. It's a loosely configured confederation of seven tiny villages: Harwich Center, East Harwich, West Harwich, South Harwich, North Harwich, Pleasant Lake, and Harwich Port.

Originally, present-day Brewster was the eighth village. The reasons behind the breakup, which occurred in the early nineteenth century, are still a matter of debate. Whether Brewster left on its own volition or was drummed out of town by Harwich is still an open question. Without a doubt, the divorce is permanent, though now quite amicable.

One of the town's first families was the Broadbrooks. This may have been a good name for the town, considering the area's plentiful water. However, the Broadbrooks family didn't like their own name. As a matter of fact, they were so unhappy with their name that they went to Beacon Hill to ask the legislature to pass a special act to shorten their family name to Brooks. It passed. Whoever said the legislature wasn't spending its time on important public business? The Brooks name lives on. The Mariners used to play ball at the Brooks School. And the Brooks Academy is now home of the Harwich Historical Society.

What makes Harwich unique is the personality of each village. When you ride through town, the differences among the villages are readily apparent. Harwich Center is the hub of Harwich's commercial life. Harwich Port links the community to the sea. Several freshwater ponds are located in the Pleasant Lake section. Along Route 39 and Chatham Road, which wind through town, there are many fine examples of popular American architecture. Greek Revival, Italianate, Federalist, Colonial, and Neo-Colonial are all represented. Just identifying the various building styles can challenge an expert.

There's something fishy about Harwich. The town was famous for its plentiful daily catch of cod, the fish that made the Cape famous. At one time, more than half of the town's workforce earned their living from the Atlantic Ocean. Unfortunately, the Grand Banks and Nantucket Sound have now been overfished. Also, large boats and whalers that harvested the ocean outgrew the town's harbors. Leisure boats and yachts now populate Saquatucket Harbor, Wychmere Harbor, and Allen's Harbor.

The Cape's first retirees supplemented their income by planting cranberries in Harwich. Other residents quickly recognized that there's cash in the cranberry business. According to a local history, everybody jumped on the bandwagon. The worst land in town was perfect for cultivating berries. Practically everyone in town had some use for the seemingly useless swampland. No more swampland was sold to unsuspecting tourists. Old sea salts became gentlemen farmers. For more than 150 years, Harwich has been bogged down in berries. Every September, the town celebrates its history with a weeklong Cranberry Harvest Festival.

Harwich is known for its sandy beaches and warm water. There are a

The singing of the pre-game National Anthem at Whitehouse Field.

number of small public beaches along Nantucket Sound. The Gulf Stream in the Atlantic runs right by town, warming the waters for swimming into mid-autumn. From Saquatucket Harbor, there are ferries, seal watches, and cruises. Tourism is now the engine that drives the local economy.

A Baseball Backgrounder

Harwich may be small, but its baseball history is big. Baseball's popularity spread through our nation's ports and railroads. Historians can measure the sport's growth in places like Harwich. Baseball has been played here since the Civil War.

The Mariners, the latest incarnation of the local team, have been playing organized ball since 1930. Harwich was never as rich as some neighboring communities. And, as a small town, it's sometimes been difficult to keep up with the Joneses of the league, like Orleans and Chatham. The team has

had only two championship seasons. Yet, year after year, the team proves that success isn't necessarily measured by number of championships.

The team has traditionally given cold-weather players a chance. Natick High's coach, John Carroll, managed a group of mostly Massachusetts players to finish the 1968 season as runner-up. The latest management team is home-grown and has strong links with Boston College. General Manager John Reid runs Boston College's baseball operations. Manager Steve Englert has been its hitting instructor and catching coach. General assistant coach Pat Mason was the Eagles' assistant baseball coach and recruiting coordinator.

Some of the Mariners' best players have come from the northeast. Former Cincinnati Red Pat Pacillo, a recent inductee into the Cape League Hall of Fame, and star pitcher Dan Merklinger played for Seton Hall. Former Cleveland Indian star pitcher Charles Nagy was a Connecticut Husky. For-

SportPix photo by Matthew Scott

The Harwich Mariners lineup is set as the team takes BP.

mer Red Sox outfielder Adam Stern is Canadian. Red Sox reliever Craig Hansen attended St. John's University.

Recently the team had quite a run of pitchers. In 2003, six of the Cape's top thirty prospects, led by Hansen, pitched for the Mariners. Two of the NCAA's greatest pitchers wore Harwich blue. The league's 2002 top prospect, Jeff Niemann, followed up his 17-0 season at Rice University by pitching 19 shutout innings during the summer. Left-hander Joe Saunders has a promising future as a starter for the Los Angeles Angels of Anaheim. For two years in a row, the Mariners were practically unbeatable with a ninth inning lead. Washington Husky Tim Lincecum, drafted 10th overall by the San Francisco Giants, was Hansen's successor as stopper. Fans who watch the College Baseball World Series got

a sneak peak of Harwich's 2006 team. Josh Horton and Matt Spencer, from NCAA runner-up North Carolina, were the heart of the offense.

A source of local pride is the late Fred Ebbett, the league's former commissioner. Nicknamed "Mr. Harwich," he's credited with keeping Cape League bats aluminum-free.

Take Me Out to the Ballgame

In 1969, during the era of cookie-cutter venues like Cincinnati's Riverfront Stadium and Philly's Veteran Stadium, the first ball was thrown at Whitehouse Field. The dimensions of its outfield are uniform. Right field and left field have exactly the same dimensions. That's about only thing that's "so seventies" about Whitehouse Field.

Located next to Harwich High, the ballpark is cut out of Cape Cod pines. This is great if you don't have allergies, but the site can be trouble for sneezers and wheezers. When you go to games, leave your allergies behind. Or at least load up on decongestants and other medication.

Whitehouse Field may be the most underrated ballpark in the Cape League. Harwich has the best of what the Cape League offers. Just a short distance from the Mid-Cape Highway, the ballpark is convenient and easy to find. Parking is plentiful. If you don't bring a blanket, there are generally good bleacher seats available along the first and third baselines. Even thought it was built many years before the Americans for Disability Act, the path to the ballpark is flat and handicap accessible. The park boasts one of the largest scoreboards in New England, named after former baseball commissioner Fay Vincent.

Unlike many of its counterparts, there are no playgrounds next to the stadium. From beginning of the game to the end, Whitehouse is all about baseball. All games are played at night. Most games start at 7:00 P.M. If your family arrives shortly after supper, there's a call for all kids. Kids and their parents gather around the Mariners third-base dugout and right before first pitch, an intern matches each kid with a player. Boys and girls accompany each starting player onto the field for introductions. The Harwich Athletic Association sometimes allows those who donate the game balls to throw out the first pitch. The balls go for about $50 a dozen. A pretty good

price for having the thrill of a lifetime. Touches like this create lifelong baseball fans.

There's generally a large contingent of scouts who sit behind home plate. But the best seat in the house is the Al Graeber Press Box, named after the team's longtime announcer who passed away at the age of 90. Volunteers, led by Peg Kelly, serve delicious food while following each pitch in the downstairs concession stand. Not counting all of the sponsors, there are more than 365 members of Harwich's Home Run Club.

In 1995, Whitehouse Field hosted the World Junior Baseball Tournament. It's also been a venue for many regional NCAA baseball tournaments. Two of the Harwich's biggest fans were Carl Yastrzemski, whose son Mike played for the Mariners, and former U.S. Speaker of the House Tip O'Neill.

Best Game (When You Think About It, How Does Someone Decide Which Game Was the Best?)

Harwich native Cody Crowell has pitched a number of the greatest games ever seen on the Cape. A four-year starter at Harwich High, Crowell led his team to three consecutive regional playoff finals. He started his senior year by pitching a complete-game two hitter while striking out 18. He struck out 12 Sandwich batters in a row. One of Crowell's best performances was his last high school game on Memorial Day of 2003. He shut-out Norton High 1-0, striking out a record 24 batters. He started the game by striking out the side in the first three innings and finished with a flourish. In the seventh, eighth, and ninth, Crowell whiffed the last nine batters he faced. One of the greatest pitchers in Cape high school history, the left-hander with a funky delivery made an immediate impression at Vanderbilt University. He's one of the few local players in the Cape's modern era to spend summers playing for the hometown team. He has had excellent years for the Brewster Whitecaps and the Harwich Mariners.

Greatest Team (Not the '27 Yankees, but Who Is?)

There are two clear choices, 1983 and 1987. Pat Pacillo, an outfielder with the 1983 and 1984 Mariners, was drafted in the first round by the Cincinnati Reds, hit 18 home runs, and helped lead the 1983 team to a long-awaited championship. Pacillo and future All-Star Cory Snyder may have formed the best hitting combination in league history. They were the Ruth and Gehrig of the Cape.

But the 1987 team might have been just a smidgen better. It had power, pitching, and defense. Future Kansas City Royal Bob Hamelin was the power behind the team. Future Red Sox catcher John Flaherty supplied the defense. But the real key to its on-field success was pitching. Charles Nagy was the ace of the staff. The league was very strong. The Harwich staff baffled great hitters like Robin Ventura and Albert Belle on its way to its second championship.

Best Player . . . in My Opinion

Cory Snyder rewrote the Cape Cod Baseball League's record book. He had 50 RBIs, 47 runs scored (third all-time), and a .764 slugging average. But what really stands out are his home runs. Snyder set the league record by slugging 22 homers. The second-best home run total in league history is 16. The most impressive power display was when Snyder hit four homers in consecutive at-bats. Snyder also twice hit three homers in a game. It will be many years before his feats will be matched. Snyder capped off his storybook season by leading Harwich to its first league championship.

Craig Hansen also deserves an honorable mention. It's easy to understand why the Red Sox broke the bank to sign him. The reliever couldn't have pitched better on the Cape as his ERA was zero. He struck out 42 batters in just 22 innings and set the league record for saves.

Round Tripper (Some Suggestions for Sightseers)

The villages of Harwich reflect old-time Cape Cod. The beaches along Nantucket Sound are sandy. Since the water is warm, summertime fun starts early and ends late. Swimming season generally stretches into September. With 17 ocean and 7 freshwater beaches, the town has one of the largest per capita beach ratios on the Cape.

Excursion boats and sport fisherman set sail from the town's five boat ramps. There are seal watches, and tours of both nature and history. There are opportunities to rake in some clams and quahogs on Pleasant Bay. If you don't know how to catch it yourself, there are many restaurants that serve fresh seafood.

Biking along the 22-mile Cape Cod Rail Trail is a fine way to enjoy the summer, even when it's too cool for swimming. Getting off on the right foot by purchasing the right bike can be an expensive. But after the initial cost, it's a pretty inexpensive, healthy hobby. The trail starts at Headwaters Drive and there's free parking at the Old Powder House near Harwich Center. The Harwich Junior Theatre is a great take for families and kids. Harwich Junior Theater is located on Division Street in West Harwich.

Places to Eat ... If You Want More Than Cracker Jack

Harwich offers a lot more than ballpark food. Local restaurants offer a diverse menu but, of course, seafood is the specialty. With eateries named Castaways, Weatherdeck, Cape Sea Grille, and The Port, what would anyone expect? One of the best-known restaurants is Seafood Sam's in Harwich Port. For dessert, there are not one, but two Sundae School Ice Cream shops in town. You can find anything you want to eat near the town's main drag, Route 28.

Sources:

The Baseball Almanac, 1995–2007.
Boston Globe, 1900–2007.
Cape Cod Times, 1990–2007.
Chatham A's Program, 2007.
Harwich Mariners Yearbook, 2007.
Glassman-Jaffe, Marcia. *Fun with the Family in Massachusetts: Third Edition*. Guilford, Connecticut: The Globe Pequot Press, 2002.
Price, Christopher. *Baseball by the Beach—A History of America's National Pastime on Cape Cod*. Yarmouthport, Massachusetts: On Cape Publications, 1998.

www.all-baseball.com
www.ballparkdigest.com
www.ballparkreviews.com
www.baseballalmanac.com
www.baseballamericaonline.com
www.capecodbaseball.org
www.capelinks.com.cape-cod/main/entry/town-of-harwich-ma-overview/%20/%20more
www.gatemen.org
www.harwichcc.com/
www.harwichhistoricalsociety.org/history.htm
www.harwichmariners.com
www.hjtcapecod.org/
http://mychatham.com/harwichhistory.html

9

MCKEON PARK

Address: High School Road, Hyannis, MA 02601

Web Site: *www.hyannismets.org*

First Game: 1935

Dimensions: LF 330 CF 400 RF 325

Directions: Take US Route 6 to Exit 6 and follow Route 132 South. Go straight through a set of lights, and then bear right at the second intersection onto Bearses Way. Go straight through a set of lights and continue about a half-mile. Bear left at the fork onto High School Road (Kennedy Skating Rink will be on your right). Continue straight through two sets of lights and a stop sign. The field is on the left side of the school building.

Home of the Hyannis Mets of the Cape Cod Baseball League

Claim to Fame

Hyannis was and still is the playground of the Kennedy clan. Jack, Bobby, Ted, and later John John sailed its waters, walked barefoot on the beach and lawn, and took in the good life from the family's compound in Hyannisport. Many cite the attention garnered by the Cape during John Kennedy's presidency as the main reason for its rapid growth in both popularity and population.

Strange but True

Beat Generation writer Jack Kerouac, author of *On The Road*, *The Dharma Burns*, and *Big Sur*, called Hyannis home in 1966. In November of that year, he married his third wife, Stella Sampas, at his house on Bristol Street. Months later the Kerouacs moved back to his hometown of Lowell, Massachusetts. After a life spent struggling with alcoholism, he died in Florida two years later at age 47. His Hyannis home sold in April 2006 for $300,000, but the new owners initially had no idea who Kerouac was.

It's an extra-innings victory for the hometown Mets at McKeon Park in Hyannis.

Who's Who in Hyannis

Rich Aurilia, Albert Belle, Kris Benson, Casey Blake, Brian Buchanon, Pat Burrell, Jeromy Burnitz, Eric Byrnes, Randy Choate, Josh Fogg, Ross Gload, Ryan Garko, Brendan Harris, Eric Hinske, Pat Hope, Ross Jones, Jason Lane, Doug Mirabelli, Matt Morris, Ron Perry Jr., Scott Proctor, J.J. Putz, Buck Showalter, John Valentin, Jason Varitek, Robin Ventura, Joe Vitiello, and John Wasdin.

About Hyannis

Hyannis is one of eight villages in the Town of Barnstable. (Cotuit, to the west, also hosts a Cape League team.) Barnstable is the Cape's largest town in population (49,000 year-round residents) and area (60 square miles), and serves as the government seat of Barnstable County. To its north lies Cape Cod Bay, while the waters of Vineyard Sound are to the south. Settled in 1639, the Cape's second-oldest town is also the economic center of Cape Cod.

Though Barnstable was founded as a farming community, the sea has always been an important resource for the town. In 1666, Nicholas Davis, one of the first settlers, built a warehouse on Lewis Bay where he pickled oysters in brine.

Hyannis has its roots in a transaction so fabled that it rivals the Red Sox' sale of Babe Ruth to the Yankees. In the early seventeenth century, Iyanno, a sachem of the Wampanoag Cummaquid tribe, is alleged to have traded colonists several square miles of land for 20 English pounds and two pair of pants. Iyanno had earlier befriended the Pilgrim settlers, helping them find a lost boy and aiding them in their search for water. The village took its name from the great native leader, and a bronze statue stands in his honor at the Village Green on Main Street.

Fishing and whaling became important industries for the town as Portuguese immigrants settled in large numbers during the 1800s. A salt works was built before 1840, which became a busy enterprise. The arrival of the railroad in the 1850s brought a wave of commercial growth, which continued after the Civil War. The shipping trade also grew briskly and by the turn of the century more than 800 sea captains called Barnstable their home port.

The trains also brought visitors and vacationers to the Cape, many seeking respite along its placid shores. In 1872 the Hyannis Land Company purchased more than 1,000 acres between Lewis Bay and Craigville Beach, which included most of present-day Hyannisport. So began the region's role as a tourist destination for the rich and famous. It was Ulysses S. Grant in 1874, long before John F. Kennedy, who was the first U.S. president known to have spent a summer in Hyannis.

The Kennedy compound had relatively modest origins. Joseph P. and Rose Kennedy purchased the Malcolm Cottage and its private beach in 1925 after previously renting it during a vacation. They later expanded the cottage to a 23-room home, including nine bathrooms and a private movie theater in the basement, providing ample room for their nine children and extended family.

Construction on Barnstable Municipal Airport began in 1928. During World War II, its runways were lengthened as the U.S. Army Air Corps used them as a jump-off point for anti-submarine patrols in the Atlantic Ocean. Today the bulk of traffic comes from small, private aircraft, but direct commercial flights connect the Cape with Boston, Providence, and New York, as well as the nearby islands of Martha's Vineyard and Nantucket. The airport is still owned by the town, and is scheduled to undergo a $45 million terminal expansion beginning in 2007.

John Kennedy's presidency brought a wave of development to Barnstable and Hyannis, though its smaller villages were spared rapid growth and retained their character. During the next 20 years, retail development on the outskirts boomed and led to the completion of the 50-store Cape Cod Mall in 1970, which has since nearly doubled in size.

Hyannis' quaint downtown shopping district suffered as customers flocked to the large, accommodating parking lots and enclosed storefronts that kept them cool and protected from the elements.

Today the downtown is making a slow but steady comeback. New shops, boutiques, restaurants, and cafes continue to pop up, and meandering pedestrians are a more common sight. Its proximity to the busy waterfront, where ferries, tour boats, and pleasure craft churn the waters, is a plus.

A Baseball Backgrounder

Baseball's origins in Barnstable date to the mid-1800s. One of the earliest written accounts of a game appeared in the *Barnstable Patriot* after the Cummaquids of Barnstable defeated the Mastetuketts of West Barnstable on November 7, 1865—nearly seven months to the day after the Confederacy's surrender brought the Civil War to a close.

Teams came and went, but baseball steadily gained popularity on the Cape over the remainder of the century. In 1883 a team from Barnstable Village beat Middleboro, 24-8, to win the regional championship of Southeastern Massachusetts.

In the 1920s, after the Barnstable County Agricultural Society decided to limit its annual baseball tournament to teams from the Cape, rivalries developed between towns. Barnstable, however, fielded teams from Hyannis, Osterville, and Barnstable Village, heightening competition between them for both talent and attendance. Osterville won the Cape title in 1922.

The following year, Arthur "Dutch" Ayer of Osterville and William J. Lovell of Hyannis joined with counterparts from Falmouth and Chatham to form a new baseball league comprising college and prep-school players, according to the *Hyannis Patriot*. With that, the Cape Cod Baseball League was born.

Hyannis, playing at Hallett's Field on Main Street, remained a member of the league until 1930, winning the 1927 championship and sharing the 1926 crown with Osterville. The team had difficulty generating public support, however. With Osterville enjoying terrific crowds, Hyannis dropped out of the league after just eight seasons.

Fast-forward to the 1970s. The Cape League had lost the Bourne Canalmen, which left just seven teams. To fill the void, Hyannis was granted a franchise for the 1976 season. Team organizers chose to name the squad the Mets in a failed effort to obtain financial assistance from the New York Mets.

The team played its first three seasons at Barnstable High School on West Main Street. Among the members of the inaugural team was league Most Valuable Player Nat "Buck" Showalter, who played error-free ball in the outfield. He won the batting crown while scoring 35 runs and knocking in 20. His .434 average remains the third-highest in the Cape Cod Baseball League's (CCBL) history. Showalter went on to manage the New York Yankees and Arizona Diamondbacks before joining ESPN as a baseball analyst.

Bob Schaefer took the helm as manager of the Mets for the 1978 season and led the team to a pair of CCBL titles his first and only two years. The success led Schaefer to join the Yankees, where he began a stellar career as a minor league manager and executive.

Though the Mets have yet to win another championship since, a number of outstanding players have honed their skills in Hyannis. Major league All-Stars Robin Ventura and Albert Belle were teammates in 1987, with Ventura posting a .370 average, second best in the league. He knocked in a CCBL-best 37 runs in 40 games while scoring 40 runs and hitting 6 homers, third highest in the league. That same year pitcher Pat Hope won 11 games while striking out 96.

In an unusual occurrence, future Red Sox All-Star catcher Jason Varitek played non-consecutive seasons for the Mets, sandwiching the 1991 and 1993 summers around a stint with Team USA in 1992. Varitek hit .263 in his first go-around in the Cape League, but returned to take the CCBL by storm.

In his second season, Jason won both the Most Valuable Player and Thurman Munson Award by hitting a league-high .371 with a .514 on-base percentage.

Varitek's backup in Boston, Doug Mirabelli, also played for Hyannis.

Take Me Out to the Ballgame

Coming off a league title in 1978, the Mets moved to their new home, McKeon Park, in time for the 1979 season. In proper fashion, they christened the field with a win and went on to repeat as champions. The field, next to the old Barnstable High School, had been the site of other baseball action since the 1930s. The building now houses Pope John Paul II High School.

The Mets, with support from the Hyannis Athletic Association, spent two years refurbishing the downtrodden field at no expense to the town. Despite the team's success, crowds continued to lag in the face of competition from other daytime pursuits nearby, namely beaches, boating, and shopping. Hoping that night baseball would prove more inviting, the team launched another fundraising campaign to purchase lights, which were installed in 1983 at a cost of $75,000.

After enduring 20 years of coastal New England weather, the lights were removed in 2003. New state-of-the-art lighting is due to be installed in 2007, supported in part by a grant from the Yawkey Foundation.

McKeon Park—named for the late John McKeon, a long-time school administrator and athletics benefactor—has seen a number of other improvements over the past several years. The

Mets have added more seating, a new backstop atop a red-brick wall, and landscaping accents.

The Mets Mart souvenir shop and adjacent snack bar behind home plate is topped by a small press box. When weather cooperates, Cape League broadcasters and other media will sit outside on the flat roof above the shop rather than inside the cramped press quarters. The shop will also place merchandise racks outside under clear skies to allow fans to choose from a variety of shirts, jackets, and accessories. The building is sided with weathered cedar shingles and surrounded by a layer of crushed seashells, lending a nautical feel.

Food offerings run the gamut, with grilled hot dogs and burgers, pizza, nachos, peanuts, and popcorn among the options.

The days of poor team support appear to be over in Hyannis. The blue bleachers behind the Mets dugout on the third-base side of the field are usually full. Other prime vantage points on the sloping hill further down the third baseline are staked out early by regulars with lawn chairs and blankets in tow. Another set of bleachers on that side sits further back from the foul line.

For those wishing to get a closer feel of the game, standing on the first-base side is an option. Prime spots to the left of the visitors' dugout are within feet of the on-deck circle. On the right side of the dugout, you'll be next to the bullpen where the pop of a fastball in the catcher's mitt resonates. Fans can also bring chairs, but the four-foot-high chain link fence will impede the view. Beware of the setting summer sun, however, which is directly in viewers' eyes as they look toward home plate and the pitcher's mound.

There is also a small set of aluminum bleachers between the building and home plate, but those seats are usually taken by pro scouts with notebooks and radar guns at the ready.

The limited parking and residential location of McKeon Park are often an issue. Those who park close to the field can expect to sit in traffic after the game as the lot slowly empties. Games held on dates when functions take place at the school can be more problematic.

Cape League games are free of charge, but a $2 donation per person is encouraged.

Best Game (When You Think About It, How Does Someone Decide Which Game Was the Best?)

In 1926, Hyannis and archrival Osterville tied for the Cape League crown, and after battling all summer both teams prepared for a one-game playoff. Hyannis was ready to send ace hurler Joe Sherman to the mound, while league power Osterville countered with Harry Vernon against his former team. However, heavy rains forced the postponement of the game.

Many players on both teams were college athletes who also excelled in football. With summer winding down, these players were being beckoned to return to campus. When the teams couldn't agree on an immediate makeup date, they agreed to share the league championship. As a result, a game that had promised to be great was never even played.

Greatest Team (Not the '27 Yankees, but Who Is?)

The 1979 CCBL champions, coached by Bob Schafer, finished 33-7-1 for an .817 winning percentage. As a team, the Mets hit .314 while scoring 348 runs, both of which remain franchise records. The team also set a record for highest team batting average (.314) and runs scored (348) in league history.

Best Player . . . in My Opinion

The key player on the 1978 and 1979 Mets championship teams was shortstop Ronnie Perry Jr., though he is recognized more for his dominance on the basketball court for Holy Cross College. Perry, who held New England's all-time college basketball scoring record until it was broken by the late Reggie Lewis, wasn't too shabby with the bat and glove.

Perry hit .357 in 1978 and .401 in 1979, finishing second in the league and earning Most Valuable Player honors the latter season. He hit .383 over his career and slugged 594, still second all-time in CCBL history. The Red Sox drafted Perry in 1978, but he returned to college.

The Chicago White Sox followed suit in 1979, making Perry their third-round selection. The pale hose had some competition from the National Basketball Association's Boston Celtics, who also drafted him. Perry signed with Chicago, playing minor league ball for a season. Injuries stymied his development and the White Sox traded him to the Minnesota Twins as part of a package for pitcher Jerry Koosman.

SportPix photo by Shannon Taylor

Mets players huddle for a pre-game rally at McKeon Park in Hyannis.

Round Tripper (Some Suggestions for Sightseers)

Compared to other parts of the Cape, Hyannis has a frenetic tempo. However there are plenty of nearby opportunities to unwind.

Barnstable's south-facing beaches (Craigville, Orrin Keyes, Kalmus, and Veterans) offer warmer water, while those to the north (Corporation, Mayflower, Chapin, Grays, and Sandy Neck) are usually less breezy.

There are numerous charter boats that embark from Hyannis for those wanting to chase cod, flounder, bluefish, or striped bass. Hy-Line Cruises is at the Ocean Street docks, while *Helen-H* is berthed at Pleasant Street.

Hy-Line also offers one- and two-hour narrated cruises in Pleasant Bay and Vineyard Sound, which provide a perfect view of majestic

Hyannisport homes including the Kennedy compound.

The John F. Kennedy Museum on Main Street features personal artifacts, photographs, and a short film narrated by Martha's Vineyard resident Walter Cronkite. The Kennedy Memorial, at Veterans Park off Ocean Street, is worth a visit. Go early to both venues, or you'll be stuck with the crowds.

Whales migrate during the summer east of the Cape, and Hyannis Whale-Watch Cruises is a great way to see them up close. Excursions depart from Barnstable Harbor and last about four hours.

Steamship Authority ferries depart from Hyannis for Martha's Vineyard and Nantucket. The high-speed passenger ferry *Flying Cloud* chops the normal two-hour transit time to Nantucket in half. Hy-Line also offers passenger service to Nantucket.

The Cape Cod Crusaders soccer team, the only pro-sports franchise on the Cape, plays a dozen home games from May to mid-August at Barnstable High School. The club is a farm team for the New England Revolution.

Under new ownership, Cape Cod Central Railroad offers scenic excursions past cranberry bogs and salt marshes from Hyannis to Sandwich and Bourne, as well as a classy dinner train service.

Some of the tastiest snacks in New England are found at Cape Cod Potato Chip Company on Breed's Hill Road, which offers free self-guided tours of its factory along with free samples.

The Cape Cod Melody Tent on West Main Street hosts nationally known musical, comedy, and entertainment acts.

Places to Eat ... If You Want More Than Cracker Jack

The best restaurant in Hyannis is the Roadhouse Café on South Street, serving steaks, seafood, and Italian specialties. There's also a more casual bistro in back, serving burgers and high-end pub fare, with live jazz Monday nights.

As good as the Roadhouse is, the Italian cuisine is no match for Ristorante Barolo on Financial Place (near the Melody Tent). A notch below but still worth a stop is Alberto's on Main Street.

Roo Bar on Main Street has the funkiest ambience and most inspired menu, and hops at night. So does Harry's on Main Street, a Cajun joint that morphs into party central when the dishes are cleared.

For some fried seafood, hit Baxter's Boat House on Pleasant Street and munch while you watch the boats ply the waters. For coffee and desserts, Left Bank Café, Caffe e Dolci, La Petite France, and Prodigal Son Café are great options.

Hyannis has a burgeoning Brazilian community, and you can savor the native flavors at The Brazilan Grill on Main Street, where skewers of succulently marinated grilled meats are brought to your table until you say "uncle." Additional upscale venues worth checking include The Paddock, The Black Cat, Tugboats, and The Naked Oyster, all of which are on the pricey side.

Chauncey's, Fazio's Trattoria, Grill 16, Penguins Seagrill, and the Duck Inn Pub, all on Main Street, are good choices, and the British Beer Company has an impressive list of imported brews on tap to go along with decent pizzas and pub fare.

Sources:

Price, Christopher. *Baseball by the Beach—A History of America's National Pastime on Cape Cod.* Yarmouthport, Massachusetts: On Cape Publications, 1998.

www.barnstablepatriot.com
www.capecodbaseball.org
www.capecodonline.com
www.hyannismets.org
www.insidecapecod.com
www.town.barnstable.ma.us

Address: 450 Aiken Street, Lowell, MA 01854

Web Site: *www.lowellspinners.com*

First Game: June 22, 1998

Dimensions: LF 337 LCF 368 CF 400 RCF 337 RF 301

Directions: From I-495 and Route 3, take the Lowell Connector. From Boston, take Route 93 North to Route 495 South to the Lowell Connector. From south of Lowell, take Route 128 North to Route 3 North to the Lowell Connector. Follow the Lowell Connector to Exit 5B, Thorndike Street. Follow Thorndike Street through the lights and go past City Hall. Take a left onto Father Morrissette Boulevard. At the first set of lights, take a right onto Cabot Street.

LOWELL, MA

EDWARD A. LeLACHEUR PARK

Home of the Lowell Spinners of the New York–Penn League, and the University of Massachusetts-Lowell Riverhawks

Claim to Fame

The Spinners have sold every seat to every game at LeLacheur Park since August 2, 1999, giving them a total of 270 consecutive sellouts through the 2006 season. The seating capacity at LeLacheur Park is 4,797.

Strange but True

The first carbonated and bottled soft drink to be widely distributed in the United States was produced by the Moxie Nerve Food Company of Lowell in the 1880s. First sold from "Moxie bottle wagons," it was originally developed in the 1870s as a patent medicine or nerve tonic, with claims that it cured, among other things, "loss of manhood." The word "moxie" would eventually enter the English lexicon with a definition of "vigor," "courage," or "skill." Once endorsed by Ted Williams, it is unknown if Moxie would have been of help to Charlie Snow in his attempts to catch a baseball.

Telephone numbers were first introduced in 1879 during a measles epidemic

Anne Haggerty Photography

Spinners players getting ready for a game at LeLacher Park in Lowell.

in Lowell. Fearing the town's telephone operators might succumb and paralyze telephone service, a Lowell doctor recommended the use of numbers for calling Lowell's more than 200 subscribers so that substitute operators might be more easily trained in the event of such an emergency. It is not known if Charlie Snow ever phoned the Moxie Nerve Food Company.

Writer Jack Kerouac, who is credited with coining the term "Beat Generation," also invented a tabletop dice baseball game. An accomplished athlete while growing up in Lowell, Kerouac developed the game at the age of six or seven and played it from 1936 until 1965. The game, which included sets of handwritten cards, included players with names like Wino Love and El Negro, and teams like

the Cincinnati Blacks and the St. Louis Whites.

Edward A. LeLacheur Park, which was named for a state representative who had been instrumental in obtaining state funding for the project, was designed by HOK, the same architects who designed Camden Yards and Jacobs Field.

Who's Who in Lowell

Through the 2006 season, 25 Spinners alumni have gone on to play in the major leagues. They are: Abe Alvarez, Tony Blanco, Jack Cressend, David Eckstein, Adam Everett, Lew Ford, Casey Fossum, Josh Hancock, John Hattig, Shea Hillenbrand, Rontrez Johnson, Matt Kinney, Steve Lomasney, Mike Maroth, Anastacio Martinez, Marty McLeary, David Murphy,

Matt Murton, Jonathan Papelbon, Hanley Ramirez, Anibal Sanchez, Freddy Sanchez, Angel Santos, Wilton Veras, and Kevin Youkilis.

Several Red Sox players have played in Lowell on rehab assignments, including Bret Saberhagen, Wily Mo Pena, Keith Foulke, and Gabe Kapler.

Corey Jenkins, a Lowell Spinner in 1996, traded in his outfielder's mitt for shoulder pads and played as a linebacker for the Miami Dolphins from 2003 to 2005.

John Hattig, a Lowell Spinner in 2000, became the first native of Guam to play in the major leagues when he appeared in a game for the Toronto Blue Jays on August 19, 2006.

Professional baseball in Lowell predates the Spinners by more than a century, with the Amateurs (the name is a misnomer; the players were paid) having been established in 1875. Since that time, more than 130 Lowell players have gone on to the major leagues.

There have been 17 people born in the city of Lowell who have played in the major leagues, 13 of them prior to 1900. The first was Charlie Snow, in 1874. The most recent were Johnny Barrett and Skippy Roberge in 1946.

Charlie Snow played in exactly one big-league game, and had a better career than the immortal "Moonlight" Graham—but only at the plate. Snow had a lone at-bat for the Brooklyn Atlantics, one more than Graham had with the New York Giants in 1905, and singled to finish his career with a 1.000 batting average. Unfortunately, Snow also had to try to play defense. A catcher, Snow was charged with three errors while failing to make a single putout or assist.

About Lowell

The fourth-largest city in the Commonwealth of Massachusetts, Lowell has a population of approximately 105,000. Established as a textile-manufacturing center at the confluence of the Concord and Merrimack rivers, Lowell was officially incorporated as a town in 1826 and became a city in 1836. Named for Francis Cabot Lowell, it is considered by many to be the birthplace of the Industrial Revolution in the United States.

Located approximately 30 miles northwest of Boston, Lowell has a large immigrant population. According to the 2000 census, the racial makeup of the city was 68.6 percent White, 16.5 percent Asian, 4.2 percent African American, 0.24 percent Native American, 0.04 percent Pacific Islander, 6.48 percent from other races, and 3.92 percent from two or more races. Lowell is home to the second largest Cambodian population in the United States.

While there is not a subway in Lowell, the Lowell Regional Transportation Authority (LRTA) provides bus service throughout the city. The Massachusetts Bay Transit Authority (MBTA) commuter rail line provides service to Boston several times each day.

The city is home to the Lowell campus of the University of Massachusetts. Other notable landmarks are the Lowell Memorial Auditorium, the Tsongas Arena, and Lowell General Hospital. The local newspaper is the *Lowell Sun*.

Notable people associated with the city of Lowell include: actresses Bette Davis and Olympia Dukakis; author

Jack Kerouac, entertainer Ed McMahon, inventor and businessman An Wang, boxer "Irish" Micky Ward, and painter and etcher James McNeill Whistler.

A Baseball Backgrounder

Lowell's first professional baseball team was the Amateurs, who began play in 1875 on a diamond at the city's fairgrounds on Gorham Street. The diamond was located on a part of the grounds that was also used as a harness racing track, where a grandstand already existed. The following year the Amateurs leased six acres of land elsewhere on the grounds, fenced it in, and erected a new ballpark on the site. The Amateurs played at the fairgrounds until the club went out of business following the 1878 season.

Lowell fielded its first minor league team in the New England League in 1887, and played at The River Street Grounds on the Centralville side of the Merrimack River. The ballpark stood between the Bridge Street and Aiken Street bridges, and the left-field fence, which bordered the river, was unusually close to home plate. The Lowell Browns hit 88 home runs in 107 games during the 1887 season, and so many balls were clearing the left-field fence and splashing into the river that a wire net was soon installed on top of the fence to keep some of the balls from being lost. The team went out of business after the 1889 season.

Lowell's next minor league team, the Indians, began play in 1891. When Bill McGunnigle, who had put the Browns together and was instrumental in getting the ballpark on River Street built, bought the franchise in 1893, he wanted to build a new park downtown in order to attract more fans. Unfortunately, the other investors in the club balked at putting up the money and the Indians lasted just 34 games before being moved to Manchester, New Hampshire. McGunnigle, it should be noted, was a former major league pitcher and is credited with having invented the catcher's mitt.

Lowell gave minor league baseball another try in 1895, but again the team folded, lasting only until July of that first season.

In 1901, minor league baseball returned to Lowell. The owner of the Lowell Tigers was Fred Lake, who would go on to manage the Boston Red Sox in 1908 and 1909 and the National League Boston Doves in 1910. Late in 1901, Lake secured an option on some land at the Atherton Grounds on Main Street, just across the city line, and began building a ballpark that is still in use today. The covered ballpark, which seated 3,500 fans, was ready in time for the start of the 1902 season. Lake named it Spalding Park in honor of A.G. Spalding, the most powerful man in baseball. Spalding had played several games in Lowell as a pitcher and as a first baseman for the Boston Red Stockings and Chicago White Stockings. A notable member of the Tigers in 1902 was Louis Sockalexis, the famed Indian star who drank himself out of the major leagues in 1899, but made a remarkable comeback.

Al Winn bought the Lowell Tigers in 1906, and built a state-of-the-art baseball park closer to downtown on a site in the lower Highlands neighborhood off Middlesex Street. Washing-

Anne Haggerty Photography

The main entrance to LeLacheur Park.

ton Park, limited by the size of the lot, was small. The right-field fence was so close to home plate that many balls hit off it wound up as singles instead of doubles or triples. However, being that it was the Deadball Era, few hitters could muscle balls over the fence for home runs. During the 1907–08 season the Tigers set a franchise record by failing to hit a home run in 91 consecutive games. The park was a masterpiece for the ages. Of the 3,500 seats, 1,500 were opera house–style seats, not benches, and were covered by a roof. The park had indoor plumbing and a locker room with hot showers for the players. For the ladies who attended the games, there was a powder room with mirrors, brushes, and combs available. Among the players to wear the team's uniform were former Red Sox third baseman Harry Lord and future Hall of Famer Jesse Burkett.

When Valere Lecourt, the president of the Laurier Social Club, bought a franchise in the New England League in 1933, he found a small, unused parcel of land on Aiken Street, at a 90-degree bend in the Merrimack River, and built Laurier Park. (LeLacheur Park would later be built on the same site.) However, the New England League went out of business and was replaced by the Northeastern League, which itself went out of business when the league's president, Roger Baker, was sentenced to six years in prison for embezzlement. With no league to play in, Lecourt was forced to fold his club in 1934.

Lowell had a minor league team for several weeks during the summer of 1947, the Orphans, which played at Alumni Field. It was a bankrupt team that the revived New England League had transferred to Lowell from Lawrence in July. But after a

20-game losing streak and drawing just 85 paying fans to a doubleheader on August 17, the city evicted the Orphans, who played the final two weeks of the season on the road.

Nearly half a century would pass before minor league baseball returned to Lowell in 1996. The promise of a new, modern ballpark lured owner Clyde Smoll and his Class A short-season New York–Penn League team from Elmira, New York. The city spent $600,000 to renovate Alumni Field and bring it up to acceptable standards for minor league ball while a new ballpark was being built. Prior to the 1997 season, Smoll sold the team to Drew and Joann Weber, who quickly established themselves as great ambassadors of the game of baseball in Lowell. LeLacheur Park opened in 1998, and while Joann Weber succumbed to a long battle with cancer in November 2006, Drew Weber retains ownership of the team.

In 2000, the Spinners were honored with two of the most prestigious awards given to minor league baseball teams: the Bob Freitas Award and the Larry MacPhail Trophy.

Take Me Out to the Ballgame

The games all sell out, but that doesn't mean you can't get into a Lowell Spinners game without an advance ticket. The Spinners sell standing-room tickets on the day of the game, and with the exception of a few times a year, they'll have room for you. Even better, the fan-friendly ushers will try to find a seat for you a few innings into the game if you request one.

The Spinners are known for creative promotions, having captured numerous awards and national exposure. Among the most unique was the "Yankees Elimination Project," in 2006, which encouraged youth baseball teams to change their names from the Yankees to the Spinners with the reward of free uniforms and the chance to play at LeLacheur Park before a Spinners game. The promotion was featured on ESPN's "Cold Pizza," CNN's "Headline News" and in *Sports Illustrated*.

The Spinners regularly feature bobblehead doll giveaways. One, with author and Lowell-native Jack Kerouac, not only attracted national media attention but also a spot in the National Baseball Hall of Fame. Other bobbleheads have included Hall of Fame baseball writer Peter Gammons and best-selling author Steven King.

Like most minor-league teams, the Spinners have mascots. However, "Canaligator" and "Allie-GATOR" aren't LeLacheur's big dogs on the block (nor is Blue the Frisbee Dog, who performs between innings at Spinners games every year). The team's official mascot is Del "Dog Man" Christman, who is the team's clubhouse attendant and sells hotdogs in the stands each game. Outside of saying that he is unique, it is easiest to direct readers to the Spinners' Web site--or better yet, to a game at LeLacheur Park to experience the Dog Man in action.

Best Game (When You Think About It, How Does Someone Decide Which Game Was the Best?)

On August 13, 2006, Jeff Farrell and Yulkin German combined for the first, and to this date only, Spinners no-hitter. Farrell, who missed his sister's wedding to start the game, went five innings. German pitched the final four innings. The game was played against Hudson Valley, with the Spinners winning 2-0.

Greatest Team (Not the '27 Yankees, but Who Is?)

In 1877 many considered the Lowell Amateurs second to only the National League champion Boston Red Stockings. Independent at the time, the Amateurs compiled a record of 11-7 against National League teams and were invited to join the major leagues in 1878. The team's stockholders unanimously turned down the invitation.

More recently, it's a close call between the 2003 and 2005 Spinners. The 2003 team featured four players who have gone on to play the big leagues: Abe Alverez, David Murphy, Matt Murton, and Jonathan Papelbon. The 2005 team, which included three first-round draft picks—Clay Buchholz, Jacoby Ellsbury, and Jed Lowrie—probably gets the nod as they finished with a better record.

Best Player . . . in My Opinion

If the pool to choose from were to include every player to ever play for a Lowell team, Hall of Famers Hugh Duffy, Joe Kelley, and Jesse Burkett would be the nominees. However, we'll only look back to 1996—the year the Spinners franchise was started—and will stick with players who have played for the team.

As several notable Spinners alumni are major-league players not yet in their prime, a good argument could be made for more than one. As players evolve over the next decade, opinions could change dramatically. The candidates are:

Dave Eckstein is a two-time National League All-Star and has played for a pair of World Series–winning teams. Adam Everett is considered one of the best defensive shortstops in the National League. Jonathan Papelbon was a 2006 American League All-Star and set the team's all-time record for saves by a rookie. Hanley Ramirez was the 2006 National League Rookie of the Year. Anibal Sanchez threw a no-hitter against the Arizona Diamondbacks in 2006. Freddy Sanchez was a 2006 National League All-Star and batting champion. Kevin Youkilis was a member of the 2004 Red Sox World Championship team. In a close—and highly subjective—decision, the winner is Shea Hillenbrand. Getting bonus points for having appeared in more games as a Spinner than any of the other candidates, Hillenbrand also has the most big-league experience with 870 games. Through 2006, Hillenbrand was a major league veteran with six seasons under his belt. Hillenbrand has been an All-Star with both the Red Sox and Blue Jays and has a lifetime batting average of .287 with 104 home runs. One of the original "dirt dogs"—a group of Red Sox players known for their hard-nosed style of play—Hillenbrand was very popular with Boston fans prior to being traded to Arizona for Byung-Hyun Kim in 2003. Hillenbrand also gets bonus points for being extremely unhappy to leave Boston, and for saying that playing for the Red Sox is "in his blood."

Round Tripper (Some Suggestions for Sightseers)

The Lowell National Historical Park is the oldest urban national park in the nation. Operated by the National Park Service, it comprises a group of different sites in and around the city related to the era of textile manufacturing in Lowell during the nineteenth century.

The Lowell Folk Festival is one of the largest folk music festivals in the United States. Featuring three days of traditional music, dance, craft demonstrations, and ethnic foods, it is presented on six outdoor stages throughout the city. It is held each year on the last weekend of July.

The Whistler House Museum of Art is the birthplace of painter and etcher James McNeill Whistler. Located at 243 Worthen Street, it has been the home of the Lowell Art Association since 1908 and is open as a museum.

The Paul Tsongas Arena hosts a number of sporting events and concerts. The primary tenant is the Lowell Devils, an American Hockey League affiliate of the National Hockey League's New Jersey Devils.

The Lowell All-Americans are part of the New England Collegiate Baseball League (NECBL), a summer league comprised of college players from throughout the United States. The NECBL starts its summer season in early June and plays an eight-week, 42-game-per-team schedule. The games are played at Stoklosa Alumni Field, on Rogers Street.

Places to Eat . . . If You Want More Than Cracker Jack

There aren't many places to eat and drink within close walking distance of LeLacheur Park, but The Brewery Exchange is just a block away at 201 Cabot Street. The Brewery Exchange features not only lunch, dinner, and libations, but also an outdoor patio and live music.

Other eating and drinking options in Lowell include Cavaleiro's Restaurant, at 573 Lawrence Street; Hookslide Kelly's, at 19 Merrimack Street; Outback Steakhouse, at 28 Reiss Avenue; Sal's Pizza, at 1201 Bridge Street; and Suppa's Pizza & Restaurant, at 94 University Avenue.

Sources:

Scoggins, Charles. *Bricks and Bats*, Lowell, Massachusetts: Lowell Historical Society, YEAR.

www.lowellallamericans.com
www.lowellma.gov/community/visitors
lowellspinners.com
www.necbl.com
www.nypl.org/press/2001/kerouac.cfm
www.thecolumnists.com
http://wikipedia.com

11

Address: 365 Western Ave., Lynn, MA 01901

Web Site: *www.northshorespirit.com*

First Game: 1940 (renovated 2002)

Dimensions: LF 320 CF 400 RF 320

Directions: From Route 195/128, get off at Route 129 (Lynnfield St.). Take the left at the sixth traffic light (Chestnut Street). Take the right at the second set of lights (Western Avenue, Route 107). Fraser Field is about 0.5 mile down the road.

LYNN, MA

FRASER FIELD

Home of the North Shore Spirit of the Canadian-American League—Independent

Claim to Fame

The old poem *"Lynn, Lynn, city of sin. You never come out the way you went in."* General Electric. Jet Engines. The first baseball game played under artificial light. Marshmallow Fluff is made in Lynn. The city was the first stop on the Rolling Stones' first United States tour.

Strange but True

It's incredible that a state senator recently proposed a ban on serving fluff in school cafeterias. Fluff is an incredibly useful product. The "What the Fluff" festival was recently organized by marshmallow cream connoisseurs to prove doubters wrong. The winner of the festival's science fair demonstrated the adhesive qualities of fluff. Other young scientists showed how fluff enhances athletic performance. "Tuna Fluffer," a new recipe that makes use of tuna fish, pickles, hot sauce, and crackers, was determined to be delicious. The festival also hosted a volcano that erupted orange fluff.

Photo courtesy of the North Shore Spirit

The North Shore Spirit first took to the field in 2003.

Who's Who in Lynn

Since it first opened, Fraser Field has seen many great ballplayers. The Boston Red Sox and Braves have staged exhibitions. Red Sox manager Joe Cronin's star-studded roster included Johnny Pesky, Ted Williams, Bobby Doerr, and Joe DiMaggio. Former New York Yankee pitcher Bump Hadley was the ace for the New England League. Ken Hill, Tony Conigliaro, Billy Conigliaro, Jeff Juden, and Harry Agannis played at the field during high school. The Double A Lynn Sailors were led by a couple of future Red Sox who were important contributors to the 1986 American League champs— Spike Owen and Dave Henderson.

Negro League barnstormers, including Satchel Paige, would regularly stop at Fraser Field before the color barrier was broken.

About Lynn

Lynn, home of Fraser Field, is one of America's oldest cities, tracing its founding to 1629. Tanneries and shoemaking were for a long period the city's sustaining industries. In fact, it is said that American Revolutionary War troops wore shoes that were made in Lynn.

Today, most of the leather and shoe companies have left the city. With a population of 90,000, Lynn is in the throes of attempting to rebuild its industrial base. Its primary industry currently is General Electric's jet engine division. Additional employment for its residents is found in the high-tech industry located in adjacent communities.

Lynn is a small pocket in a relatively affluent North Shore area. Nearby towns such as Swampscott, Marblehead, and Manchester are among the wealthiest in Massachusetts. There are great sightseeing opportunities in the area. Scenic Marblehead, historic Salem, Ipswich, Rockport, and fishing center Gloucester are places not to be missed. There are also a large number of ocean beaches to visit.

Lynn has been called the "City of Firsts" in a recent campaign. "Lynn Firsts" include:

- First iron works (1643)
- First fire engine (1654)
- First American jet engine
- First woman in advertising and mass-marketing, Lydia Pinkham
- First baseball game under artificial light
- First dance academy in the United States
- First tannery in the United States
- First air mail delivery in the United States

A Baseball Backgrounder

Locals have many fond memories of Fraser Field's first professional team. From 1946 through 1948, the Lynn Red Sox played in the Class B New England League. The Sox won three regular season pennants. But even before Fraser Field was built, the city by the sea already had a great baseball history. The first catcher's mask worn in an actual game was donned in Lynn in 1877. Babe Ruth, Arky Vaughn, Satchel Paige, Johnny Pesky barnstormed in Lynn. Ted Williams had two doubles against the Lynn Frasers. Before Jackie Robinson, a player named Bud Fowler broke the color barrier for the Lynn Live Oaks in 1878. In 1927, the Lynn professional team worked with local engineers from General Electric to install lights that would facilitate baseball's first professional night game, which was finally held in Lynn on June 24 of that same year.

Nostalgia for the good old days brought Lynn back into organized baseball by the early 1980s. Lynn had two teams in the Class AA Eastern League. The Lynn Sailors, affiliated with the Seattle Mariners, played at Fraser from 1980 until 1982. The Sailors had a very good team. Dave Henderson, Spike Owens, Harold Reynolds, and Bud Black played in Lynn. The Lynn Pirates only lasted one year—1983. The independent Massachusetts Mad Dogs, managed by George "Boomer" Scott, were the field's tenants from 1996 until 1999.

After a four-year hiatus, in 2003 team owner Nicholas Lopardo helped the reemergence of organized baseball at Fraser Field. A North Shore resident and business executive, his acquisition of the Waterbury, Connecticut, franchise, as well as much funding for improvements to Fraser Field, set the stage for the return of organized baseball in Lynn. The North Shore Spirit took the field for the 2003 season.

The Canadian-American League has only a single player on a big-league roster, relief pitcher Ken Ray of Atlanta who is a product of the North Shore franchise. Ray made his big-league debut in 2006, striking out Barry Bonds.

While located in the City of Lynn, the team has been dubbed the "North Shore Spirit" to identify itself with the many communities north of the City of Boston commonly referred to as the North Shore. All the cities and towns are located adjacent to or near the Atlantic Ocean.

Take Me Out to the Ballgame

Like some other minor league parks in New England—such as Holman Stadium in Nashua, New Hampshire—Fraser Field is a product of the Depression Era Works Progress Administration (WPA). The WPA was an attempt by the Roosevelt administration to improve the economy. The idea was that federal monies would be diverted directly into local economies through financial support for local civic projects such as buildings and sports facilities.

The City of Lynn benefited through the subsidized construction of a dedicated baseball facility, Fraser Field, and an adjacent stadium devoted exclusively to football, Manning Bowl. Thus, the City of Lynn was the recipient of a total outdoor sports complex that, at the time, was virtually unrivaled in the New England area. Manning Bowl was recently demolished, but, of course, the refurbished Fraser Field continues as an active sports venue.

Among the various facilities that house the minor and independent leagues in New England, Fraser Field has consistently hosted the most baseball activity since World War II. The park, as the home of the 1946–1949 Lynn Red Sox of the New England League, was a host to integration pioneers Roy Campanella and Don Newcombe of the Nashua Dodgers. In fact, Hall of Fame catcher Campanella smashed his first professional home run at Fraser Field.

Construction of the field was completed in 1940, and it was just a year later that the United States became an active combatant in World War II. With the onset of wartime, baseball became a casualty of the war. As to be expected, war-related activities took precedent over non-essential matters such as sports and entertainment. Players and future players alike were drafted or enlisted in the armed services. The manpower needed for the war effort was simply not available to organized baseball. In fact, during the war years, several governing bodies considered eliminating professional sports altogether. The idea was rejected because many believed professional sports were good morale builders for armed service personnel and civilians alike.

Besides manpower shortages, baseball was negatively impacted by strict gasoline rationing, which precluded fans from getting to many of the parks, and even made it impossible for teams to hire buses to transport players from one park to another.

So, Lynn had its brand-new ballpark—Fraser Field—but was forced to wait until the post-war years to attract its first professional franchise. The

Photo courtesy of the North Shore Spirit

Fans enjoying some summer baseball at Fraser Field.

Lynn Red Sox of the newly organized New England League started playing at the field in 1946.

From 1940 to 1946, Fraser Field was used primarily by local high school and amateur teams. And, actually, this activity continues today.

Interestingly, Fraser Field has an important place in the history of women's baseball. In 2004, the park was the scene of the National Women's Baseball League's first national championship tournament.

If for no other reason, Fraser Field merits a visit because of its age—it's more than 75 years old. Like some of the older stadiums, it was built especially for baseball and, with its outstanding sight lines, is a great place to watch a game. Foul territory is relatively small, placing you close to the action.

The field underwent an updating in 2002 with the financial help of local sports benefactor and North Shore Spirit owner Nicholos Lopardo.

More than $2 million was spent on improvements to make Fraser Field a more fan-friendly place. Lopardo purchased the Waterbury, Connecticut, Spirit in 2002 and moved the team to Lynn. There had been a number of complaints—particularly from the previous baseball tenant—that the park was woefully in need of some serious work. One of the first things Lopardo did was to get the necessary repairs underway through his funding.

Besides new seating, artificial turf was installed, concessions were upgraded, the grandstand roof was repaired, and finally a new center field giantron was installed in place of an antiquated scoreboard.

The cantilevered roof of the grandstand is unique, eliminating the need for supporting columns. And it frees the grandstand area of any viewing encumbrances.

Fraser Field has a single number adorning the leftfield wall—number 25. This is in honor of baseball slugger Tony Conigliaro, who attended St., Mary's High School in Lynn.

Tony C., as he was known, and his younger brother Billy were local baseball heroes. Although neither played professionally here, both made it to the big leagues with the Red Sox. Tony was well on his way to major-league slugging records when he was struck down by a beanball in 1967, while he was playing with the Red Sox. He never really recovered his batting prowess. At age 20, he had won the American League home run championship. Conigliaro was the youngest player ever to reach the 100-home-run mark. The beaning seemed to affect both his eyesight and his overall health. He passed away at age 45 having suffered a number of physical problems.

Photo courtesy of the North Shore Spirit

More than $2 million was spent to make Fraser Field the great park it is today.

Best Game (When You Think About It, How Does Someone Decide Which Game Was the Best?)

We have to turn the clock back to 1940 and the park's inaugural game for Fraser Field's most unusual game. The game was unusual more for what didn't occur rather than what did happen.

Both the local big-league teams—the Red Sox and the Braves—were invited to play the inaugural game against a local semipro team. The Red Sox declined the invitation since they would be on a road trip. But the Braves, who were in town and had an open date, strangely enough turned down the invitation. The excuse: the Braves said that while it was an "off" date, they preferred not to go up to Lynn on their downtime.

Fortunately for Lynn officials, the Pittsburgh Pirates were going to be in Boston to play the Braves the next day, and they agreed to take part in the inaugural game. Thus, neither of the Boston teams could or would play, while a team from out of state with no connection to the local baseball scene agreed to make an appearance.

The game itself involved a home run by Pirates' outfielder Vince DiMaggio, older brother of Joe, who played for the Yankees, and Dom, who played for the Red Sox. Usually, of course, a home run has the hitter trotting around the bases at half-speed. But since Fraser Field had no outfield fence, Vince had to leg it out. As a footnote to the game, Braves manager Casey Stengel did put in an appearance while, of course, his team was nowhere to be found.

Greatest Team (Not the '27 Yankees, but Who Is?)

Local fans have seen plenty of great amateur and professional baseball. Shortly after the end of the World War II, when the old New England Baseball League was reorganized, Lynn was lucky enough to secure an affiliation with the hometown Boston Red Sox. The Lynn Red Sox were sensational, winning three consecutive pennants. Their general manager was the young Dick O'Connell, who later took the reigns of the Red Sox. O'Connell was the architect of the Red Sox' Impossible Dream in 1967 and the 1975 American League champions.

The team's best-known player was Dale Long who homered in eight consecutive games for the Pittsburgh Pirates. The Lynn Red Sox' main rivals were the Nashua Dodgers, led by Roy Campanella and Don Newcombe. A couple of African-American players on the Nashua team voiced their displeasure about race-baiting from some of the Lynn players, so Nashua general manager Buzzie Bavasi decided to do something about it. He challenged Lynn to a put-up-or-shut-up fist fight after a game at Fraser Field. Cooler tempers eventually prevailed. Despite this, the team's on-field achievements speak loudly. Winning three consecutive pennants is an amazing accomplishment, particularly considering the personnel turnover in minor league baseball. The North Shore Spirit, Fraser Field's present tenant, has been a perennial contender for the Canadian-American League championship.

Best Player ... in My Opinion

While Tony and Billy Conigliaro were not born in Lynn, they certainly qualify as North Shore natives who have played in the major leagues. Both grew up in nearby Swampscott and played high school baseball at St. Mary's of Lynn. They are the only brother duo from Massachusetts to make their way to the majors. Neither Tony nor Billy had particularly long careers—but they did have flair. Tony's exploits and beaning incident were big news locally, while Billy's personality often made the headlines. Both spent time with the Red Sox, which added to their luster locally.

Not as well known as the Conigliaros was catcher Jim Heqan, born and bred in Lynn and considered one of the top all-time receivers. Jim also was the father of Mike Hegan, a major league first baseman. A good field, no-hit type, Jim Hegan nevertheless was a five-time member of the American League All-Star team and was a frequent battery-mate of Hall of Famer Bob Feller. He caught three no-hitters and was a member of the 1948 World Champion Indians, where he spent most of his time in the majors.

No doubt the best all-around athlete from Lynn and the North Shore was Harry Agganis, the "Golden Greek." He was a football all-American quarterback at Boston University in the early 1950s. At a time when players were rarely, if ever, drafted in their junior year of college, he was Paul Brown's first-round draft choice for the Cleveland Browns. Later, it is said the Browns offered a huge signing bonus to Agganis. The bonus was $25.00. The Browns' offer was topped by the $35,000 offer from the Red Sox to play baseball. Agganis accepted the Red Sox' money.

Agganis—a promising left-handed-hitting first baseman—had a tragically brief career with the Red Sox. He led American League first basemen in fielding average and assists in his rookie season. His second and final year, 1955, he was only 25 games into the season when he passed away at the age of 26. As a schoolboy baseball star at Lynn Classical High School, Agganis played a number of games at Fraser Field.

Other North Shore natives who played in the big leagues include pitchers Irving "Bump" Hadley and Josh Fogg, both born in Lynn, and Cy Perkins from Gloucester. Hadley played from 1926 to 1941, mainly with the Yankees. He was best-known for his beaning another Bay State native—Hall of Fame catcher Mickey Cochrane of Bridgewater. The beaning ended Cochrane's great career. Hadley played on four straight Yankee pennant-winning teams. After baseball, he was a well-known sportscaster in the Boston area.

Josh Fogg is, at this writing, with the Colorado Rockies. He has six years of big-league experience. Cy Perkins spent 17 years in the big leagues as a catcher from 1915 to 1934.

Round Tripper (Some Suggestions for Sightseers)

The City of Lynn is not known as a mecca of hotels and motels. But there is an ample stock of places to stay close by. Route US 1, just a short drive away, has a good supply of overnight accommodations. Smaller bed and breakfasts and inns can be found in Rockport and Gloucester.

Lynn Woods is currently the largest municipal park in New England. Supposedly there's still buried treasure at the park. High Rock Tower—a stone observation tower with a great view of Nahant and Boston—is the highest point in the city.

Lynn is part of Greater Boston and it's just a stone's throw away from all of the North Shore's greatest attractions. In Essex, Crane's Beach is one of the East Coast's most picturesque sanctuaries and is a great place to get away from it all and experience nature. Salem is the next town over. The Salem Witch Museum and the Peabody Essex Museums are prime attractions. There are all kinds of public beaches along the jagged coast of Gloucester and Rockport. Lynn is a great starting point for enjoying the great North Shore.

Places to Eat . . . If You Want More Than Cracker Jack

As for eating, fresh fish is the mainstay at Anthony's Hawthorne in Lynn and Anthony's Pier 4 in Swampscott, which is part of the well-known and highly-regarded Boston chain. The nearby town of Essex attracts locals to its many excellent seafood restaurants including the Village Restaurant and Woodman's, where the fried clam was allegedly invented. Both Essex and Ipswich are famous for their fried clams.

Seafood is unequaled in the area, but if it isn't on your menu drive over to Route 1, where the towns of Peabody, Danvers, Lynnfield, and Saugus offer everything from Italian to Chinese.

Sources:

The Baseball Almanac, 1995–2007.
Boston Globe, 1900–2007.
Society of American Baseball Researchers. *The Northern Game—and Beyond.* Boston: Cambridge Prepress Services, 2002.

www.all-baseball.com
www.ballparkdigest.com
www.ballparkreviews.com
www.baseballalmanac.com
www.baseballamericaonline.com
www.canamleague.com
www.ci.lynn.ma.us/
www.northshorespirit.com

12

Address: 78 Eldredge Park Way, Orleans, MA 02653

Web Site: www.orleanscardinals.com

First Game: 1912

Dimensions: LF 300 CF 434 RF 312

Directions: Take Route 6 East to the Orleans Rotary. Continue on Route 6 for 3.6 miles to the traffic light at Brackett Road. Turn right onto Brackett Road and continue 0.8 mile to the end of the road. At the end of Brackett, turn left onto Nauset Road. Take the first right onto Cable Road. Nauset Regional High School is on your left.

ELDREDGE PARK

Home of the Orleans Cardinals of the Cape Cod Baseball League

Claim to Fame

Eldredge Park is considered one of the most picturesque ballparks in the United States. Nauset Beach is one of the most beautiful beaches.

Strange but True

Baseball fans at Eldredge were among the first to hear about Lindbergh's successful landing in Paris in 1926.

Who's Who in Orleans

Jeff Conine, Carlton Fisk, Nomar Garciaparra, Todd Helton, Jason Michaels, Chad Moeller, Jay Payton, Ben Sheets, Mark Teixeira, Frank Thomas, Kelly Wunsch, Russ Adams, Aaron Boone, Scott Proctor, and J.T. Snow.

About Orleans

In many ways, Orleans is the Cape's crossroads community. It's unusual for a town to have both north and south coasts. But Orleans has them. On a clear day, northern beachgoers can see the tip of Provincetown from Skaket

SportPix photo by Matthew Scott

Fans on the berm down the first base line in Orleans.

Beach. Nauset Beach, one of the Atlantic's best beaches, defines the town's southern parameter. Orleans is considered to be either the last town in the Mid-Cape or the first town in the Lower Cape Region.

Settlers from Europe were not Orleans' original residents. For hundreds of years, present-day Orleans was inhabited by Nauset Indians. The relationship between the Native Americans and the newcomers from England was generally harmonious. The demise of the Native American was caused by diseases, such as small pox that were imported from Europe.

Orleans was once part of Eastham. But, after more than a century, Orleans' citizens had it up to here with Eastham. In 1797, citizens of South Parish declared their independence and started their own town. Drawing inspiration from the Revolutionary War, the town's incorporators named their new town Orleans to honor French allies who cinched an American victory at Yorktown.

Like many other Cape Cod communities, Orleans' livelihood has depended upon the riches of the Atlantic Ocean. The town was once famous for its massive salt works. Salt was needed to preserve fish and food. A large supply and nationwide demand created the community's first cottage industry. Large salt works were located along the shoreline.

At one time, whalers and merchants were the heart of the local economy. Times have changed. Today's journeys are considerably shorter, safer, and much more pleasant. No more around-the-world trips, risking life and limb to feed, clothe, and heat a nation. Rock Harbor once had a thriving commercial maritime industry. Many sport fishers now call Orleans home port.

The many shipwrecks Orleans has had along its coastline are legendary. Local men helped organize the U.S. Life Saving Service, the predecessor to the Coast Guard. Orleans has also seen war. British marines launched an attack on Rock Harbor in December 1814. In local waters, a German U-Boat attacked a tugboat, the Perth Amboy, and four barges during World War I.

Certain things remain the same. Shell fishing has been a constant. Oysters, quahogs, and little necks continue to be harvested. Tourism, for more than a century, is what drives the community's engine. The first tourists came by railroad. Now they come by car via the Mid-Cape Highway. When President John F. Kennedy signed the bill creating the Cape Cod National Seashore, Orleans' future as a tourist destination was assured. Orleans is all about the outdoors. There are plenty of ways to fish, boat, swim, bike, or golf in town and around the Cape.

A Baseball Backgrounder

Orleans has one of the Cape's richest baseball traditions. While they dominated the Cape League in the 1940s and 1950s, Orleans set the standard for the Cape League. A key element of summer baseball's success has always been recruiting. While other teams relied on local talent, Orleans was one of the first franchises to fill its rosters with college players. The Cape League has changed, but great teams from Orleans have been a constant.

Generations of fans have seen first hand most of the area's greatest players. Eldredge Park has always been one of the baseball's top venues. At one time, hometown boys represented hometown teams. The Cape League's rosters were, at one time, mainly made up of those who were New England born and bred. Now, the best 19–20 year-olds from all over the country summer on the Cape. Orleans had some of best teams in each era.

The key to Orleans' success is the commitment of its citizens. For the better part of a century, having quality baseball at Eldredge Field has been a source of community pride. When Eldredge Field wasn't up to snuff, townspeople rolled up their sleeves to fix it. In 1966, the town allotted more than $30,000 to upgrade the facilities as well as build tennis courts and construct a bandstand at the park.

To ensure that twilight wouldn't bother batters, the configuration of the field was changed. Left field, which was once home plate, is the sun field (where the setting sun makes it difficult for outfielders). The Cardinals were one of the first teams outside of the majors to have their own bullpen cart. In the late 1970s and early 1980s, when Eldredge Field was getting frayed, the community, once again, stepped forward.

There's nothing second class about baseball in Orleans. Cardinals fans know there's more than one way to skin a cat. Winning teams from Orleans have had a variety of formulas for baseball success. Orleans had quite a run of power-hitting first basemen. Four great major-league first basemen—Jeff Conine, Frank Thomas, Todd Helton, and J.T. Snow—put a big hurt onto opposing pitchers. Future Hall of Famer Thomas used Auburn teammate Bo Jackson's bat to win the Cape's annual home run hitting contest. Gold Glover J.T. Snow still holds the league record for 21 putouts in a game, which he accomplished against Cotuit. Louisville Slugger first-team freshman Eric Berger, from Arizona, was recently signed to play first base. A couple of Red Sox greats, Carlton Fisk and Nomar Garciaparra, played for the Cardinals.

The Cardinals have recently had a strong California connection. Orleans manager Kelly Nicholson coaches Loyola High School of Los Angeles in the spring. Both Nicholson and his pitching coach, Chris Beck, have many similarities. Both have played and been pitching coaches for Loyola of Marymount University. In 2000, Nicholson worked with some of the top hurlers in the country as Team USA's pitching coach. Loyola High School has consistently been one of the top scholastic baseball teams in the Golden State.

Recently, Orleans has produced some of the league's best pitching staffs. In 2002, under Nicholson's guidance as pitching coach, the Cardinals produced its all-time team best ERA, 2.11. The next year, the Cardinals had a league-leading ERA of 2.36, striking out 397 batters in 401 innings. In 2005, Beck's first year with the Car-

dinals, Orleans had a 2.22 ERA, once again leading the league in pitching. According to Coach Nicholson, pitching out of jams is the sign of a good pitching staff. The team recently welcomed the largest player in Atlantic Coast Conference history to the Cape. Andrew Brackman of North Carolina State, who has a record of 6-10, was Orleans' stopper.

The Cardinals haven't just won with hitting and pitching. Orleans knows how to play small ball. Coach Nicholson places a priority on stealing bases, hitting behind the runner, and great defense. The 2005 Cape League champions set records for steals. They were led by quicksilver All-American shortstop Emmanuel Burris, a Kent State graduate who was a first-round pick of the San Francisco Giants.

Take Me Out to the Ballgame

Philanthropist Lewis Winslow Eldredge's generous donation to local youth is the pride of the community. The ballpark has consistently received rave reviews as one of the country's best summer parks. One of the most important aspects of the ballpark is its fan friendliness. Eldridge Park is accessible, located near downtown Orleans, on the campus of Nauset High. The games sometimes draw as many as 7,000. But even when there's a big game, fans can generally find good seats. Parking is plentiful. When the parking lot at the high school is full, the team has access to a nearby field.

A signature feature of Eldridge Park is a large berm beside first base. With

SportPix photo by Bill Vaughn

The Cardinals mascot entertaining some young Orleans fans.

things for kids to do while the adults follow the game. There's a large, safe, state-of-the-art playground in the left-field corner. Tennis players, skateboarders, and soccer players generally continue to play during the games.

At the field, a mascot named Mr. Cardinal walks around the park, greeting fans and signing autographs. Kids get a kick out of buying novelties at the ice cream truck. Souvenirs can be purchased behind home plate at Ed Mooney's "Bird's Nest," which also serves as the press box.

Despite all of the fanfare, the park has a few imperfections. It's impossible to get a good view of the field behind home plate. Watch out for broken windshields if you

the bricked buildings of Nauset High as a backdrop, thousands can comfortably sit on the sculpted terraces and cheer for the home team. The berm may be baseball's biggest, larger than any bleacher berms. Some fans bring lawn chairs, but if you arrive early a good old-fashioned beach blanket should provide sufficient seating.

Sometimes small kids get bored with baseball. Luckily, there are many park behind left field. Thank goodness, pitchers say, for wooden bats and heavy night air. The park is short down the right-field and left-field lines, which measure 312 and 300 feet respectively. It pays for pitchers to let hitters try to hit the ball to the spacious 434-foot centerfield and let outfielders do the heavy lifting.

The field looks great in the day. But the park really lights up at night. July wouldn't be quite the same without night baseball in Orleans.

Best Game (When You Think About It, How Does Someone Decide Which Game Was the Best?)

Some of the greatest games in Cardinals history have been played against archrival Chatham. All signs pointed to 2005 being Chatham's year. No other team had so many individual stars. The star-studded roster had the league's batting champion, the home run champion, and most outstanding pitcher. Eight of Chatham's players were named All-Stars. But one thing stood in its way—the Orleans Cardinals.

Picking and choosing one great game from another is impossibly difficult. But no win may have been any sweeter than Orleans' Eastern Division series victory over the Chatham A's. The Cardinals won two games on the same day.

The three-game series had a little bit of everything. Chatham looked like it was in the driver's seat after winning an exciting 11-inning marathon. The tide turned for the Cardinals.

It happened right after Chatham's Garrett Bussiere hit a long home run to give Chatham a 2-1 lead going into the fourth inning. With Chatham's best pitcher, Robert Woodward, was on the mound, things looked bleak for the visiting Cardinals. But then the fog, which Chatham is famous for, rolled in, enveloping the field and causing the game to be suspended until the next day.

The fog seemed to give the Cardinals time to regroup. When they next took the field, the Cardinals were smokin'. Pinch hitter Robert Petit hit a two-run double to give Orleans a lead. After drawing a walk, Emmanuel Burris forced an errant pickoff and ultimately scored a poor throw on a grounder to the shortstop. Orleans won the game 5-2, forcing a deciding night game hours later.

In Game 3, Chatham grabbed the early lead. But Orleans responded, holding a five-run lead. Chatham came back. But a great throw from left fielder Chris Petit nipped a Chatham baserunner at home and saved the day. After Chatham's Derrick Lutz threw behind batter Brett Pill, the managers barely averted a major fistfight late in the game. Two different pitchers had already hit Pill, so tempers flared. Chatham defeated Orleans four out of six games in the regular season. Orleans had a great regular season but had their hands full with Chatham. The Cardinals' two victories in one day were stunners.

Greatest Team (Not the '27 Yankees, but Who Is?)

In many ways, these are the good old days for the Orleans Cardinals. In 2003 the Cardinals were the 11th team in the league's history to go undefeated in the playoffs. Orleans, capturing their 10th title since the end of World War II, was one of the few teams to lose in the finals and come back the next season to win a championship. Many observers ranked 2003 as one of the team's best. Cesar Nicolas was the playoffs' Most Valuable Player, hitting .312 with three home runs and four RBIs in the post season. That year, for the first time, the Cape League's final was broadcast nationally on College Sports TV. The 2003 team was good, but many say the 2005 team was better.

In 2005, manager Kelly Nicholson's first Cardinals team rewrote the record book. Team records for most wins (30), best July record (19-7), stolen bases (111), and earned run average (2.22) were set. The stolen base mark was originally set in 1984. And the ERA mark stood for more than three decades. Emmanuel Burriss, who had 37 stolen bases, led the "Go-Go" Cardinals.

In the first inning, the key play of the championship series' deciding game occurred. An infield hit by Long Beach State's Robert Perry kept the inning alive. The hit was characteristic of the team's scrappy play. Loyola of Marymount's Chris Pettit took advantage, pulling a liner just inside the third baseline for a three-run home run. The winning pitcher was Orleans starter Brad Meyers, who only gave up one run in 12 1/3 playoff innings. Meyers, who shared the series' Most Valuable Player award, also attended Loyola of Marymount. Do we detect a trend here?

Meyers shared the Most Valuable Player award with leadoff hitter Emmanuel Burriss. Burriss was 4-for-6, reached base five times, and scored three runs in the deciding game. Burriss' ground-ball, two-run single put the game out of reach early. The Cardinals' closer, Steven Wright, finished off the Bourne Braves for its 11th championship.

Best Player . . . in My Opinion

There are many great candidates for this honor. Who to choose? Mark Texiera, Mo Vaughn, Frank Thomas. This is just a small sampling of worthy candidates. What a dilemma!

Three recent inductees to the Cape Cod Baseball League Hall of Fame deserve consideration. Comparing players from different eras is difficult. There's a good argument in favor of each player.

No one will ever match the accomplishments of Roy Bruninghaus, an outfielder for the Cardinals throughout the 1930s, 1940s, and 1950s. His playing career began in 1933 and ended in 1955. He attended Holy Cross, where he was signed to play in the Red Sox farm system. Bruninghaus was a pitcher, outfielder, and first baseman. A perennial All-Star and long-time captain, he was the glue that held together the Orleans team that won six championships.

Some Red Sox fans may remember Jim Norris. After spending 1969 and 1970 with Orleans, Norris had a very good career in the majors with the Cleveland Indians and the Texas Rangers. Norris was a perfect two-for-two, being named to two All-Star teams and playing for two playoff contenders. The Maryland alumnus was the league's Most Valuable Player in 1969, and finished off his career by batting .421 in the 1970 playoffs. He was named to the Cape Cod League's all-time 50th anniversary team.

San Francisco first baseman Lance Niekro—nephew of former Brave Phil

Niekro and son of late Astros player Joe Niekro—set many team hitting records. Niekro set records for most hits, longest hitting streak, most runs batted in, most total bases, and most home runs. A Triple Crown winner, Joe's son made his family proud when he was inducted into the league's Hall of Fame.

A couple of other players who deserve special recognition are Texas first baseman Mark Teixeira, who won the league's Most Valuable Player award, and catcher Matt Wieters from Georgia Tech. The backstop, following in the footsteps of other Georgia Tech alums Nomar Garciaparra and Jason Varitek, captured the Robert A. McNeese Award as the best pro prospect. It was the sixth time a Cardinal won this award.

Round Tripper (Some Suggestions for Sightseers)

If you visit Orleans, you'd better like the beach. A couple of the East Coast's most spectacular beaches are just a short drive from downtown Orleans. Nauset Beach on the southern side of the Cape Cod National Seashore may be the area's most popular beach. There are more than 1,000 parking spaces at its lots. The wavy, windy beach is perfect for surfing and windsailing. For sports fishing and pleasure excursions, few ports can match what's offered at Rock Harbor on the other side of town. Fleets of vessels hunt big-game fish like bass, bluefish, and tuna.

If you want to get out of the sun, check out the Jonathan Young Wind-mill, located on Route 6A on the Town Cove. It was originally built in the 1700s and is now operated by the town's historical society. Cape Cod was once known for its windmills. This is one of the last real windmills in existence on the Cape. Snow's Department Store at 22 Main Street is a local institution. A trip to Snow's will never bore the kids because there's a massive model railroad, with all of the bells and whistles, in the middle of the store. Orleans is accessible to all of the attractions of the lower Cape, including the Cape Cod National Seashore, which runs all the way to the tip of Provincetown.

Places to Eat . . . If You Want More Than Cracker Jack

One of the best places on the Cape to grab a cup of coffee or a snack is the Chocolate Sparrow. It takes real skill to brew a great cup of coffee. The staff at the Chocolate Sparrow has discovered the secret to success: great organically grown coffee, fresh chocolate, great desserts, and snacks. The Chocolate Sparrow has won many awards for their coffee, dessert, and chocolate. Because they open early and close late, it's always a convenient place to grab a bite to eat, access wireless Internet access, and check the daily paper. The Chocolate Sparrow can be found at 5 Old Colony Way in Orleans. The phone number is 508-240-2230.

Another interesting place to eat or stay is at the Orleans Inn, right near the rotary on Route 6A. The restored Victorian-Era inn is practically in the water. Boats and birds are part of the backyard landscape. There are many other dining choices in town. The Lobster Pot and Cooke's are famous restaurants that are right down the street. Captain Elmer's, at 18 Old Colony Way, is closer to downtown. Orleans is one of the few towns on the Cape to actually have fast-food chains. There's a Papa Gino's and Wendy's. One of the better places to get an affordable yet hearty meal is the Hearth 'n Kettle.

Sources:

The Baseball Almanac, 1995–2007.
Boston Globe, 1900–2007.
Cape Cod Times, 1990–2007.
Chatham A's Program, 2007.
New York Times, 1890–2007.
Orleans Cardinals Program, 2006–2007.
Glassman-Jaffe, Marcia. *Fun with the Family in Massachusetts: Third Edition*. Guilford, Connecticut: The Globe Pequot Press, 2002.
Price, Christopher. *Baseball by the Beach—A History of America's National Pastime on Cape Cod*. Yarmouthport, Massachusetts: On Cape Publications, 1998.

www.atlanticleague.com
www.all-baseball.com
www.ballparkdigest.com
www.ballparkreviews.com
www.baseballalmanac.com
www.baseballamericaonline.com
www.capecodbaseball.org
www.capecodcommission.org/pathways/trailguide.htm#orleans
www.capecod-orleans.com/
www.orleanscardinals.com
www.orleanshistoricalsociety.org/windmill.htm
www.orleansinn.com/history.html
www.sabr.org
www.town.orleans.ma.us/document.ccml?34,7,2232,cc2232,,,Doc,page.html
www.whalewatch.com/

13

Address: 105 Wahconah Street, Pittsfield, MA 01201

Web Site: *www.pittsfielddukes.com*, *pittsfieldelms.org*

First Game: 1892

Dimensions: LF 334 CF 374 RCF 400 RF 333

Directions: From the Massachusetts Turnpike (Route 90) take Exit 2. Take Route 7 North into Pittsfield. At the rotary, proceed halfway around to North Street. Proceed on North Street until Berkshire Medical Center. Take left onto Wahconah Street. One-quarter mile down the street on left is Wahconah Park.

From the north, take Route 7 South until Wahconah Street. Proceed on Wahconah Street until you reach 105 Wahconah Street and Wahconah Park will be on the right.

PITTSFIELD, MA

WAHCONAH PARK

Home of the Pittsfield Dukes (New England Collegiate Baseball League) and the Pittsfield Elms (Vintage)

Claim to Fame

Historic Wahconah Park is one of the last wooden ballparks in the country. Pittsfield was the site of the first inter-collegiate baseball game in history. A record from 1791 of a game played in Pittsfield is the oldest written account of a baseball game.

Strange but True

During a two-week tour of New England in September 1902, President Theodore Roosevelt's carriage was involved in a terrible head-on collision with a trolley in Pittsfield. The president's bodyguard was killed and Roosevelt almost got into a fistfight with the trolley driver. The driver pled guilty to manslaughter and was sentenced to six months in jail.

Who's Who in Pittsfield

Bobby Bonds, Jim Bouton, Larry Bowa, A.J. Burnett, Bobby Doerr, Hugh Duffy, Carlton Fisk, Lou Gehrig, Ken Griffey Jr., Bill Lee, Mike Lowell, Sparky Lyle, Greg

Maddux, Joe Morgan, Jamie Moyer, Thurman Munson, Satchell Paige, Raphael Palmiero, Herb Pennock, Jim Rice, Cal Ripken Sr., Curt Schilling, Mike Schmidt, John Smoltz, Casey Stengel, Jim Thorpe, Tim Wakefield, Earl Weaver, Ted Williams, and Don Zimmer.

About Pittsfield

Pittsfield's founding may prove that real estate speculation is the world's second-oldest profession. In 1738 Pittsfield's founder, Colonel Jacob Wendell, purchased 24,000 acres of prime real estate in the Berkshires. The Colonel never visited western Massachusetts and made the purchase sight unseen. The city's original name was Pontoosuck, which in Mohican means "a field or haven for winter deer." What was good enough

for winter deer was good enough for colonial settlers, Wendell figured. But his ambitious plans to subdivide and develop the land never worked out.

Nevertheless, Pittsfield grew. By 1761, a group of 200 residents decided to give their community a permanent name. The Township of Pittsfield was named after British Prime Minister William Pitt, who was very popular for his support of America.

The Revolutionary War was a time of growth for Pittsfield. At the turn of the eighteenth century, the Township of Pittsfield had more than 2,000 residents. A great source of the city's wealth has always been its location, on the banks of the mighty Housatonic River. The river powered the lumber mills, grist mills, and textile mills, which all fueled the beginnings of the Industrial Revolution.

Photo courtesy of Paul Healey

A hitter digs in at venerable Wahconah Park.

If Pittsfield's first town team had a nickname at the time, it would have been the "Lambs" or the "Sheepherders." Pittsfield owed its early prosperity to sheep. Pittsfield's baseball team was once named the "Electrics," in recognition of the town's electric industry. An enterprising resident imported the first Merino sheep from Spain to Pittsfield. The sheep quickly adjusted to their home in the new world. Merino sheep produce high-quality wool, which sparked a nationwide growth in textile manufacturing. Today, Pittsfield's opportunities in the manufacturing industry have declined.

Another important factor in Pittsfield's growth was General Electric (GE). William Stanley built the world's first electric transformer in the town. Pittsfield's workers have provided electricity to millions of people. Stanley's business was the first piece in the puzzle that built multinational giant GE. Pittsfield's fortunes have risen and fallen with GE. Still located in Pittsfield is GE Advanced Materials (plastics), but, because of changes in the electric and aerospace industry, a GE workforce that was once more than 13,000 now adds up to less than 700 workers.

Pittsfield may be inland, but the town has a strong connection to the sea. Herman Melville penned his famous epic *Moby Dick* at his Pittsfield home. The humpbacks of nearby Mount Greylock inspired Melville's descriptions of the great white whale.

Arts, culture, and baseball are key components of Pittsfield's post-industrial future. Tanglewood, the summer home of the Boston Symphony Orchestra, is located in neighboring Lenox. The Berkshire Museum is a great place to visit. And the Colonial Theatre is a pristine example of turn-of-the-century theatre architecture. These are just a few examples of what the city has to offer.

At the same time, Pittsfield hasn't forgotten about its favorite game: baseball. Historian John Thorne's recent discovery of the oldest written account of the game has inspired the nation. Pittsfield initiated "The Art of the Game," to celebrate Pittsfield's baseball heritage. The Berkshire Museum recently had an exhibit about the Red Sox–Yankee rivalry.

A Baseball Backgrounder

Practically everything that can happen in baseball has occurred at Pittsfield's Wahconah Park. According to the city's official records, baseball has been played at the site of the grand old ballpark since 1892. But, truth be told, it seems like hardball has always been played there.

Where did baseball really start? Maybe the answer is Pittsfield. Historian John Thorne may have recently discovered baseball's Rosetta Stone in the dusty archives of Pittsfield's city hall. His discovery is proof positive that our nation's first baseball addicts may have been the men and women of the Berkshires. There's still plenty of speculation about baseball's origins. But there's no doubt that by 1791, playing baseball on Pittsfield's green had become much more than a game. To many homeowners near the makeshift ballpark, baseball was a public nuisance. Baseball and glass windows have always been a bad mix. Neighbors near the green had to stay alert for stray balls from the diamond. After years of being on the losing end of local ballgames, homeowners finally decided enough was enough. The town fathers put an end to baseball. Selectmen stepped in, passed an ordinance, and banned baseball from being played on the town common.

In 1858, another major milestone in baseball history occurred. Pittsfield, located halfway between Amherst College and Williams College, was chosen to serve as a neutral venue for the first intercollegiate baseball game ever played. The event was also the first double header—the opener was a baseball game and the finale was the first American intercollegiate chess match in history. Amherst challenged Williams to an old fashioned game of hardball. Williams accepted the Amherst's challenge and countered with a chess match, a "trial of mind as well as muscle." Amherst won at both sports. It was the beginning of one of collegiate sport's greatest rivalries.

Baseball has endured in Pittsfield. Construction of the original Wahconah Park in 1892 brought baseball's modern era to the Berkshires. The first game took place in August 1892. The teams were from Pittsfield and Albany. It didn't take long for it to become a hardball haven. Ladies and gents paid 25 cents to see the great Holy Cross Crusaders play a group of local all-stars. At the time, the Crusaders were one of the greatest collegiate teams in the country. The home team, according to the game's promoters, had "been selected from the best players in the county" and was "the strongest team that has yet contested for Berkshire baseball honors." Holy Cross outfielder Lou Sockalexes, the first Native American to play big league ball, was the most famous participant. Sockalexus was billed, as "the heaviest hitter and fastest baserunner in the country." But today he is known as the original "Cleveland Indian." The Cleveland Indian's Web site claims the team was named after the Penobscot.

Take Me Out to the Ballgame

Wahconah Park, as we know it, was built in 1919. The ballpark and its surrounding 50-acre site were donated to the city. It has been home to many different professional teams. Pittsfield's first professional franchise, a member of the New York State League, lasted only a month. Its second team, the "Hillies," played in the Eastern League until mid-1930. The Mets have had a team here. So did the Cubs, the Astros, the Washington Senators, the Milwaukee Brewers, and the Red Sox. Future Red Sox fan favorite, George "Boomer" Scott, won the Triple Crown as a young third baseman for the Eastern League Pittsfield Red Sox. Another New Englander, Hall of Famer Carlton Fisk, later became the team's catcher. Mark Grace, Shawon Dunston, and Greg Maddux learned the ins and outs of professional ball for the Cubs' Double A team. Hometown boy and former Texas Ranger Tom Grieve was the first draft choice of the old Washington Senators and played for their affiliate.

Photo courtesy of Paul Healey

View of the grandstands and wooden bleachers at Wahconah.

Wahconah Park has had almost as many renovations as tenants. In the Roaring Twenties, the grandstand was repaired. During the Great Depression, a 1,300-man crew re-graded the baseball field. After World War II, the city installed eight light towers and built a new scoreboard. At the beginning of the Cold War, Pittsfield invested in new toilets, concessions, a locker room, and a new grandstand. And, to celebrate the nation's bicennentenial, the federal government spent $700,000 to contain the overflowing banks of the mighty Housatonic River.

For many years, the ballfield's spacious outfield was 352 to left field, 362 to center field, and 333 to right field. But the dimensions, like many other things about the ballpark, are now different. Now, a 430-foot drive is needed for a home run over the right-center-field fence. Great center- and right-field play is important at Wahconah.

The ballpark has seen many changes, but the old plastic owls in Wahconah's grandstand have always been there. The city has welcomed countless sports heroes, musicians, and fans. But the nesting birds that once inhabited the ballpark were not wanted. What a mess! Installing the owls was an inventive solution to a frustrating problem.

The sunsets are another unique feature of Wahconah. While most ballparks face east, not Wahconah. The historic ballpark is one of the few ballparks that face west. That's because

Photo courtesy of Paul Healey

Wahconah is a step back to a simpler time for baseball fans.

there was no night baseball when it was built. Builders didn't consider how the setting sun could impact a game. For many years, it was the only stadium in organized ball to have both "rain delays" and "sun delays."

The famous sun delays occur when the glare of the setting sun shines directly into the eyes of the hitter, catcher, and umpire at home plate. In 1989, management built a large mesh fence and planted trees in centerfield to block the sun. Since then, sun delays have been rare. There were no sun delays in either 1996 or 1999, and there were just two in 1998.

Many times, Wahconah's days seemed to have been numbered. In 1942, the owner of the Pittsfield Electrics had plans to build a new ballpark

on Dalton Street. In 1946, the night baseball and a new scoreboard gave the ballpark new life. The last affiliated team, the Pittsfield Astros, moved to Troy, New York. But several independent leagues have tried to make Wahconah work. The last professional team to call it home was the Berkshire Bears of the Canadian-American League. Former major leaguer Jim Bouton tried to bring professional baseball back to the Berskhires. Unfortunately, he wasn't successful.

Under the stewardship of the Pittsfield Dukes of the New England Collegiate Baseball League, Wahconah's future looks much brighter. Former Red Sox general manager Dan Duquette owns the club, drawing inspiration from spending summers following George Scott, Billy Conigliaro, Sparky Lyle, Carlton Fisk, and the old Pittsfield Red Sox. The Dukes regularly draw more than 1,500 a game.

The city recently took an important step toward ensuring the ballparks' future by submitting an application to have Wahconah Park and 18.2 surrounding acres placed on the National Register of Historic Places. The next step is to expand the parking lot from 225 to 500 spaces. Plans are also on the drawing board to eliminate the persistent flooding from the Housatonic River. More renovations to the restrooms, grandstand, and clubhouse are planned.

In 2005, more than 50,000 people stepped through the gates of the park for cultural and sporting events. The Bob Dylan/Willie Nelson concert drew one of the largest crowds of the summer—10,000 people. The last time Wahconah was in the national spotlight was July 3, 2004. A live vintage baseball game, 1886 style, featuring the Hartford Senators and the Pittsfield Hillies was broadcast by ESPN Classic. The wooden bleacher seats can bother your back. And, in some rows, there's very little legroom. But every fan's seat is practically on top of the action. The sightlines are close. And there's still great baseball being played. If you visit the park, you get a good idea about what baseball was really like around the turn of the century.

Despite its flaws, Wahconah continues to serve its intended purpose. The park is not just for the professionals who play the games, but for the people who go to watch the games. High school baseball, football, and soccer are played at the field. It has hosted Pittsfield's state champion 14-year-old Babe Ruth All-Star. And a couple of old football foes, Pittsfield High School and Taconic High School, have renewed their rivalry at Wahconah Park. With everything going on, it's looking more certain that the community will continue to enjoy the ballpark through the new millennium. When visiting Wahconah, don't forget to try a hot dog. Wohrle's Hotdogs are the best in the Berkshires.

To raise some extra cash, the owners of the Hillies organized a big raffle for a house off of Dalton Avenue. There was one problem with the contest: it was totally illegal. Holding unlicensed sweepstakes was illegal in Massachusetts. Eager to make good, the management agreed to refund every penny collected—$15,252.51 to be specific. Anyone who asked for one got a refund. But many ticket holders didn't bother to ask for a refund. The Hillies therefore pocketed a cool $10,941.92. The best donnybrook came on August 22, 1971. Maybe this is how a former National League batting champion got the nickname "Maddog." While with Pittsfield of the Eastern League, Bill Madlock was suspended for the entire season for his involvement in a brawl. It all started when Madlock was nearly beaned in the head by pitcher Bob Cluck. An enraged Madlock broke from the restraint of home plate umpire Ken Kaiser and charged the mound, setting off a war. White Sox scout Deacon Jones, who was in the stands, said, "It was the best fight I've seen in my many years in baseball." The Pittsfield police had to come onto the field to restore order, and arrested one player. Several witnesses claimed Madlock had swung a bat and hit a Waterbury player in the arm. Later, the league shortened his suspension. League President Roy Jackson stated: "As I reconstruct the picture, there was no actual swinging of the bat over his head, but there was some swishing of it back and forth. I want to be fair about it. [Madlock] has served a 14-day suspension and has paid a $75 fine. That's a reasonable penalty. I feel that he has learned his lesson."

Best Game (When You Think About It, How Does Someone Decide Which Game Was the Best?)

Thousands of players have played at Wahconah Park. So it's difficult to pick the best game. But there's no doubt that the old stadium's defining moment occurred on July 3, 2003. It was an evening where the old stadium became the center of the baseball world. Wahconah was the host of a live, nationally broadcast vintage baseball game between the Hartford Senators and the Pittsfield Hillies. The contest was played strictly by the book. The 1886 Rulebook, that is.

The game was very civil. Umpires were treated with the utmost respect. Batters could request "Gentleman's Rulings," asking pitchers to throw the ball high or low. All balls out of play had to be returned to the umpire. Three strikes was an out, but batters walked after seven balls.

More than 6,000 fans attended, the largest crowd ever to watch baseball in Pittsfield history. Tim Robbins and Susan Sarandon were among the fans. The game proved some things about the game are the same: Pitching has always been the key to winning baseball. The hometown Hillies started strong, holding a seven-run lead, but couldn't hold the fort. Pitcher, manager, and owner Jim Bouton lost the game. The Senators won 14-12. But the real winner was Pittsfield and baseball.

Greatest Team (Not the '27 Yankees, but Who Is?)

For four years, starting in 1985, the Pittsfield Cubs of the Eastern League produced some incredible baseball talent. Jamie Moyer, Darrin Jackson, Mike Brumley, Jerome Walton, Gary Varsho, Dwight Smith, and Hector Villaneuva are alumni who had long careers as major leaguers. The Cubs finished in second with two future Hall of Famers, Raphael Palmeiro, who was the league's Most Valuable Player, and all-time pitching great Greg Maddux, who finished 4-3 with a 2.89 ERA. The next year, future great Mark Grace was the Pittsfield Cubs' second straight Most Valuable Player award winner, leading the league with 101 RBIs.

A close second was the mid-to-late sixties Pittsfield Red Sox, who actually won more games than the Cubs. The "Boomer," George Scott, won the Triple Crown. Reggie Smith played second base. Massachusetts resident Billy McLeod was the ace of the 1965 Eastern League champions. The accomplishments of the Pittsfield Red Sox set the stage for Boston's "Impossible Dream" season. In 1969, Hall of Famer Carlton Fisk got off to a rocky start as a professional catcher, leading Eastern League catchers in errors.

Best Player . . . In My Opinion

Many great players are part of Pittsfield's baseball history, but the greatest of them all may have been Hall of Famer Frank Grant. Many historians believe he was the best African-American player of the nineteenth century. Little about Grant is known, but his accomplishments on the field speak for themselves.

Right after the Civil War, baseball was integrated. In 1886, Grant played second base, batting .325, for Meriden, Connecticut, in the Eastern League. When that team folded, he was signed by Buffalo, where he led International League in home runs with 11 while batting .340 and stealing 40 bases. Grant endured terrible racism. Other players would slide into second base, feet first, to injure the second baseman. Grant started wearing shin guards to protect himself from the sharpened spikes of his opponents. In 1888, the color barrier reappeared. Blacks were banned from organized ball. Grant finished out his last year in the majors with a flourish, batting .346. By 1890, Grant was out of organized ball and relegated to the sandlots of segregation.

Round Tripper (Some Suggestions for Sightseers)

There are plenty of great summer activities in the area. Tanglewood, the summer home of the Boston Symphony Orchestra, is located in neighboring Lenox. If classical music doesn't appeal to you, how do you feel about the theater?

The Colonial Theatre, built in 1903, is considered one of the greatest turn-of-the century playhouses in the world. It was designed by world-renowned architect and critic J.B. McElfatrick, who also rebuilt the Metropolitan Opera House of Philadelphia, the National Theater in Washington, D.C., and more than 300 other venues across the country. The Colonial has hosted a number of great events, including the stage debut of former Red Sox general manager Dan Duquette in *Damn Yankees*.

If you want to get away from the hubbub of the city, why not try what is called the "City of Peace?" Hancock Shaker Village, located on 1,200 acres within the beautiful Berkshires, is a 20-building compound with many fine examples of American craftsmanship. There are many educational programs and tours regularly offered. There's plenty of room to roam. The Round Stone Barn is a famous example of the elegant simplicity of Shaker design. Hancock Shaker Village is located on Route 20 in Pittsfield, Massachusetts, just west of the junction of Routes 20 and 41.

Arrowhead, Herman Mellville's home, is another great tourist attraction. And if that's not enough, just go outside. There are plenty of opportunities to enjoy the beauty of the Berkshires.

Places to Eat . . . If You Want More Than Cracker Jack

If you visit the Berkshires, try some Italian eateries. Many Italians immigrated to the Pittsfield area to work in the factories, bringing along their fine-dining traditions. The Highland Restaurant, located at 100 Fenn Street, has a long tradition of fine, affordable dining. Belissimo Dolce, has opera music, delicious pastries, and real cappuccino. Trattoria Rustica on McKay Street features fresh mozzarella and baked bread. Elizabeth's Borderland Café at 76 North Street is another good choice for Mediterranean dining.

Sources:

The Baseball Almanac, 1995–2007.
   Berkshire Eagle, 1999–2007.
Glassman-Jaffe, Marcia. *Fun with the Family in Massachusetts: Third Edition*. Guilford, Connecticut: The Globe Pequot Press, 2002.
Pietrusza, David. *Baseball's Canadian-American League*. Jefferson, North Carolina: McFarland, 2005.

www.all-baseball.com
www.ballparkdigest.com
www.ballparkreviews.com
www.baseballalmanac.com
www.baseballamericaonline.com
www.berkshireeagle.com
www.canamleague.com
http://ci.bridgeport.ct.us/
www.davidpietrusza.com
www.digitalballparks.com/
www.easternleague.com/history.htm
www.hancockshakervillage.org
www.nlbpa.com/grant__frank.html
www.pittsfieldelms.com
www.pittsfield-ma.org/history.asp
www.pittsfieldramadainn.com
www.pittsfieldweb.com
www.sabr.org
www.state.ma.us
www.thecolonialtheater.org
http://www.wahconahpark.com

14

WAREHAM, MA
CLEM SPILLANE FIELD

Address: 54 Marion Road, Wareham, MA 02571-1428

Web Site: *www.gatemen.org*

First Game: 1930s

Dimensions: LF 318 LCF 365 CF 400 RCF 365 RF 330

Directions: The field is located directly behind the Town Hall parking lot.

From Cape Cod, take 25/495 North from Bourne Bridge and follow to Exit 1 (Route 195 West). Take Exit 21 (first exit) to Route 28, Cranberry Highway. Turn left at end ramp onto Route 28 South. Follow signs to Blue Hospital to the traffic lights at Route 6/Marion Road. Turn right at the traffic lights and continue 0.2 miles. Viking Drive is just after Wareham Town Hall on the left.

From Middleboro/Boston, take 25/495S to Exit 1 (Route 195 West). Follow above directions from this point.

From New Bedford/Providence: Follow Route 195 East to Exit 21 (Wareham/Route 28). Take a right at the top of the ramp. Follow above directions from this point.

Home of the Wareham Gatemen of the Cape Cod Baseball League

Claim to Fame

Wareham is called the "Gateway to the Cape." The Tremont Nail Factory was the oldest continuously operating nail factory in the country. Onset Beach has many rare examples of Victorian architecture along its shoreline.

Strange but True

The world's most extensive collection of thermometers is housed in Wareham. The curator of the museum, the "Thermometer Man," can tell you how hot it is, anywhere in the world, and is conversant in Celsius, Kelvin, and Fahrenheit.

Who's Who in Wareham

Over the years, Wareham has had quite a few distinguished alumni. At the end of 2006, 34 Gatemen had made it to the big leagues. The list starts with Barry Zito, Ben Sheets, Lance Berkman, Jeremy Sowers, Nick Swisher, Andy LaRoche, Matt Murtyn, and David Murphy. Some other alumni include Doug Glanville, Mo Vaughn, Chuck Knoblauch, Pete Incaviglia, Bob Tewksbury, and Walt Weiss. The bottom line is that Wareham, like other teams on the Cape, has produced a large number of quality future major leaguers.

About Wareham

Wareham isn't really on Cape Cod. While every other Cape Cod community is in Barnstable County, Wareham is in Plymouth. It's one of the last stops for tourists before the Cape. Nevertheless the town's architecture, activities, and character is pure Cape Cod. While the summer population swells, Wareham has many fulltime residents. With soaring housing costs, commuters to Boston and Providence have discovered the affordable housing in town. In many ways, the "Gateway to the Cape" has become a bedroom community.

The town was originally incorporated in 1739. But even before the Europeans arrived, Native Americans would camp out on its offshore islands during the summertime. The town's motto, "NEPINNAE KEKIT," means "summer home" in Wampanoag. The town's first name was "Webquish." How they decided upon "Wareham" is somewhat of a mystery. The original Wareham is not an Atlantic seaport—it's located on the banks of the Puddle River. Maybe the colonists had a rich benefactor named Lord Wareham. No great battles have ever been fought in Wareham, Massachusetts—unlike Wareham, England. The closest it ever came to war was during the War of 1812, when 200 British ma-rines stormed through the center of town on a search and destroy mission against a cotton factory.

Like many other coastline communities, the local economy was based on fishing and shipbuilding. But Wareham has a long industrial history. Cranberries are now grown in bogs where iron was once harvested. Blast furnaces fired away along the Weweantit River. Wareham businesses were the first to start the mass production of nails. The last, the Tremont Nail Company, recently packed up its bags and moved to another Massachusetts location. Recently purchased by the town, the seven-acre former factory site is being preserved for posterity.

Just before the Civil War, the transportation revolution sparked a summer tourism boom. The new railroad opened up the town to the rich and famous. Old Victorian hotels, like the Oak Crest and Anchor Inn, had a great oceanside view. In its heyday, musicians like Tommy Dorsey, Cab Calloway, and Duke Ellington would regularly appear at local nightclubs. But the good times didn't last forever.

The automobile age brought about the end of Wareham's golden era. Great Victorian houses along the shoreline were sometimes forgotten. Many were left intact. Meanwhile, other local industries, such as cranberry growing, flourished. Wareham was rediscovered in the 1980s, when local preservationists decided that it made sense to rehabilitate Onset Village.

Despite the passage of time, the town retains a strong sense of tradition. Shipbuilding continues at Cape Cod Shipbuilding Company. While the old New Orleans style steamboats have been retired, Onset is the embarkation point for tour cruises and deep sea fishing trips. Wareham is a diverse, racially mixed community. There's a large Cape Verdean population. A highlight of the summer is the annual Cape Verdean summer festival. Musicians come from all over the world to celebrate the culture of the small islands off the African east coast.

A Baseball Backgrounder

Wareham's baseball history has been a rollercoaster ride. Teams from Wareham have played in several different leagues. At one time, its main rivals were mostly from southeastern Massachusetts, not the Cape. The town's main rival was Carver. Former Hall of Fame catcher Mickey Cochrane, nicknamed "Black Mike," played for Middleboro against Wareham.

Against every competition, Wareham has had its share of success. When the Cape Cod League was first organized, it was on top. Wareham captured its first Cape Cod Baseball League crown in 1930 and was the toast of the town. Local residents feted the champions with a banquet at the Old Colony Inn. Marchers celebrated by having a great parade through the center of town. Appreciative fans raised enough money to give each player a gold watch. These days, players who received lavish gifts would be ineligible to play collegiate ball. But in those days, winning players enjoyed the spoils of war.

Cranberry king John Decas ran the team from 1976 until 1983. The 1983 team had a winning record, but not enough players stayed to put together a team for the playoffs. Only 12 players, including 10 pitchers, were on the post-season roster. Decas concluded there was no sense in continuing if Wareham couldn't field a competitive team. He suggested that the next best team take its place. The league and the Gatemen had a big misunderstanding. Cape League headquarters rejected the Decas' proposal and the Gatemen decided not to participate in the playoffs. This created a firestorm. There was some talk that Wareham would be kicked out of the league. Over the winter, fences were mended. But there were some tough times until the late 1980s.

A group of new volunteers, led by John Wylde and John Claffey, changed the Gatemen forever. More money was raised. Facilities at Spillane Field were updated. John Wylde turned himself into one of baseball's greatest scouts, personally attending games all across the country. The new management approach worked wonders. The team quickly moved up in the standings. Other teams quickly took notice of the Gatemen and made necessary adjustments to stay competitive. A rising tide lifts all ships. And the quality of play for the whole Cape improved.

Wareham quickly climbed to the top of Cape League standings. The team had some great stars, like Walt Weiss and Pete Incaviglia. But the 1988 team is credited with bringing back baseball in Wareham. Former Red Sox player Mo Vaughn and former Yankee Chuck Knoblauch led the Gatemen to the championship. Over the past two decades Wareham has won five championships and more games than any other Cape team.

Don Reed was one of the Cape's greatest managers. And current manager Cooper Farris is considered to be one of the best hitting teachers in baseball. In his year on the Cape, the three best hitters on the Cape were Gatemen. The team achieved an all-time high average of .261, while winning another Cape League championship. Ryan Beggs, the Gatemen's pitching coach, tutored some outstanding staffs. His first two years, 2001 and 2002, in Wareham were record breakers. The first year his staff set the team's all-time best ERA 1.84. His second year was better than the first, setting another record with a miniscule 1.81 ERA.

Many of Wareham's best-known players have been hitters. Houston Astros star Lance Berkmen hit .352 in 1996. Chuck Knoblauch had 61 hits in 1994. And Walt Weiss set the team's all-time doubles record at 19. But recently, pitching has been very strong. Red Sox first-round draft pick Daniel Bard had a 1.25 ERA, leading the league in strikeouts and innings pitched. Bard left the Cape in a blaze of glory, striking out 8 of the last 11 batters he faced. Nobody has ever seen a more promising young left-hander than Cleveland Indian Jeremy Sowers who had 1.52 in 2002.

For many years, the organization's main mission has been to prepare collegiate players for professional baseball. By any measure, the all-volunteer organization has been a rousing success. In 2003, three of the top four prospects on the Cape, Wade Townsend, Andy LaRoche, and Jeremy Sowers, played here. In 2005, the majors drafted 25 former Gatemen. In 2006, 34 alumni were invited to participate in major league spring training camps.

Wareham has one of the Cape League's largest followings. The whole community has taken particular pride that several of its players have been drafted by the Red Sox. Georgia Tech slugger and Red Sox draftee Matt Murton led the team to two championships. His teammate David Murphy quickly moved through the farm system and played outfield for the Red Sox. Justin Masterson from San Diego State landed a temporary roster spot with the team and made the best of it. In 2005, the sidewinding right-hander became Wareham's closer. Red Sox scouts took notice and drafted the Gateman, who had a great professional debut for the Lowell Spinners. There's also a bit of an old Ivy League connection. Steffan Wilson, Ben Crockett, Shawn Haviland, and Lance Salsgiver are recent Harvard men who've played for Wareham. In 2006, there were four non-roster invitees from the Ivies.

If you don't go to the games, you can read all about the Gatemen. The Gatemen were one of the first teams in amateur ball to keep detailed statistics about their players, and one of the first to have its own play-by-play broadcast team. The team also pioneered the use of a state-of-the-art scoring system. The team's yearbook editor, Dotty Tamagini, produces one of the best media guides in baseball.

SportsPix photo by Bill Vaughan

The managers and umpires going over the ground rules.

It's the only team with a regular beat man from a large daily paper. Readers can regularly check on the team's comings and goings in the *New Bedford Standard-Times*.

Take Me Out to the Ballgame

Spillane Field is one of the Cape's greatest attractions. Located on the campus of Wareham High, the old ballpark is comfortable and convenient. It's an easy ride for off-Cape baseball fans, just a short drive away from I-195. Wareham is a regional team, drawing fans from all over southeastern Massachusetts. Large contingents from New Bedford and Plymouth are among the most fervent fans.

The Gatemen's home is the only enclosed ballpark on the Cape, with large grandstands beside first and third base. The perch behind home plate is reserved for the scouts and media. Downstairs, there's a large concession stand and souvenir store. The best seat in the house is reserved for John Wylde. And why shouldn't it be? He's not just team president and general manager, but is also its voice. For many years, he's been the team's public address announcer. Spillane Field has ground-level seating underneath the third base grandstand. This may the best-protected area in baseball. Fans are completely safe from stray foul balls. If this were the majors, you'd have to pay big bucks to sit there. But this being the Cape, this choice location is completely free. These seats go fast so get to the park early if you want to get first dibs. Don't forget to bring your lawn chair.

When the grandstands fill up, there's usually overflow seating in the outfield bleachers. Even at a tender age, many Cape League pitchers

Yarmouth-Dennis takes BP before a game at Clem Spillane Field.

throw just as hard as the major leaguers. There's a ledge in right field where fans can see, up close and personal, the home-team bullpen. Generally, this writer observed more scouts, scorebooks, and formatted scouting reports at Wareham than at any other Cape League ballpark. Scouts don't just work for professional teams. Agents hire their own birddogs to check out local talent. It's another example of big-business baseball.

The infield, some rivals say, gives the Gatemen a competitive advantage. While most ballparks have clay infields, Wareham does not. The Gatemen's infield is made of ground-up seashells. Groundballs at Gatemen games can take some strange bounces.

The atmosphere at its games is very similar to a minor-league game. The team is extremely interested in providing educational opportunities for local youth. Wareham High School's DECA Program (Distributive Education Classes of America) manages the food concession area. Students learn about what it takes to succeed in business while enjoying baseball.

While the Spillane Field may be old, it's still one of the best. Running a Cape Cod League team is more than a summer commitment. Volunteers work during the off-season to make the great ballpark better. In 2000, a new infield was installed. The next year, the outfield, which also is used as a football field, was re-sodded. The drainage system was replaced. Handicapped access was improved. More toilets were installed. Six new light posts were recently added. There's also a new sound system. The story of the Wareham Gatemen is one of continuous improvement. The upkeep of Spillane Field is one of the volunteers' greatest legacies.

Best Game (When You Think About It, How Does Someone Decide Which Game Was the Best?)

The 2001 Cape Cod League champions were a star-filled team. The Gatemen swept most of the Cape League's major honors. Florida Marlins/Texas A&M outfielder Eric Reed led the league in batting. Matt Murton was the regular-season Most Valuable Player. Chris Leonard, with a 6-0 record and an 0.98 ERA, was the pitcher of the year. Red Sox draft choice Ben Crockett—2000's best pitcher—was also on the staff. The playoff's Most Valuable Player, Toronto Blue Jays infielder Aaron Hill was 8 for 20.

But winning a championship is a total team effort. If the bottom of the order hadn't come through, Chatham would have been champion. In the final game of the championship series, Wareham's best two pitchers weren't able to put Chatham away. Ben Crockett, the starter, left the deciding game with a lead. But Chris Leonard couldn't hold it. Chatham tied the game in the eighth.

The winning rally started in the bottom of the ninth. Keith Butler led off with a single. Catcher Rusty Meyer's sacrifice moved Butler to second. Eric Reed's groundout moved the winning run to third. Then it was all up to shortstop Paul Henry. He quickly got behind with a 1-2 count before fighting off several pitches. Then it happened. Henry hit a topper to third base. The ball just barely stayed in play. Keith Butler scored. The big hitting Wareham team won the championship by "playing little ball"—an unlikely ending to a great series.

Greatest Team (Not the '27 Yankees, but Who Is?)

The 1988 team is considered to be one of the Cape's greatest teams. Its record, 29-13-2, speaks for itself. No other team in Cape League history has been better. The key to the 1988 team was depth. The Gatemen featured a lethal combination of speed and power. Mike Weimerskirch led the team with 25 stolen bases. Future major league star Chuck Knoblauch had 23 stolen bases, 17 doubles, and hit .361.

Imagine all of the RBI opportunities for Mo Vaughn! The skinny Seton Hall first baseman had 17 doubles and many RBIs. The team had it all, and was easily able to win another Cape League championship.

Best Player . . . In My Opinion

There are many deserving candidates for the honor. Chicago Cubs outfielder Matt Murton led the team to two championships. In his first year, he won a Most Valuable Player award and led the league in RBIs. In his second, the Georgia Tech great hit .400 and won the All-Star Game's home run derby. Mo Vaughn was one of the Cape's first big draws. At the Cape, the future Red Sox player showed the right stuff. Fans always loved Mo. Mo was the 1988 playoffs' Most Valuable Player. Chock Knoblauch was Mo's teammate. Also, don't forget about star left-handed pitcher Barry Zito, who was the ace of the pitching staff in 1997 and 1998. His pitching partner in 1998 was Brewer ace Ben Sheets.

Only Haverill, Massachusetts, native Carlos Pena, though, has had a whole page of the Gatemen yearbook completely devoted to him. The Wareham Gatemen and the Cape are grateful they gave the Northeastern University star a chance. Pena hit .318 and led the league in homers (eight) and runs batted in (33) and was named the league's Most Valuable Player.

Pena has had a successful career as the starting first baseman for the Detroit Tigers. In 2006, Pena had the thrill of a lifetime—hitting a walk-off game-winning home run for his hometown Red Sox. According to John Wylde, "his love of the game was infectious and he carried the team to the [Cape Cod Baseball League] championship in 1997."

Round Tripper (Some Suggestions for Sightseers)

Wareham is kid friendly. The tides at Onset Beach aren't wavey. There are bathrooms, places to change, fast-food eateries, and a good amount of parking. If you want to get a break from the sun, set sail on a Cape Cod Canal cruise. See how the Cape Cod Canal was built. Get a seaside view of Mass Maritime College. Weather permitting, two-hour jaunts are very pleasurable. The boat ride is long enough for Cape connoisseurs, yet brief enough so that kids won't get bored. A great take for day trippers. Hy-Line has three daily trips in the summer. Call 508-295-3883 or access *www.hy-linecruises.com* for more information.

There are great attractions along Route 6 and 28. Water Wizz Water Park is just a short drive from the Bourne Bridge. There aren't too many water parks in New England, but this is, by consensus, considered the best. The wave pools and slides are thrilling. The park opens after Memorial Day. For more information contact 508-295-3255 or go to *www.waterwizz.com*. Cartland has kiddie rides, mini-golf courses, bumper boats, and mini-race cars. It's a great place for kids to learn the joy of frenzied movement. Their phone number is 508-295-8560.

Places to Eat . . . If You Want More Than Cracker Jack

Route 6, the old highway to the Cape, has plenty to offer. There are Burger Kings, McDonalds, Subways, Papa Gino's—all of the usual fast-food choices. Despite the growth of chains, there are many local hangouts that are easy to find. The area's specialty is fish. Throughout Wareham, there are plenty of fish shacks where tourists can sample the best local fish. Nearby New Bedford is the largest scallop harvester in the country. If you like fried foods, try the scallops or the clams.

Some of the best-known spots for fish are Barnacle Bill's Restaurant, at 3126 Cranberry Highway; Clam Shack Creamery, at 3249 Cranberry Highway; Bowl Restaurant Seafood, at 3013 Cranberry Highway; and Uncle Sam's Diner at 189 Main Street. There's Portuguese, Italian, New Age, Chinese, and good old American cuisine offered. Wareham offers tourists a diverse dining experience.

Sources:

The Baseball Almanac, 1995–2007.
Boston Globe, 1900–2007.
Cape Cod Times, 1990–2007.
Wareham Gatemen Media Guide.
Glassman-Jaffe, Marcia. *Fun with the Family in Massachusetts: Third Edition*. Guilford, Connecticut: The Globe Pequot Press, 2002.
Price, Christopher. *Baseball by the Beach—A History of America's National Pastime on Cape Cod*. Yarmouthport, Massachusetts: On Cape Publications, 1998.

www.508ma.com/wareham/
www.all-baseball.com
www.ballparkdigest.com
www.ballparkreviews.com
www.baseballalmanac.com
www.baseballamericaonline.com
www.capecodbaseball.org
www.gatemen.org
www.nefan.com

15

WORCESTER, MA

HANOVER INSURANCE PARK AT FITTON FIELD

Address: 1 College Street, Worcester, MA 01610

Web Site: *www.worcestertornadoes.com*

First Game: 1905 (completely renovated in 2005)

Dimensions: LF 332 LCF 357 CF 385 RCF 372 RF 313

Directions: From the Massachusetts Turnpike (I-90), take Exit 10 to I-290 East toward Worcester. Take Exit 11 (College Square/Southbridge Street) off I-290. Cross over to the right lane immediately after coming off ramp to College Square. Take the first right (before the traffic light) onto College Street. Take the first left onto Fitton Avenue.

Home of the Worcester Tornadoes of the Canadian-American League and the Holy Cross Crusaders

Claim to Fame

On June 12, 1880, J. Lee Richmond of Worcester's National League pitched the first perfect game in the history of major league baseball. Ted Williams' first professional home run was hit at Fitton Field.

Strange but True

The city is home to the American Sanitary Plumbing Museum. It's difficult to understand how someone came up with an idea for this museum. Everything you ever wanted to know about handling waste, but were afraid to ask, is here. There are all kinds of plumbing devices to see. Antique showerheads, water heaters, bath tubs, basins, and toilet-paper dispensers are all on display. The museum is an unforgettable experience. Items from the museum were part of an exhibit at the Massachusetts Institute of Technology called "The Process of Elimination: the Kitchen, the Bathroom, and the Aesthetics of Waste."

Photo courtesy of Worcester Tornadoes

A night game at Fitton Field.

Who's Who in Worcester

Former Red Sox catcher Rich Gedman; J. Lee Richmond; Ted Williams; Babe Ruth; Lefty Grove; Joe Cronin; Hall of Famer John Gibson Carlson; the winningest major league pitcher in the nineteenth century, Jesse Burkett; Babe Ruth; Lou Gehrig; Mark "the Bird" Fidrych; Philadelphia Athletic's shortstop Jack Barry; former Met Ron Darling; Yankee Tanyon Sturtze; Millville's Gabby Hartnet; Hank Greenberg; and Casey Stengel.

About Worcester

Bostonians sometimes think Worcester is somewhere near Los Angeles. But it's really just a stone's throw away from Boston, about 50 miles west of downtown. The community's first name was "Quinsigamond," but early settlers found the name too difficult to

say, never mind spell. So the name was changed to "Worcester," which translates as "station or camp under the hill" or "war castle." The origins of the name of the Commonwealth's second-largest city are unclear. Scholars speculate the city's name commemorates the victory of Oliver Cromwell and the Puritans over Charles II.

If you ever visit Worcester, the first thing you'll notice are the hills. A long-standing topic of local debate is which hills, exactly, are the seven hills of Worcester. The heights of Worcester are too steep for skateboarding, but it would be a good venue for the death defying stunts of ESPN's *X-Games*. The city boasts plenty of hospitals with fully equipped trauma units. One tip: Before driving around Worcester, be sure to check your brakes.

Worcester has more than its share of firsts. Worcester-based Professor Albert A. Michelson was named America's first Nobel Prize Winner, for calculating the speed of light. In 1914 Dr. Robert H. Goddard of Clark University invented the first liquid fuel rocket. There were also many things invented in Worcester: the monkey wrench, the typewriter, and the steam calliope. The first national women's suffrage convention was held in the city. Elm Park, founded in 1854, was the first public park in the country. Resident Harvey Ball, who recently passed away, invented the smiley face. The first reading of the Declaration of Independence was by Isaiah Thomas on July 14, 1776, from the porch of the Old South Meeting House. Diners and street lunch carts were first created in Worcester and Valentine's Day greeting cards were first mass marketed in the city as well. The first bicycle ever made in our country was in Worcester. And who can ever forget the contributions of Worcester resident Henry Perky, who invented shredded wheat?

Worcester is the only city to be visited by George Washington, Abe Lincoln, Sigmund Freud, and Abbie Hoffman. While in town, Freud and Lincoln both gave speeches about psychoanalysis. In his speech, Lincoln psychoanalyzed the conditions that enslaved millions of Americans. Washington traveled to Worcester twice, the first being on his way to Boston to assume command of the Continental Army. The second time he was in town Washington received the thanks of grateful citizens for leading our country through the Revolutionary War.

After the War of 1812, Worcester became a large manufacturing city. The city was once an important component of a great transportation system. The Blackstone Canal connected Worcester to the seaport of Providence. Much of the canal was eventually filled in or covered. Some remnants of the loch system and canal structures can be seen along Blackstone in the Blackstone River and Canal Heritage State Park in the area around Uxbridge. The State Park operates in conjunction with the Blackstone River Valley National Heritage Corridor. The Boston and Worcester Railroad was the first incorporated railroad in Massachusetts. On July 4, 1835, Worcester celebrated the arrival of its first locomotive.

The wire industry was once Worcester's greatest. It could be argued that wire produced in Worcester held together our country. Wire was needed for fencing, telegraphs, telephones, and electricity. One factory once produced more than 1,500 tons of hoopskirt wire per year.

A Baseball Backgrounder

There's something new at one of New England's oldest ballparks. Worcester's venerable Fitton Field has witnessed some incredible events over the years. But can anything compare to its 100th year? It has been 71 years since New England's second-largest city had its own professional team. In 2005, Worcester's wait was over. A totally renovated Fitton Field was ready for the June debut of its newest team, the Tornadoes.

When you think about the city's history, it's hard to believe that it took so long for Worcester to rejoin the world of professional baseball. Worcester was once a member of the National League. On June 12, 1880, J. Lee Richmond threw the first perfect game in major league history, a 1-0 victory over Cleveland at the old Worcester County Agricultural Fairgrounds. But, when the major league team folded, the hits kept on coming as Lou Gehrig, Babe Ruth, and Ted Williams played against Holy Cross at Fitton Field. Holy Cross College has had a great baseball history of its own. Its first future major leaguer, Thomas Cahill, played for its first varsity team in 1886. Another great player was Lou Sockalexus. A member of Maine's Penobscot tribe, Sockalexus is widely acknowledged to be the first Native American to play major league ball. Holy Cross has developed some great managers and coaches as well. The local Little League baseball organization is named after Hall of Famer Jesse Burkett, who had two stints as the Crusaders' skipper, 1898 and 1917–20, and compiled a 100-20-1 record.

A couple of former Holy Cross players brought their life lessons and winning tradition to the Red Sox. Catcher "Wild Bill" Carrigan managed the Red Sox to two consecutive World Series titles in 1915 and 1916. And in 1917, another former great Crusader, Jack Barry, managed the Sox and led the Holy Cross Crusaders to a miracle NCAA baseball championship.

Holy Cross is known for basketball. But, once upon a time, baseball made the school famous. Baseball and football match-ups between Holy Cross and Boston College were incredibly popular, particularly during the Roaring Twenties. Whenever pitcher Owen Carroll took the mound, it was more than a game, it was an event. More than 20,000 fans packed Fitton Field to see the ace defeat the Eagles three times in a row. Carroll was paid a bonus of $20,000 to sign with Ty Cobb's Detroit Tigers. Almost 30 years later in its final regular-season game of the 1952 season, Holy Cross defeated Boston College 13-3, on the way to Omaha where the team won the NCAA championship.

True to this tradition, the Worcester Tornadoes took the Canadian-American League by storm in 2005. Former Red Sox catcher and hometown hero Rich Gedman was named the Tornadoes' first manager and following in the footsteps of former Red Sox Jack Barry and Bill Corrigan, Gedman brought fundamental baseball back to Worcester. Gedman hired another old Red Sox pal, left-hander Bobby Ojeda, as pitching coach. Worcester native and former Red Sox left-handed pitcher Ed Riley came out of retirement to help get the expansion team off to a good start.

Many experts didn't like the Tornadoes' chances for success, and on June 12, trailing New Jersey 7-2 in the eighth, Worcester's on-the-field fortunes looked bleak. Injuries had taken a toll on the team. No regular players were left on the bench, and an injury

Young Tornadoes fans with the team mascot.

to center fielder Alex De Los Santos, forced Gedman to bat the pitcher.

Then *it* happened. Worcester rallied by scoring four runs in the eighth and tied the game in the ninth on former Montreal Expo Yohanny Valera's single. Closer Dave Byard had one at-bat the whole year but made it count. In the 10th, he laid down a textbook bunt that moved Alex Nunez to second. Outfielder Lucas Taylor then singled to give Worcester a dramatic win, the first of a five-game winning streak. After losing a game, the Tornadoes won another nine in a row. The Tornadoes breezed to win the first-half South Division title on July 11.

With a playoff spot secure, a quartet of local residents provided pitching and punch to Worcester's lineup. Milford's Chris Colabello, an Assumption

alumnus, hit .320 with eight home runs and 31 RBIs and Leominister's Keith Beauregard hit .471 (16 for 34) in his first nine games and finished with a .338 average, 3 home runs, and 27 RBIs. Left-handed reliever Greg Montalbano of Westboro, the former Red Sox 2001 Minor League Pitcher of the Year, went 2-2 with a 3.13 ERA, fanning 28 in 23 innings. Westminster's Chris Shank helped buoy the bullpen, allowing just 14 earned runs in 39 1/3 innings of relief (3.23 ERA).

A key factor in Worcester's championship was that bullpen. The 6-foot-10 Steve Palazzolo went 2-1 with a 3.15 ERA. Left-hander Dallas Mahan had a 4-2 record with a 4.21 ERA. The stopper was former Met farmhand Byard, who allowed just three earned runs in August and just two hits in the playoffs, where Worcester would prove that its strong start was no fluke. The Tornadoes lost their first playoff game but stormed back in their second. Facing a four-run deficit at home, the Tornadoes scored six runs in the sixth inning against the New Haven Cutters. Third baseman Zach Strong and Danilo Reynoso provided home run thunder.

By the time they reached the championship series opener in Quebec, nothing could stop the Tornadoes. Worcester swept the first two games at Quebec. Rain delayed the start of the third and deciding game of the championship series until 9:30 P.M., but it was well worth the wait for Worcester. Third baseman Zach Strong hit his fourth home run of the playoffs, giving Worcester a 5-4 lead in the fifth inning. And the Tornadoes never looked back. Since coming to town, the Worcester Tornadoes' performance has exceeded every expectation. They are a winning team, a division winner, and a playoff contender. The team had a three-game sweep for its first-ever professional championship. For a great sports community like Worcester, 2005 was indeed a grand return to professional baseball.

Take Me Out to the Ballgame

Worcester native Earnest Thayer authored one of the most famous poems in American history, "Casey at the Bat." Ever since it was written, there's been plenty of speculation about the identity of the real Casey. But where was the real Mudville? Maybe the Worcester County Agricultural Fairgrounds on Highland and Russell streets. Worcester's National League entry had really bad facilities. Imagine sharing the same field with circuses, horse pulling, and other kinds of farm activities. Mudville would have been an appropriate nickname for Worcester's original multi-purpose baseball facility. Fitton Field is a long way from Mudville.

The first game ever played at Fitton Field was on Patriots Day in 1905. A crowd of 6,200 cheered the Crusaders to an 8-5 victory over Brown University. The game wasn't cleanly played, but had plenty of action. There were 10 errors, 13 strikeouts, and 16 hits.

Many times, Worcester came close to getting professional baseball. However, there was always a major league impediment: the agreement among affiliated baseball teams to reserve minor league territories. All rights were exclusively held by the Pawtucket Red Sox. Undeterred, Worcester tried to lure the Pawtucket Red Sox to Central Massachusetts, but when the PawSox decided to stay in Rhode Island, Worcester was left out in the cold.

For years, Worcester's baseball future was blowing in the wind. That all changed when a group of local business people were shooting the breeze around developer Alan Stone's kitchen table. Purchasing a team franchise in the independent Canadian-American League was an easy choice. The biggest challenge was finding a suitable home for the team. Stone's group fell in love with

Holy Cross. The proximity to Route 290, the parking, and the historic setting were perfect.

After a whirlwind romance between the school, the city, and the owners, the Tornadoes went to work. Starting in mid-March 2005, the historic stadium was totally revamped. The developers started with only a field and a few bleachers. The company that had built a new baseball stadium for the University of Virginia was hired and the Cavaliers' plans were modified for the Crusaders.

It took a combination of ingenuity, luck, and old-fashioned elbow grease to get Fitton Field ready for opening night and the home opener came off with a few hitches. The late-May debut of the new Fitton Field was delayed until June 6th. As fans filed into the stands, fences in front of the dugout were still being installed. Up until first pitch, construction workers were still putting the final touches to the stadium. With just 45 minutes to spare, Worcester's new baseball team was ready to call Hanover Insurance Park at Fitton Field home.

The Holy Cross campus has a spectacular view overlooking Worcester. Fitton Field is in a valley, tucked between an underpass and the football field. Fans can always see and hear the traffic from Route 290. On a not-so-clear day, a large sign for Rotman's, "New England's Largest Furniture and Carpet Store," dominates the left-field skyline. There's very little foul area. There are no skyboxes. And until 2006 the scoreboard was somewhat primitive. Nevertheless, the new baseball park is a great fit. The Worcester Tornadoes have consistently played to 85 percent capacity, without a lot of group sales or season tickets.

Best Game (When You Think About It, How Does Someone Decide Which Game Was the Best?)

On June 12, 1880, Lee Richmond of Worcester's National League team pitched the first perfect game in the history of professional baseball. But what may have been most amazing was that it was the second game Richmond pitched that day. Just hours before hurling the gem against Cleveland, Richmond caught a train to Providence and pitched a game for Brown University's senior class. Richmond was quite a workhorse. He pitched 591 innings in 74 games. Over the next two years, Richmond pitched almost 900 innings. Predictably, too many pitches spoiled Richmond's arm and he retired by the age of 26.

Greatest Team (Not the '27 Yankees, but Who Is?)

The 1952 Holy Cross Crusaders are one of the most remarkable teams in college baseball history. Jack Barry, in his 40th year as the coach of the Crusaders, led his team to their only trip to the College World Series in Omaha, Nebraska. It was the only team in NCAA history to win seven consecutive games, while facing elimination, for a national championship. It was also the only team from the northeast to win a national title. Ronnie Perry Sr. starred for the Crusaders basketball National Invitation Tournament winners and the baseball team.

Best Player . . . in My Opinion

There's little debate about this issue. Jack Barry was the greatest figure in Worcester's baseball history. He was the starting shortstop for Holy Cross at Fitton Field's first game, on Patriots Day of 1905. As part of Connie Mack's famous "$100,000 infield," Barry started on four Philadelphia Athletics world championship teams. After the 1914 season, Barry was sold to the Red Sox, leading them to 1915 and 1916 World Series championships.

In 1921, Barry returned to Worcester to stay. Over four decades, his teams won 627 and lost 151 for a .8057 percentage. He guided the Crusaders to 10 Eastern Championships, 2 regional titles, and an incredible NCAA national championship in 1952.

Second best may be Lou Sockalexis, a Penobscot Native American from Maine, who was one of the greatest players in college baseball history. After playing ball for Holy Cross and Notre Dame, he was signed to play right field for Cleveland's National League team. In 1897, he became the first Native American to play Major League Baseball. Sockalexis could hit, but his fielding caught up with him. After a strong rookie season, the former Holy Cross student rode the bench

and was released two years later. The Cleveland Indians have consistently claimed that the Indians' name is in honor of Sockalexis, but this may be more fiction then fact. There's really very little evidence that the Indians were named after Sockalexis. He didn't play long enough with Cleveland to establish a following and the name was just one of several choices. It seems the Indians might have been given their nickname after a contest was held by a Cleveland newspaper.

Round Tripper (Some Suggestions for Sightseers)

Worcester has many interesting offerings for the whole family. The Higgins Museum houses one of the greatest collections of armor in the Western Hemisphere. John Woodman Higgins, the founder of the museum, was fascinated with knights and chivalry and started collecting armor while visiting Europe during the 1920s. The exhibits feature the gamut of human armor, from ancient to modern. The collection has been on display since 1931. All kinds of interesting activities are offered, including realistic reenactments of life in a Roman legion camp

The EcoTarium is a modern name for one of Worcester's oldest institutions. It was founded in 1825 and has had a number of name changes. Despite this, the mission of the museum remains the same. It's a great place for families to have a hands-on experience with science and nature.

Places to Eat ... If You Want More Than Cracker Jack

There are more than 300 hundred places to eat in Worcester, but the city is best known for its diners. Worcester is home to some of the first diners in the country. Some of the best are Kenmore Diner, 250 Franklin Street; Boulevard Diner, 155 Shrewsbury Street; Miss Worcester Diner, 300 Southbridge Street; and Parkway Diner, 148 Shrewsbury Street.

Another cheap eating place is George's on Grafton Street. It's a pita bakery on Grafton Street that opens each morning at around 2 A.M., so it is a great place to go after a late night of studying or partying. If you like hot dogs, you can get the real thing at George's Coney Island Hot Dogs at 58 Southbridge Street. George's, in business since 1918, practically invented hot dogs served in steamed buns.

A couple of other recommendations are near Worcester Polytechnic Institute. The Sole Proprietor on 118 Highland Street serves fresh seafood and has achieved recognition for its dining excellence. Tortilla Sam's, at 107 Highland Street, serves authentic Mexican food at reasonable prices. Lebanese on 1143 Highland Street features Middle Eastern cuisine, pastries, baked goods, and live entertainment.

Sources:

Boston Globe, 1900–2007.
Worcester Telegram, 1900–2007.
Glassman-Jaffe, Marcia. *Fun with the Family in Massachusetts: Third Edition*. Guilford, Connecticut: The Globe Pequot Press, 2002.

www.all-baseball.com
www.ballparkdigest.com
www.ballparkreviews.com
www.baseballalmanac.com
www.baseballamericaonline.com
www.brocktonrox.com
www.canamleague.com
www.clui.org/clui_4_1/lotl/lotlv10/sanitary.html
www.ecotarium.org
www.geocities.com/Athens/2088/worc.htm
www.higgins.org
www.holycross.edu/athletics/
www.sabr.org
http://travel.explorenewengland.com/restaurants
www.worcesterhistory.org/
www.worcestertornadoes.com
www.worcesterweb.com/index.html?worcester1.htm

16

Address: 210 Station Avenue, South Yarmouth, MA 02664

Web Site: *www.ydredsox.org*

First Game: 1949

Dimensions: LF 346 CF 352 RF 338

Directions: Take US Route 6 to Exit 8, and head south on Station Avenue. Follow for 1.4 miles and turn left at Dennis-Yarmouth High School. Red Wilson Field is at the rear of the parking lot.

YARMOUTH, MA
RED WILSON FIELD

Home of the Yarmouth-Dennis Red Sox of the Cape Cod Baseball League

Claim to Fame

Cranberries are native to the bogs of Cape Cod, but the idea of cultivating them as a crop didn't emerge until 1816. That's when Henry Hall of Dennis village discovered the wild plants, when covered by windblown winter sands, generated more bountiful harvests with larger berries. Before long bogs across the Cape and Southeastern Massachusetts were being farmed using this practice. Today there are nearly 40,000 acres of cranberry bogs in production nationwide, including Hall's original bog off Route 6A.

Strange but True

Anthony Thacher arrived in Yarmouth in 1639, and, along with John Crow and Thomas Howes, was one of the town's first three land-grant settlers. He came hoping for a fresh start to a life torn apart by tragedy. Before he decided to leave his native Great Britain and rebuild his life in the New World, he had already lost five of his nine children as well as his wife. Remarried,

SportPix photo by Matthew Scott

Scouts and spectators share a close-up view of the action behind home plate.

he and his remaining four children boarded a ship that sailed westward in April 1635.

In August, shortly after their arrival in Massachusetts, tragedy struck the family again. They boarded a passenger bark sailing from Newburyport to Marblehead. Joining them was Anthony's cousin, who brought along a wife and six children. Sailing into a violent storm as she rounded Cape Ann, the vessel broke apart after striking rocks near an offshore island. Of Thacher's entire family, only he and his second wife survived the incident. The island was later named for Thacher.

The Thachers made their way to Cape Cod four years later, along with a one-year-old son. The boy, John Thacher—who settled in Yarmouth—would eventually father 21 children of his own and became the assistant to the governor of the Massachusetts Bay Colony in 1691. John Thacher's home still stands on Route 6A across from the Yarmouth Port Post Office.

Who's Who in Dennis and Yarmouth

Mark Angelo, Steve Balboni, Alan Benes, Craig Biggio, Mike Bordick, Michael Bourn, Cal Burlingame, Scott Downs, Jeff Duncan, Morgan Ensberg, Todd Greene, Matt Guerrier, Brad Hawpe, Jim Hubbard, Luke Hudson, Philip Humber, Joe Jabar, Justin Lehr, Lou Lamoriello, Mike LaValliere, Cody McKay, Mike Mordecai, Mickey Morandini, David Newhan, Denny Neagle, Russ Ortiz, Steve Parris, J.J. Putz, Britt Reames, Don Reed, Steve Smyth, Cory Sullivan, Mark Sweeney, Bobby Valentine, Mark Watson, Justin Wayne, Matt Wise, and Jason Young.

About Dennis and Yarmouth

The two mid-Cape towns are partly separated by the Bass River, which empties south into Nantucket Sound and, at six miles long, is the longest tidal river on the East Coast. While the European discovery of the Cape is commonly attributed to England's Bartholomew Gosnold in 1602, Viking explorer Leif Eriksson is said to have sailed up the river some 600 years earlier and set up a camp, according to local lore, though no evidence has been found to support the claim.

A variant of that legend identifies Eriksson's brother, Thorvald, as the visitor, and tells that he and his entourage encountered Native Americans at Bass Hole along the north coast of present-day Yarmouth. The story goes that during an ensuing battle between the groups, Thorvald was killed and buried at the beach. However, his grave has never been found.

The lands around the river were once home to several Wampanoag tribes, including the Pawkunnawkut, the Hokanums, and the Cummaquids. In 1638 pilgrim Stephen Hopkins, a *Mayflower* passenger, built the first house in Yarmouth, near Mill Lane. Native American relations with British settlers were, by all accounts, cordial and cooperative, but hostilities that rose off-Cape eventually spread to the peninsula.

Three villages—Yarmouth Port, West Yarmouth, and South Yarmouth—make up the 28-square-mile town of Yarmouth, which has a year-round population of about 25,000. Dennis, comprising Dennisport, West Dennis, South Dennis, East Dennis, and Dennis Village, has about 17,000 people over its 22 square miles.

Both towns were initially one and the same. Yarmouth was named for the British port city where many of the Dutch pilgrims had passed through on their way to America. In 1793 the community split along church parish lines, and residents of the eastern parish chose to name their new town after Reverend Josiah Dennis, its resident minister for 38 years. His 1736 home is preserved as an historic site along with a one-room schoolhouse.

Farming and fishing were the primary vocations of early settlers. As the nation was declaring its independence in 1776, Captain John Sears came up with a way to evaporate moisture from saltwater, which he patented in 1799. The discovery led to the country's first commercial salt works on the east banks of Sesuit Creek in present-day East Dennis, which produced salt for leather tanning and fish preserving.

In 1815, on the west side of the creek, Asa Shiverick's shipyard began building and launching vessels. His first boat was a schooner, but Shiverick's yard went on to build brigs, several more schooners, and eight clippers that sailed the globe as merchant ships. Shiverick's was the only shipyard on the Cape to build such large vessels.

Soon the shipping trade took hold in both towns, as merchants, coopers, and sail makers did brisk business. In Dennisport, the Union Wharf Packing Company thrived in the 1850s, while Yarmouth Port became home to dozens of sea captains. About 50 of their stately homes lined Captain's

Row, many of which remain as private residences today.

As tourists began flocking to the Cape in the early 1900s, hospitality and entertainment venues took hold including the Cape Playhouse in Dennis. Its opening show in 1927, *The Guardsman*, starred Basil Rathbone (of the early Sherlock Holmes films). Over the ensuing decades many future stage and screen stars performed at the playhouse in their early days, including Humphrey Bogart, Gregory Peck, Ginger Rogers, Lana Turner, and Bette Davis (reputedly discovered while she worked as a summer usher.) In 1958 Henry Fonda took the stage, performing with his 20-year-old daughter Jane.

When the Mid-Cape Highway (US Route 6) was extended across Dennis and Yarmouth, it split both towns into discernible halves. The north, along Cape Cod Bay and Route 6A, remains largely bucolic, quaint, and serene. To the south, scenic attractions remain along Nantucket Sound and the Bass River, but the over-developed areas along Route 28, replete with garish tourist traps and competing eyesores, tend to overwhelm the senses.

A Baseball Backgrounder

Organized baseball in Dennis and Yarmouth didn't take off until after World War II. The towns had separate teams, with the Dennis Clippers playing at Ezra Baker Field in South Dennis. In Yarmouth, the Indians hosted games at Simkins Field on Route 28 across from the town hall.

In 1958, the Indians beat the Sagamore Clouters, 4-3, to win Yarmouth's first Cape League championship. Yarmouth would win another crown in 1960.

Through the rest of the 1960s and most of the 1970s Yarmouth and Dennis both struggled. Among the standouts was Joe Jabar, who went 7-4 for Yarmouth in 1965 with 74 strikeouts while completing 9 of his 14 starts. He started the 1965 Cape League All-Star Game for the eastern division. Jabar spent the next two seasons with Chatham, compiling perfect 7-0 records each year, and was inducted into the Cape League Hall of Fame in 2003. In 1967, the last year the Cape League allowed high school players, a swift 17-year-old kid from Stamford, Connecticut, named Bobby Valentine patrolled center field for Yarmouth.

A decade later the teams did the exact opposite of what Dennis and Yarmouth had done two centuries earlier; whereas the towns had split in 1793, the Dennis and Yarmouth teams merged in 1977.

The communities had long shared a regional school district and since town money from Dennis was helping to fund the high school and field where the combined squad would be playing, it was agreed to give the team a combined name, the Yarmouth-Dennis Red Sox, or the Y-D Sox for short.

In its inaugural season, Y-D finished in third place but reached the championship series against Cotuit. Slugging first baseman Steve "Bye Bye" Balboni hit .271 with a league-leading 13 homers and 38 RBIs to earn the league's Most Valuable Player award.

During the five-game title series, Balboni socked 6 home runs in 5 games while driving in 16, but the Kettleers took the crown in the deciding game, 8-3.

During the late 1980s, the Red Sox saw plenty of star power. In 1986, University of Maine's Mike Bordick teamed with future Houston Astros player Craig Biggio. Infielder Mike Mordecai and pitchers Steve Parris and Denny Neagle were standouts in 1988.

Don Reed became manager in 1987, and ushered in the first sustained success in nearly three decades. Through four seasons with Y-D, he compiled a 98-64-4 record. Following up on a championship-round loss in 1987, Reed led the Sox to three straight division titles and a pair of league titles in 1989 and 1990. Future pro Mark Sweeney was a key player for both championship clubs. Reed, who also managed for Wareham, was inducted into the Cape League Hall of Fame in 2004 as the winningest manager in Cape Cod Baseball League (CCBL) history.

While a number of great players graced the diamond for Yarmouth-Dennis in the 1990s, including Alan Benes, Todd Greene, David Newhan, Cody McKay, Russ Ortiz, Britt Reames, Luke Hudson, Scott Downs, Morgan Ensberg, J.J. Putz, and Brad Hawpe, the team did not taste another title until 2004.

Take Me Out to the Ballgame

The field's namesake, Merrill "Red" Wilson, played seven seasons for Yarmouth in the Cape League from 1956 to 1962, helping the Indians to a championship in 1958 and winning the league's Most Valuable Player award in 1961. He also managed the Y-D Red Sox until 1974, and again from 1979 through his retirement in 1986. His 16-year tenure remains the longest of any manager in the history of the league.

Inducted into the CCBL's Hall of Fame as part of its initial class in 2000, Wilson logged 257 wins during his managerial career, the third most in CCBL history. However his contributions since the mid-1950s as a teacher and coach at Dennis-Yarmouth High School, where the park is located, were just as large a factor in the field being named in his honor.

The team began playing at the high school field in 1977. Bleachers line both the first and third baselines. The flat terrain provides great spectator views from just about anywhere around the diamond, and there are plenty of great spots to plant a couple of lawn chairs or spread out a blanket. The high school offers ample parking, including a large lot next to the field.

The field is one of four Cape League venues without lights, and home games start at 5 P.M. Because the field is well inland, it lacks the refreshing sea breezes that sweep across other CCBL parks. Sponsors and volunteer organizations often set up tents and kiosks on the shaded grounds near the field, providing a nice spot to cool off from the late-day summer heat.

A concession stand behind home plate offers burgers, dogs, pizza, and ice cream. Nearby, the Grand Slam Shop sells an array of team souvenirs, from hats and t-shirts to key chains and baby bibs.

Cape League games are free of charge, though a donation of $2 per person at each game is encouraged.

Best Game (When You Think About It, How Does Someone Decide Which Game Was the Best?)

On August 13, 2006, the Red Sox won their second CCBL championship in three years. Whereas Y-D won the 2004 crown in an epic road battle with the Commodores (see the Falmouth chapter for details), the 2006 finale against Wareham wasn't so much a great game as it was a great event. The outcome was never really in doubt, but the high-energy crowd of 8,272 fans who crammed the perimeter of Red Wilson Field generated the exciting buzz.

Michael Taylor drew a bases-loaded walk in the first inning off Wareham's Jeremy Bleich, scoring Evan McArthur. Meanwhile Sox starter Terry Doyle tossed four perfect innings with six strikeouts.

The Sox played small ball in the last of the fourth, as Luke Sommer's bunt single scored Buster Posey from third. Sommer later scored on a suicide squeeze by Jordan Pacheco.

The Gatemen got on the board in the fifth as Brad Suttle crushed a Doyle fastball, sending it sailing over the fence in right. Wareham tried to rally, putting two men on with one out, but Doyle bore down and whiffed Steffan Wilson and Beamer Weems to end the threat and keep the score at 3-1.

David Robertson came on to pitch for Y-D in the seventh, following a stellar outing by Doyle (6 IP, 2 H, 1 BB, 9 K on 86 pitches). The Sox tacked on a pair of insurance runs in the bottom half of the inning on a walk, a hit, and a stolen base as they took advantage of two Wareham throwing errors. Four of the Sox' five runs were unearned.

Robertson finished things off with authority, tossing three perfect innings and seven strikeouts and garnering the Cape League Championship Most Valuable Player award while Dennis-Yarmouth again earned the Arnold Mycock CCBL Championship Trophy.

Greatest Team (Not the '27 Yankees, but Who Is?)

All six of the Yarmouth and Y-D championship teams have been evenly matched, but the 2006 squad set a club record for wins with a 28-16 mark. Eight Sox players made the East division All-Star team, including starters Doyle (5-1, 2.89 ERA), Nate Boman (3-2, 2.94) and Donnie Hume (4-0, 2.40) and reliever Joshua Fields (27 Ks and 5 BBs in 17.1 IP). Offensive honors went to shortstop Posey (.345 OBP, 34 R) and second baseman Brad Emaus (.366 OBP, 6 HR, 28 RBI), while left fielder Sommer and catcher Danny Lehmann were named All-Stars largely for their stellar defense.

Best Player . . . In My Opinion

In 1987, future big-leaguer Mickey Morandini was the Cape League's

SportPix photo by Matthew Scott

The Grand Slam Shop marks the entrance to Red Wilson Field.

Most Valuable Player after leading the CCBL in batting average, hits, doubles, runs, total bases, and stolen bases. His performance for Y-D earned him a slot on the U.S. national team at the 1988 Olympic Games, and he was inducted into the Cape League Hall of Fame in 2005.

Like all CCBL players, Morandini held down a summer job during his stint on the Cape. For Mickey, it was painting homes, something he apparently was not too skilled at. With tongue in cheek, Morandini alluded to his lack of handiwork during his induction ceremony. "I apologize to anybody in Yarmouth or Dennis who had to have their house repainted the next summer," he told the crowd.

Round Tripper (Some Suggestions for Sightseers)

There are several don't-miss spots in Dennis and Yarmouth, beginning with the Bass Hole Boardwalk near Grays Beach in Yarmouth Port. It extends 860 feet across lush, unspoiled tidal marshes, with a set of benches at its northern end. Also near the boardwalk is the two-and-a-half-mile Callery Darling Nature Trail.

While in Yarmouth Port, check out the history of the village at several sites within walking distance of the village common. They include the Captain Bangs Hallet House Museum (an old sea captain's home built in 1840), the Winslow Crocker House, and the Edward Gorey House (home to the eclectic twentieth-century playwright, author, and illustrator). Also worth a look are the Yarmouth New Church, which fronts the common, and the tiny Kelley Chapel, about 100 yards down a nature trail originating near the Yarmouth Port Post Office.

Take the family to Taylor-Bray Farm, off Route 6A east of Yarmouth Port, where sheep, highland cattle, and a diverse garden can be found. The 22-acre farm was settled by Richard Taylor in 1639 and remained with his descendants until 1896 when brothers George and William Bray, who had worked for the Taylors, purchased the site. The town purchased the land for historic preservation in 1987.

In West Yarmouth, the 1710 Baxter Grist Mill, on the shore of Mill Pond off Route 28, is powered by a water turbine, which replaced the paddle wheel in 1860 due to persistent problems with freeze-ups. Also in West Yarmouth, the Yarmouth Boardwalk extends from Meadowbrook Lane (off Route 28) through swamp and marsh to secluded Swan Pond.

In South Yarmouth on River Street sits the Judah Baker Windmill, built in 1791 and refurbished in 1999. The surrounding park includes a small beach along the Bass River. On North Main Street, the 1809 Quaker Meeting House is still open for Sunday services at 10 A.M. The grounds include a cemetery and a one-room schoolhouse.

In Dennis Village, start at the 30-foot, stone-and-mortar Scargo Tower, which sits atop Scargo Hill off Route 6A, the highest point on the mid-Cape. A wooden tower, built in 1874, once stood on the site as one of Cape Cod's earliest attractions (tourists paid five cents). After it was destroyed by a fire, the existing stone tower was built in 1901. Climb the winding stairs and survey Scargo Lake and Dennis Village below. Weather permitting, the view extends north across Cape Cod Bay to Provincetown.

The Josiah Dennis Manse, a 1736 saltbox where the town's namesake lived, still stands at the corner of Whig Street and Nobscusset Road in Dennis Village. Period exhibits include a maritime history wing and a 1770 one-room schoolhouse.

In South Dennis, the tiny Gothic-style Village Library on Main Street is worth a look. The South Dennis Congregational Church, known as the sea captain's church, contains the nation's oldest working organ.

The 26-acre Cape Playhouse Center for the Arts includes the original Cape Playhouse, the Cape Cod Museum of Art, and the Cape Cinema. Actress Shirley Booth, who won an Oscar (for *Come Back Little Sheba*) and an Emmy (for her portrayal of the title character in the sitcom *Hazel*), donated both awards to the playhouse, where they remain on display.

Dennis is also the southwestern terminus of the 22-mile Cape Cod Rail Trail, a paved path for cyclists, pedestrians, in-line skaters, and even the occasional horseback rider. It starts near the intersection of Route 134 and US Route 6, where parking and trail maps are available. The trail, following the same route plied by passenger trains as early as 1873, winds through scenic vistas and nature preserves in Dennis, Harwich, Brewster, Orleans, Eastham, and Wellfleet. An overhaul of the western end of the trail was completed in June 2006. The eastern end, from Nickerson State Park in Brewster to South Wellfleet, is undergoing rehabilitation until mid-June 2007.

For beachgoers there are several options in both towns. Daily parking permits in Yarmouth are $12 on weekdays and $15 on weekends. In Dennis, daily permits are $10. To the north, Chapin, Corporation, and Mayflower beaches are in Dennis Village, but Chapin Beach lacks lifeguards and rest rooms. Gray's Beach, at Bass Hole, is the only Yarmouth public beach on Cape Cod Bay. To the south, Parker's River, Sea Gull, and Bass River beaches in Yarmouth face Nantucket Sound, as does and West Dennis Beach in West Dennis, a popular spot for windsurfers and kite boarders.

While most of what Route 28 offers is over-the-top in its blatant pandering to tourists, kids will enjoy Zoo-Quarium in West Yarmouth, with a sea lion show, petting zoo, pony rides, and a touch tank. In South Yarmouth, Pirate's Cove is one of the more elaborate miniature golf courses on the Cape.

Places to Eat . . . If You Want More Than Cracker Jack

The one sure-fire hit is Captain Parker's Pub on Route 28 in West Yarmouth. You won't find better clam chowder anywhere on Earth, and they've got a trophy case to prove it. Expect crowds, but it's worth the wait.

Step back in time at Hallet's, a quaint country drugstore in Yarmouth Port built in 1889. The soda fountain, with swivel stools and a marble counter, still serves creamy concoctions. The Hallet family still runs the store, and even opened a museum on the second floor.

The Lighthouse Inn in West Dennis offers twists on traditional New England cuisine from a bluff overlooking Nantucket Sound. You can't miss the bright red rooftop light tower, which warned approaching ships during the nineteenth century.

Quiet, high-quality dining can be found at the Red Pheasant Inn on Main Street in Dennis, and at the Old Yarmouth Inn on Route 6A in Yarmouth Port, which was established in 1696 and is the oldest inn on Cape Cod. The contemporary Abbicci, on Route 6A in Yarmouth Port, serves the best Italian cuisine in either town, and you can sample complimentary tapas selections weekdays from 4 to 6 P.M.

Nearby is Oliver's on Route 6A, which specializes in seafood. Anthony's Cummaquid Inn in Yarmouth Port, operated by the Athanas family of Boston's Pier 4 fame, offers pricey waterfront dining., The Yarmouth House, on Route 28 in West Yarmouth, and 902 Main, on Route 28 in South Yarmouth, also stand out.

Chapin's Restaurant in Dennis offers a great location just off Chapin and Mayflower beaches, and features a seasonal outdoor raw bar. Ardeo Mediterranean Taverna in South Yarmouth offers Greek and Italian cuisine. In Dennisport, the Ebb Tide, the Ocean House, and the Oyster Company Raw Bar & Grill are all great choices.

To keep kids occupied while avoiding the fast-food scene, Christopher's on Route 28 in South Yarmouth and Clancy's in Dennisport both fit the bill. Budget-minded diners can hit Skippy's Pier 1, Heath 'n Kettle, Seafood Sam's, Doyle's, and the Longfellow Tavern, all on or near Route 28 in South Yarmouth. The Pancake Man, a Cape Cod breakfast tradition, is nearby. Also along Route 28 are Ninety-Nine, Giardino's, O'Shea's, Molly's and Sundancers, all in West Yarmouth.

For a cool treat in Dennisport, two great options are the Sundae School Ice Cream Parlor, set in a rustic mid-1800s barn, and Kream 'n Kone on the banks of the Swan River. The latter offers 24 soft-serve flavors, seafood rolls, onion rings, and tasty fried clam strips for those wary of whole bellies.

Sources:

Perley, Sidney. *Historic Storms of New England.* Beverly, Massachusetts: The Salem Press Publishing Company, 1891; reprinted by Commonwealth Editions, 2001.
Price, Christopher. *Baseball by the Beach—A History of America's National Pastime on Cape Cod.* Yarmouthport, Massachusetts: On Cape Publications, 1998.

www.capecodbaseball.org
www.capecodhistory.us
www.capecodonline.com
www.capeplayhouse.com
www.hsoy.org
www.insidecapecod.com
www.mass.gov/dcr/parks/southeast/ccrt.htm
www.taylorbrayfarm.org
www.town.dennis.ma.us
www.yarmouth.ma.us
www.ydredsox.org

Address: 20 America's Cup Avenue, Newport, RI 02840

Web Site: www.newportgulls.com

First Game: 1908

Dimensions: LF 315 LCF 365 CF 395 RCF 315 RF 285

Directions: From the north, take I-95 South from Providence to Exit 9. Take RI-138 East toward Newport Bridge. Travel over two bridges. At the end of Newport Bridge, follow signs toward "Scenic Newport." At the second traffic light, turn right onto America's Cup Avenue. Drive 0.3 miles, and the field will be on your left.

From the south, take I-95 North to Exit 3. Take RI-138 East toward Newport Bridge. Travel over two bridges. At the end of Newport Bridge, follow signs toward "Scenic Newport." At the second traffic light, turn right onto America's Cup Avenue. Drive 0.3 miles, and the field will be on your left.

CARDINES FIELD

Home of the Newport Gulls of the New England Collegiate Baseball League

Claim to Fame

The America's Cup, the Tennis Hall of Fame, Newport's many mansions, and the United States Naval War College.

Strange but True

Newport was once a favorite port-of-call for many of this country's most notorious pirates. William Kidd, Calico Jack Rackham, and Thomas Tew were once among the city's most honored citizens.

Who's Who in Newport

Former major leaguer Frank Corridon, also known as "the Father of the Spitball," is from Newport. Yogi Berra, Phil Rizzuto, Bob Feller, Satchel Paige, Larry Doby, and Luke Easter have played at Cardines Field.

About Newport

Newport has an important place in United States history. It was originally founded as a refuge from religious intolerance. The city's original settlers were born and bred Bostonians who had differing views about worship than the ruling Puritan class. Religious dissent wasn't tolerated in Massachusetts. Newport's founders chose to challenge the powerful elite, but discovered that it was impossible to fight City Hall. Better to move than fight.

In 1636, the group first settled near Portsmouth, Rhode Island. But they quickly found that there wasn't enough room in the area to satisfy everyone. Just three years after Portsmouth's founding, a group led by William Coddington and Nicholas Eaton decided to strike out on their own and move south to the tip of Aquidneck Island. They founded a small fishing and farming village at present-day Newport.

The city's first families quickly learned that they had discovered the key to wealth and prosperity: religious tolerance and a deep seaport. These principles were embedded in the Newport Town Statutes of 1641. It was a happy coincidence that some of the city's most talented members were its religious dissidents. A group of Jewish immigrants from Spain and a large contingent of Quakers planted deep roots in colonial Newport. The Touro Synagogue, the oldest Jewish house of worship in the United States, was organized in the area. By 1700, more than half of Newport's population was Quakers.

Before the Revolutionary War, Newport was one of the British Empire's most important seaports. The town was also full of bootleggers. Sugar and West Indian molasses were shipped to rum refineries in the city's wharves. Great prosperity brought great sins.

Newport was once a northern outpost for the slave trade. Slave auctions were held at the Old Brick Market. Many of the slaves are buried in the Common Burial Ground. One of the most popular city residents was a pirate named Thomas Tew. But eventually, the long arm of British justice finally reached Newport. Many of the pirates were imprisoned and hanged. Some are now buried on nearby Goat Island.

Local merchants made a fortune, but the good times didn't last. Newport felt, first hand, the ravages of the Revolutionary War. The city paid dearly for its resistance to the British. One of Newport's residents, William Ellery, signed the Declaration of Independence. In the fall of 1776, the British began a three-year occupation of the city. Most of the population, supporting the American cause, abandoned Newport, which left the town in enemy hands. When the British left, the French—under General Rochembeau—came to the rescue. The French were very popular visitors. The fleet stationed in Newport helped Washington apply the finishing touches at America's victory at Yorktown. By the time the war ended, Newport's population had gone from more than 9,000 to less than 4,000.

Even though it lost much of its economic base, Newport still retained some of its importance. For many years, Newport was one of Rhode Island's two state capitals. The city soon recaptured its glory by reinventing itself as a summer resort. Samuel Ward McAllister, creator of "the Four Hundred" social list, purchased Bayside Farm in

Photo courtesy of Newport Gulls

A view of action from behind the plate in Newport.

the 1850s. Rich and famous robber barons, like Cornelius Vanderbilt, built "cottages" along Rhode Island's jagged coast that were bigger than castles. Today, the mansions are one of the city's most famous attractions.

The city has always had a close connection with the United States Navy. Besides being the former residence of Commodore Oliver Hazard Perry, it has been a port-of-call for the Atlantic and the home of the U.S. Naval War College

On September 12, 1953, Newport hosted what many have considered the social event of the century—the wedding of John Fitzgerald Kennedy and Jacqueline Bouvier. Kennedy lived at Hammersmith Farm, and the couple was married in St. Mary's Church. Newport has another presidential claim: Dwight Eisenhower's "summer White House" was at Fort Adams.

A Baseball Backgrounder

The southern Rhode Island city is known for its sports. The city's most famous sporting event was the America's Cup. The Brittania silver metal trophy is emblematic of yachting greatness. From 1930 until 1983, the New York Yacht Club reigned over its home port, Newport. It seemed that the United States' 130-year reign of sailing supremacy would never end. But in 1983, *Australia II* took the America's Cup, defeating *Liberty*. The United States has subsequently retaken the cup, but the great competition has never returned to Newport.

Despite the loss, Newport still has a sporting life. The Newport Casino is the home of the Tennis Hall of Fame and an annual professional tournament. Recently, the Newport Country Club hosted the annual United States

Photo courtesy of Newport Gulls

The Gulls in the field during a game at Cardines Field.

Open Ladies Golf Tournament. And, of course, there's always world-class polo. There's nothing like spending a sunny Sunday afternoon at the polo matches and enjoying a scrumptious cucumber sandwich or two. Matches take place at the Glen Farm, which is six miles north of downtown Newport. Teams from all over the world come to town to play polo.

For more pedestrian tastes, there's always been baseball. Like many other New England communities, Newport has a rich baseball tradition. The first organized games were played at Morton Park and Freebody Park. At the turn of the century, Newport had a franchise in the old New England league. Occasionally, major-league teams would take a short detour to play a game for local fans. The city was a little too small and the leisure activities too diverse to support minor-league baseball.

Newport has one of the oldest amateur baseball leagues in the country, the George L. Donnelly Sunset League. Since opening day in 1919, local men have been getting together to play some good old-fashioned hardball at Cardines Field. During World War II, many former major leaguers played in the Sunset League. Bob Feller, Phil Rizzuto, and Yogi Berra are some the Sunset League's most prominent alumni. Games between the Twilight League's All-Stars and famous Negro League teams, like the Baltimore Elite Giants, Boston Royal Giants, and the New York Black Yankees, were a Wednesday night tradition.

In 2001, the Newport Gulls flew into town. They immediately established themselves as one of the New England Collegiate Baseball League's (NECBL) flagship franchises. The Gulls, like other teams in the league, recruit nationally from every major conference. The Gulls have already won the 2001, 2002, and 2005 championships. In addition, former Gulls players have gone on to join the Baltimore Orioles, Chicago Cubs, St. Louis Cardinals, Detroit Tigers, Philadelphia Phillies, and Boston Red Sox.

Pawtucket native Chris Iannetta was the first former Gull to make it in the majors. Everywhere he's played, the catcher has made an immediate impact. The North Carolina alumnus was named to the NCAA all-tournament team in the Starksville Regional tournament and was selected to the NECBL All-Star team. On August 16, 2006, Iannetta, played his first game as a member of the Colorado Rockies, and recorded his first major-league hit against the San Diego Padres.

Take Me Out to the Ballgame

Cardines Field is a cozy little bandbox in downtown Newport. The hitters and fans love it, but the pitchers can take it or leave it. Since it's just 285 feet down the right-field line, homes behind right field might as well be painted with a bull's-eye. The ballpark's history dates back to 1908, when a group of railroaders for the old New York–New Haven railroad started their own baseball league at the site. At first, the neighborhood must have been happy that a group had found a new use for the buggy, swampy piece of land, but the excitement was short lived. Stray balls led to broken windows, which caused many complaints. Soon after, upon the orders of management, the baseball league was disbanded.

In 1919, baseball returned to stay. Since then, the George S. Donnelly Sunset League has been the ballpark's main tenant. While the ballpark still has its original backstop, the wooden bleachers weren't built until 1936. Since then, the City of Newport has owned and operated the stadium.

Cardines has an old-time feel. The ballpark is tucked away between Newport's downtown and residential areas. Many consider Cardines Field a close cousin of Ebbets Field and Fenway Park—maybe it's because of the small dimensions, or maybe it's because fans are so close to the action. Comparisons may be made because of all the ballpark's nooks and crannies.

At one time, Cardines Field was in danger of being torn down to be replaced by, of all things, a parking lot. Fortunately, the city came to its senses. Ron MacDonald organized the "Friends of Cardines Foundation" to spare the old park from extinction. With every year, there's another improvement. A lighting system, a new concession stand, a bathroom, bleachers, and a locker room have recently been added.

Best Game (When You Think About It, How Does Someone Decide Which Game Was the Best?)

Accounts of many games are irretrievably lost. Great visiting teams, like the Baltimore Elite Giants, the New York Black Yankees, and the House of David, didn't have regular beat writers. Barnstorming teams, led by all-time greats like Satchel Paige, didn't keep track of wins or losses. During World War II,

Photo courtesy of Newport Gulls

The Gulls mascot getting the young fans into the action.

many former professionals, like Bob Feller and Yogi Berra, played at Cardines Field. Yet detailed descriptions of games sometimes weren't recorded.

Since the Gulls came to town, Team USA—a collection of the United States' best young players—has been a regular visitor. Perhaps the best game was a contest between Team USA and the Newport Gulls played in 2005. Team USA was, of course, the heavy favorite. In the top of the first, the national team jumped out to a seemingly insurmountable six-run lead. But the bullpen held Team USA at bay. The Gulls climbed all the way back and made it a game.

In many ways, it was the finest hour for outfielder Cyle Hankerd, who is probably the Gulls' all-time greatest player. The Southern California student hit two home runs against Team USA. His second home run tied the game at 6 in the bottom of the eighth.

However, Team USA responded. Third baseman Josh Rodriguez hit a home-run in the top of the ninth to give Team USA a hard fought 7-6 win. It was a memorable game for Newport and the NECBL. The game proved that the NECBL is one of the nation's best amateur baseball leagues.

Greatest Team (Not the '27 Yankees, but Who Is?)

The Newport Gulls have already won the three league championships. In 2001, the original Gulls had four of the leagues' top prospects. The team was led by first baseman Mike Bohlander from Pace, left-handed pitcher Joel Kirston from Los Angeles' Pierce Junior College, third baseman Kainoa Obrey from Brigham Young, and outfielder Billy Graiser from St. John's.

Most knowledgeable observers agree that the 2005 champions were the best. Cyle Hankerd fell just short of winning the Triple Crown, but walked away with every other major award in the league. He was the New England Collegiate League's Most Valuable Player and top offensive player. He won the batting and home run titles. And the outfielder batted .500 in the playoffs. The 7-6 loss to Team USA is further proof of the strength of the team.

Since 2001, the quality of play in the NECBL has vastly improved. Just look at the pedigree of the 2006 team. Newport is attracting top players from top programs. Third baseman Chris Dominguez played for Louisville; first baseman Jim Murphy is from Washington State. The Gulls' two best current pitchers are from Virginia and Washington.

Best Player . . . in My Opinion

Many historians believe Newport native Frank Corridon is the inventor of the spitball. Truth be told, he wasn't the first to throw it. Since baseball was first played, there have been accounts of spitballs in the game. But Corridon did make the pitch popular. He wouldn't have ever made it to the major leagues without the pitch. The spitball was Corridon's ticket to majors. .

Corridon had a good minor-league career as a pitcher for the Providence Greys but seemed unable to make it to the majors. On a rainy day the pitcher discovered the pitch that would be the key to his success. The answer to all of his problems was as simple as a ball in a puddle. Corridon noticed he could make a wet baseball do anything he wanted. After trying out his pitch in the bullpen, Corridon was ready to try it in an actual game. The spitball worked like a charm. Batters were baffled. Corridon was quickly promoted to the majors.

In the baseball world, it's impossible to keep a secret. Word about the miracle pitch spread. Spitballs were thrown by some of the most famous pitchers in the game, including several Hall of Famers such as Jack Chesbro, Urban Shocker, and Burleigh Grimes. For many years, spitballs were perfectly legal—and yes, respectable. Foreign substances on baseballs weren't banned because they were seen as giving an unfair advantage—they were banned for sanitary reasons. Baseball owners were concerned that spitting on balls caused the spread of disease. That's the real reason why the spitball was banned in 1920.

Round Tripper (Some Suggestions for Sightseers)

Located on the tip of Aquidneck Island, the City of Newport isn't just a playground for the rich and famous. The city's seaport is steeped in history. Many of Newport's original colonial buildings still stand. Massive mansions dominate the shoreline. Along the city's ancient cobblestone streets, there are plenty of fascinating shops, galleries, and museums. Newport also has a great nightlife.

The heart of the city is the sea. The coastline is scenic. If you get bored with the beaches, there's sea kayaking, SCUBA diving, hiking, fishing, and sail boarding. Popular land sports are lawn tennis, golf, polo, and croquet. Newport is the home of the International Tennis Hall of Fame and the yearly inductions are hosted at the Newport Casino. The annual professional tennis tournament—the courts have closely cut grass just like Wimbledon—is a highlight of the social season. Another must-see is the world-famous Newport Jazz Festival, held every August.

The Newport Preservation Society owns many of the "Gilded Age" castles that are located on Bellevue Avenue. For a modest sum anyone can see many of the city's best-known stately homes. For example, the Breakers, the Elms, Marblehouse, and Rosecliff are now open for public tours. There are dozens of vacation alternatives. Landlubbers can learn how to sail or build an America's Cup–style yacht. You can even spend a week on Rose Island to learn all the ins and outs of lighthouse keeping. The bottom line is that Newport gives you plenty to do and see within a short ride of Boston, Providence, and Hartford. For more information, go to *www.GoNewport.com.*

Places to Eat ... If You Want More Than Cracker Jack

Newport isn't just a great place to live,

work, and play. It's also a great place to eat. Imagine a place where you can try homemade pâté de foie gras and then, just across the street, you can scarf down a Coney Island dog with celery salt. That's what's unique about dining in downtown Newport. For seafood, there are several great restaurants near the wharf—Christie's, Dave's, and the Chart House are the best known. The Brick Alley and the Cheeky Monkey are more informal. Many of the city's most famous restaurants are located along Thames Street, right near Newport Harbor. Ben's Chili Dogs on Broadway is a great little hot dog joint. There are also a number of excellent English and Irish pubs. If you're in the mood for ice cream, try the famous "Awful-Awful" from the Newport Creamery. Short for "Awful Big, Awful Good" these shakes won't disappoint on either claim.

Sources:

The Baseball Almanac, 1995–2007.
New York Times, 1890–2007.
Society of American Baseball Researchers. *The Northern Game—and Beyond.* Boston: Cambridge Prepress Services, 2002.

www.all-baseball.com
www.ballparkdigest.com
www.ballparkreviews.com
www.baseballalmanac.com
www.baseballamericaonline.com
www.cityofnewport.com
www.davidpietrusza.com
www.necbl.com
www.nefan.com
www.newportchamber.com
www.newportgulls.com
www.sabr.org

Address: Ben Mondor Way, Pawtucket, RI 02860

Web Site: *www.pawsox.com*

First Game: 1942

Dimensions: LF 325 LCF 375 CF 400 RCF 375 RF 325

Directions: From the north, take Route 95 South to Exit 2A in Massachusetts (Newport Avenue/Pawtucket). Follow Newport Avenue for two miles and take a right onto Columbus Avenue. Follow Columbus Avenue for 0.50 mile. Turn right after the traffic light onto George Bennett Highway. Follow George Bennett Highway for 0.30 of a mile. At the traffic light, turn left onto Division Street and follow signs for game parking.

From the south, take I-95 North to Exit 27, 28, or 29 and follow directional signs to McCoy Stadium. All exits lead to available game day parking lots.

From the east, take Route 195 West to I-95 North, then follow the directions for a southern approach.

From the west, take Route 146 South to Route 295 North to I-95 South, then follow the directions for a northern approach.

MCCOY STADIUM

Home of the Pawtucket Red Sox of the International League

Claim to Fame

Slater Mills was the first large-scale cotton mill in the country. It was a harbinger of the Industrial Revolution. Hasbro's headquarters is in Pawtucket. The longest game in professional baseball history took place at McCoy Stadium.

Strange but True

This isn't strange, but very unique. A longtime resident of the city, Elizabeth Johnson, built and compiled a whole library about Pawtucket history in the basement of her house. Johnson's house is in a working-class neighborhood just blocks away from the McCoy Stadium. The museum is a magnificent storehouse of historical information. Historians, scholars, and even the Library of Congress, have consulted with Mrs. Johnson about Pawtucket and Rhode Island history.

Who's Who in Pawtucket

Just look at this list of Pawtucket Red Sox alumni: Don Aase, Andy Abad, Izzy Alcántara, Bronson Arroyo, Steve Avery, Marty Barrett, Rod Beck, Todd Benzinger, Wade Boggs, Oil Can Boyd, Ellis Burks, José Canseco, John Cerutti, 1992; Roger Clemens, Tony Conigliaro, Cecil Cooper, Wil Cordero, Jim Corsi, Brian Daubach, Bo Diaz, Gary DiSarcina, Dennis Eckersley, David Eckstein, Mark Fidrych, Carlton Fisk, John Flaherty, Scott Fletcher, Jeff Frye, 1999; Nomar Garciaparra, Rich Gedman, Alex González, Mike Greenwell, Mark Guthrie, Bill Haselman, Scott Hatteberg, Dustin Hermanson, Ken Hill, Sam Horn, Bruce Hurst, Byung-Hyun Kim, Gabe Kapler, 2005–06; Jon Lester, Fred Lynn, Steve Lyons, Ramón Martínez, Willie McGee, Lou Merloni, Wade Miller, Kevin Mitchell, Bill Mueller, Tim Naehring, Trot Nixon, Tomo Ohka, Bobby Ojeda, John Olerud, Jonathan Papelbon, Carl Pavano, Dustin Pedroia, Dick Pole, Paul Quantrill, Manny Ramirez, Jim Rice, Ken Ryan, Bret Saberhagen, Calvin Schiraldi, Curt Schilling, Aaron Sele, Earl Snyder, Matt Stairs, Bob Stanley, Jeff Suppan, John Valentin, 1991–94, Jason Varitek, Mo Vaughn, Tim Wakefield, David Wells, Mark Whiten, Kevin Youkilis.

Fans in Pawtucket are enterprising in their attempts to get an autograph.

About Pawtucket

Pawtucket is the fourth-largest city in America's smallest state. Located along the banks of the Blackstone River, many historians have called it the "Birthplace of the American Industrial Revolution." There were once two Pawtuckets. Pawtucket East is now part of Rehoboth, Massachusetts, while Pawtucket West was once part of North Providence. For many years, the city of 72,644 people has been at the forefront of our country's economic development.

The key to its early growth was its location. Its waterfalls powered the community's early growth. By 1671, Pawtucket already had its own iron works. Soon more small factories were built along the river. The river's strong currents inspired Samuel Slater to build our country's first textile mill. Slater Mill, built in 1790, was a technological breakthrough. It was the first commercialy venture to mass produce cotton yarn using water-powered machines. Other mills were soon established throughout Rhode Island and New England. Thousands of men, women, and children were once employed in New England's textile industry. In many ways, Pawtucket was the United States' first high-tech area.

Like many other Northern industrial cities, Pawtucket's fortunes declined after World War II. The textile industry still lives. Specialty textiles, lace, nonwoven, and elastic woven materials are still being manufactured. Pawtucket boasts more than 300 different industries, including jewelry and silverware, in approximately 300 small factories. The city is the corporate headquarters for Hasbro Toys, the world's second-largest toymaker. Mr. Potato Head's hometown is Pawtucket.

With the post-Industrial Era upon us, Pawtucket looks to its past to build its future. Some two-dozen former textile mills now form an arts district. The community offers cost affordable artist lofts. Many tourist and recreational sites, including those of Providence, are nearby. Like Old Man River, Pawtucket's still rolling along.

A Baseball Backgrounder

The Pawtucket Red Sox have a rich history but its real story is almost as old as baseball itself. The city of Pawtucket was incorporated in 1886. But long before that, teams from the area have played organized baseball.

In September 1870, a large group of fans witnessed the Monitor Base Ball Club of Pawtucket play its archrivals, the Eagle Base Ball Club of Central Falls, Rhode Island. The game took four hours to play. After five innings, the game was called due to darkness. It must have been quite a game. With impending darkness and facing certain defeat, the Pawtucket side rallied with an incredible 21 runs in the top of the fifth and then survived a seven-run inning by Eagle to eke out a hard-fought 34-33 win.

Meanwhile, just south of Pawtucket, some of the best baseball in the land was being played in Rhode Island's capital. The Providence Grays, a member of the National League from 1878 until 1888, had a brief but glorious history. In its first seven years in the league, Providence never finished lower than third. The Grays won two pennants, in 1879 and 1884, as well as baseball's first "World Series." Some of the greatest players in the history of baseball, including Hall of Famers George Wright, Harry Wright, and "Old Hoss" Radbourn, played for Providence.

Radbourn won 59 games during the regular season and led the 1884 team. But winning the National League wasn't enough for Old Hoss. He took matters into his own hands in the World Series, winning all three games for the Grays against the New York Metropolitans of the American Association. Harry Wright, the Grays' manager in 1882 and 1883, was one of the sport's greatest innovators. He invented pitching rotations, relief pitching, the doubleheader, batting practice, platooning, spring training, and patented scorecards.

Wright also developed another invention that has particular significance to every baseball fan. Wright founded a new team, the Providence Reserves, in 1888, to prepare young players to play in the big leagues. Many historians believe that the Providence Reserves were baseball's first minor-league team.

Despite their success, the Grays disbanded because of financial problems just one year after becoming baseball's first world champions. Providence later joined the Eastern League, the predecessor of today's International League, and had many successful teams.

Over the years, Providence has had baseball franchises in the Eastern League, International League, and New England League. They've been named the Grays, the Chiefs, the Clamdiggers, the Braves, and the Rubes. Other southeastern New England cities, like Attleboro and Taunton, Massachusetts, and Newport, Woonsocket, Cranston, and Pawtucket, Rhode Island have had professional teams.

Local industrial leagues, such as the Manufacturer's League in Pawtucket, the District Manufacturer's League in Woonsocket, and the Blackstone Valley League in central Massachusetts, also flourished.

Hall of Famers like Nap Lajoie and Woonsocket's Gabby Hartnett first played organized baseball in local industrial leagues. Many other great players, too numerous to mention, including former Brave and Pawtucket native Chet Nichols, former Paw Sox manager Joe Morgan, and Mike Roarke, played for local factory teams.

Boston and Pawtucket have always had a close relationship. It was natural for the first professional team at McCoy was a Boston affiliate. However, the first parent club for Pawtucket wasn't the Red Sox, but the Braves.

One of Pawtucket's greatest assets has always been its proximity to Boston. Braves executives didn't have to go out of their way to see top prospects play in person. To Braves management, fielding a minor league team in Pawtucket was a no-brainer. The Blackstone Valley was always a great source of talent for the Braves. Many local standouts, like pitcher Chet Nichols, infielder John Goryl, ex-Cardinal pitcher Max Surkont, ex-White Sox and Orioles general manager Roland Hemond, and ex-Paw Sox and Red Sox manager Joe Morgan, have been part of the Braves organization.

Photo courtesy of Bill Chapman

McCoy Stadium is one of the finest ballparks in the minor leagues.

Professional baseball finally came to Pawtucket on May 9, 1946. The Pawtucket Slaters played in the Class B New England League against teams from all over New England. Hometown hero Joe Krakowski, pitching the opener, led the Slaters to a 5-3 triumph over the Lawrence Millionaires. The most important event of the 1946 season may have occurred the next night, at the Slaters' second home game.

That evening Hammond Pond Stadium was an important stop along the long road to desegregate baseball. According to the schedule, the Pawtucket Slaters hosted the Nashua Dodgers, Brooklyn's farm team. But according to history Hammond Pond Stadium is one of the first places where Branch Rickey helped break baseball's color barrier. Anybody who attended the game had to agree that two former Negro League stars, Don Newcombe

and Roy Campanella, who played for Nashua, belonged in the majors. Pitcher Newcombe spun a seven-hit shutout and slammed two hits against the Slaters. Hall of Famer Roy Campanella, Nashua's catcher and cleanup hitter, was just as impressive. "Campy" hit the ball hard and called a great game behind the plate.

Take Me Out to the Ballgame

McCoy Stadium is Triple A's oldest ballpark and recently celebrated its 60th birthday. To baseball fans all over New England, going to see the PawSox at McCoy Stadium never grows old.

During the Depression, minor league baseball almost went under, losing many minor teams. The Providence Grays didn't survive the crash and, throughout the 1930s, Rhode Island was without minor league baseball.

Despite the country's struggles and hard times, Rhode Islanders still had a strong appetite for professional baseball. But there was one big problem: The Ocean State didn't have a suitable venue for professional baseball.

Mayor Thomas McCoy of Pawtucket, a strong advocate of Roosevelt's New Deal and a big baseball fan, had the perfect solution, or at least he thought he did. He proposed to have the city build a new ballpark on an underutilized swampy lot of land that was once a man-made reservoir named Hammond Pond. Today's McCoy Stadium is located smack-dab in the middle of the old reservoir.

Mayor McCoy had great plans for the stadium, which was originally named Hammond Pond Stadium. The development was supposed to be a one-of-a-kind sports complex surrounded by athletic fields and tennis courts. The ballpark was originally designed to have 20,000 seats, with every modern amenity. Outside of the major leagues, Hammond Pond Stadium was to be one of the finest athletic facilities in the country. The total cost for the land was $39,455. According to most estimates, the federal government, through the Works Progress Administration, planned to just spend $500,000.

Work on the project began in 1936. But from the beginning, nothing went right. Original plans went through a number of changes. The original concrete piers for the stands sagged. The men who laid sewer lines sank into quicksand. For two years, two crews of 125 men worked day and night, for more than one million hours draining, excavating soil, and filling the pond.

Costs quickly mounted. Criticism of Mayor McCoy grew. Before long, it was obvious that Hammond Pond Stadium's costs wildly exceed all estimates. Stadium plans needed to he scaled down. When it opened, Hammond Pond Stadium seated only 5,500 instead of 20,000. At its completion in 1942, Pawtucket's stadium was probably the most expensive in United States history. The total cost was $1,462,339.35—more expensive than large stadiums that were recently built at the University of Michigan, Notre Dame, and Ohio State. The fair market value of famous baseball stadiums, like Fenway Park, Braves Field, and the Polo Grounds, didn't come close to the high price of Hammond Pond Stadium.

To top it off, the final days of the stadium's construction were just as controversial as the first. Two weeks before opening night, the commission supervising Hammond Pond Stadium's construction ran afoul of the law. The War Production Board banned the use of all vital materials, like metal, for baseball stadium construction. But somehow, no one got the message to those putting the finishing touches on the stadium. Despite the ban, the builders were able to lay their hands on the last bit of steel needed to finish the ballpark's fence. McCoy's dream had become, according to critics, McCoy's folly.

Despite the high cost of Hammond Pond Stadium, the community enjoyed their new ballpark. In 1942, Pawtucket didn't have a professional team. So Pawtucket's local semi-pro team, the Slaters, which played in the New England League, also known as the New

England Victory League during the war, was the stadium's first tenant.

More than 6,000 jammed the stadium on its opening night on July 4, 1942. There were no Fourth of July fireworks due to wartime restrictions. Nevertheless, dignitaries from all over the state attended the celebration. Ceremonies started in the early afternoon with the induction of 14 teenage boys from Pawtucket into a naval aviation squadron. Local radio stars, singing all kinds of music, put on a great show. Fourteen drum, fife, and bugle corps, from Providence, Pawtucket, Cumberland, and Bristol, performed. Admission was free with the purchase of a 25-cent defense stamp. There was such a rush for defense stamps that ticket sellers couldn't keep up with the demand. Before the first pitch was thrown on July 5, Eugene Eraser, president of the New England League, presented a pennant to Mayor McCoy and Donat Maynard, manager of Pawtucket's semi-pro team, to commemorate the Slaters' 1941 New England League championship season. The New England League champions celebrated opening night in style. Pounding out nine hits against former New York Yankees pitcher "Bump" Hadley, the Slaters defeated the Lynn Erasers by a 4-2 score.

Through the war years, there was no professional ball at the stadium. Nevertheless, some of the best baseball around was played at Hammond Pond Stadium. Many major leaguers who were stationed at local military bases would play for local semi-pro teams at the stadium. To hide their identity, major leaguers didn't gener-

ally use their real names. Yogi Berra, under the assumed name "Joe Cusano," played for the Cranston Firesafes. Playing first base and batting behind Campanella, Walter Alston, the future Dodgers manager, lofted a long three-run homer over the stadium's center-field fence in the eighth inning—the first professional home run ever hit in the ballpark.

For his mighty clout, Alston was rewarded with a big prize: 100 baby chicks. Nobody knows what ever happened to those chicks. But there was one thing for sure: Alston would be too busy with the Dodgers to ever manage a chicken ranch. Nashua beat the Slaters by a score of 3-0.

Through the 1940s, McCoy Stadium was a favorite stop for major-league teams on the way to Boston. Local fans have seen the Boston Braves, the Boston Red Sox, the Philadelphia Phillies, and even Leo Durocher and the Brooklyn Dodgers. Some say a crowd of more than 6,000 people attended an exhibition game between the Slaters and Casey Stengel's New York Yankees.

On June 6, 1946, Hammond Pond Stadium was dedicated and given today's name, McCoy Stadium, in honor of Mayor McCoy, who had recently died. Despite Pawtucket's success, the New England League went out of business after the 1949 season, and the Slaters disbanded. For many years, McCoy was without professional baseball. But in 1966, professional baseball returned when Cleveland moved its Double A farm team to Pawtucket.

In 1970, the Pawtucket Red Sox first took the field as a member of the

Photo courtesy of Bill Chapman

The grounds crew works to prepare the McCoy field for another Paw Sox game.

Eastern League. Since then, for more than 30 consecutive years, Pawtucket has been part of the Boston farm system and a full-fledged member of Red Sox Nation. Triple A baseball soon followed. The Louisville Colonels, the Red Sox International League affiliate, didn't have a suitable place to play the 1973 season. So the city of Pawtucket stepped up to the plate and, since then, the Pawtucket Red Sox have been part of the International League.

On the field, the Pawtucket Red Sox were an immediate success. In their first year in Triple A, the Paw-Sox defeated Tulsa of the American Association to win the Little World Series. Despite their on-field success, the Pawtucket Red Sox at first had difficulties at the box office. Without its current owner, Ben Mondor, Pawtucket would have lost the team. When Mondor purchased the team in

1977, the park was dirty, dilapidated, and not a good place to bring a family. Attendance was low and the team was deeply in debt.

But pretty soon, things turned around under Mondor's leadership. With a lot of elbow grease, not to mention a large infusion of capital, McCoy came hack to life. It became a safe, affordable place to bring a family. Word about the PawSox spread quickly, and the rest is history. The PawSox have had so many great players, and so many great games, it's difficult to know where to start.

There's an annual Little League parade, the Rhode Island State High School Championships, college tournaments—and the gold-medal-winning U.S. Olympic team played Taiwan McCoy. Even vintage baseball teams, playing under nineteenth-century rules, have been held at McCoy.

McCoy knows how to rock. It has hosted the Allman Brothers, Louis Armstrong, Ella Fitzgerald, Gene Autry, and other musicians. In 1948, Harry Truman's campaign caravan stopped at McCoy. On the Fourth of July, there are always spectacular fireworks to celebrate our country's birthday. McCoy may be the oldest park in Triple A, but the $16 million spent in renovations during 1999 have made it like new. To meet National Association guidelines, McCoy's capacity is now 10,031. There's a bird's-eye view of the field from the new entry tower near the ballpark's entrance. And the new grassy berm in left field is a great place to enjoy an afternoon of baseball.

More than seven million fans have watched the grand old game at the grand old ballpark. It seems like every year means another franchise attendance record. After all of the struggles and controversy McCoy survives and thrives.

Best Game (When You Think About It, How Does Someone Decide Which Game Was the Best?)

One event that will never be forgotten is the "longest game in the history of baseball" between the PawSox and the Rochester Red Wings. The eight-hour, 25-minute, 33-inning marathon, which began on April 18, 1981, will always be the stuff of baseball legend and lore. A worldwide audience saw the completion of the game on July 23, 1981.

Eleven professional records were set and still stand. There were milestones reached in all kinds of categories, including innings played, time, putouts, at-bats, plate appearances, strikeouts, and assists. Cal Ripken, as was his habit, played every inning. With three other teammates, the former Orioles shortstop set the record for most plate appearances—18. The game even made it to Cooperstown—where it has its own exhibit at the Hall of Fame.

There have been many other great games at McCoy. A memorable pitching match-up was between Mark "the Bird" Fidrych against Dave Righetti of the Columbus Clippers on July 1, 1982. For most franchises, an event like the "World's Longest Game" would be more than enough. But not for the PawSox. Two future Red Sox hurlers pitched perfect games. On June 1, 2000, Tomu Ohka threw a 76-pitch masterpiece against the Charlotte Knights. Bronson Arroyo duplicated the feat on August 10, 2003 against Buffalo.

Greatest Team (Not the '27 Yankees, but Who Is?)

The PawSox have had many great players but have won only two championships. Pawtucket's first year in the International League was one of its best. The 1973 team, led by Cecil Cooper and Dick Pole, won Pawtucket's first Governor's Cup and its only Junior World Series championship. Jim Rice and Fred Lynn joined the PawSox late in the season and had an immediate impact. Rice hit .378 with four homers in just 10 postseason games.

Owner Ben Mondor's only championship team was in 1984. The PawSox defeated the Maine Guides, who represented Old Orchard Beach, to win the Governors' Cup. The team had Roger Clemens and "Oil Can" Boyd early in the year, but they were quickly called up to the majors. The team was led by a scrappy bunch of journeymen including Chico Walker, Steve Lyons, Kevin Romine, and Marc Sullivan. Each of the players had respectable careers with the Red Sox but were never stars. The team's best pitchers were Mike Rochford, Dennis Burtt, and Mike Brown.

Best Player . . . in My Opinion

Two of the greatest Red Sox players, Jim Rice and Fred Lynn, helped bring championship gold to Pawtucket. After helping the PawSox win the 1973 World Series, Jim Rice had one of the greatest years anybody has ever had in International League history. While the 1974 team finished in the second division, Rice's performance for the PawSox was first class. He was the International League's Triple Crown winner, Rookie of the Year, and Most Valuable Player. Thinking back, it's amazing that, for most of the year, the Boston Red Sox kept Rice down in the minors for seasoning. Carlton Fisk, Rick Burleson, Cecil Cooper, Dwight Evans, Juan Beniquez, Rick Miller, and Fred Lynn also played on the 1974 team.

Roger Clemens' stay was much briefer. After being drafted by the Red Sox, the future Hall of Famer shot through the farm system like a rocket. Clemens made just seven appearances for Pawtucket compiling a 2-3 record with a 1.93 ERA. Many Red Sox

greats—Jim Rice, Fred Lynn, Carlton Fisk, Rick Burleson, Roger Clemens, Wade Boggs, Mo Vaughn, John Tudor, Bruce Hurst, and Nomar Garciaparra—have played for the PawSox. One of the most famous aspects of the park is the murals of great Red Sox players that can be found throughout the park.

The most famous Providence player was Babe Ruth. In 1914, the Red Sox sent a then- skinny young left-handed pitcher from Baltimore named Babe Ruth for a bit more seasoning in Providence. From the beginning, Rhode Islanders new that Babe was something special. In just six weeks of play, he helped lead the Grays to the International League pennant.

Round Tripper (Some Suggestions for Sightseers)

Pawtucket has two first-class attractions: the Pawtucket Red Sox and the Slater Mill. When the Pawtucket Red Sox aren't playing, tourists can step back into history by visiting the old Slater Mill. Like many other historical sites, tourists can get hands-on experience about life in the early days of the Industrial Revolution. Actors provide realistic demonstrations of factory life.

Located where the Blackstone River empties into the Narragansett Bay, there are many things to see at the historic complex. There's a dam, a power canal, and a riverside park. Original operating machinery is located in the Wilkinson Mill (circa 1810). There are guided and self-guided tours. The site is the crown jewel of the Blackstone River Valley National Heritage Corridor. The museum is open every day during the summer and on weekends in the spring and fall.

Places to Eat . . . If You Want More Than Cracker Jack

You know you're in the Ocean State when you're eating a meal of clam cakes, stuffed quahogs, and red Manhattan clam chowder. Wash it down with a coffee milk. Only Autocrat syrup will do. Top it off with a frosty "Awful-Awful" shake or cabinet from Newport Creamery or a frozen lemonade from Dell's. Now you're eating like a real Rhode Islander.

While Pawtucket doesn't have a lot of fancy restaurants, there are many places to have a real Rhode Island dining experience. There are plenty of pizza shops, Chinese restaurants, and American Diners. While in town, here are a few choices. There are several diners near McCoy Stadium. The Riverside Kitchen is a real Greek diner serving New York weenies and heaping helpings of fish and chips. Real Coney Island dogs, Ocean State style, are served with mustard, celery salt, onions, and a special meat sauce. If you want to get a true Rhode Island experience, flavor your fried foods with vinegar.

One of the nice things about Pawtucket is that it's easy to feed a family of four for under $25 bucks. If you want something more upscale, Providence is just a short ten minute drive from Pawtucket. Accessing great places to eat before and after a PawSox game couldn't be easier.

Rhode Island

Sources:

The Baseball Almanac, 1995–2007.
Boston Globe, 1900–2007.
Boston Red Sox Media Guides, 1995–2006.
Pawtucket Red Sox Yearbooks, 1990–2006.
Society of American Baseball Researchers. *The Northern Game—and Beyond.* Boston: Cambridge Prepress Services, 2002.

www.all-baseball.com
www.ballparkdigest.com
www.ballparkreviews.com
www.baseballalmanac.com
www.baseballamericaonline.com
www.espn.com
www.milb.com
www.mlb.com
www.pawsox.com
www.sabr.org

19

Address: 500 Main Street, Bridgeport, CT 06604

Web Site: *www.bridgeportbluefish.com*

First Game: May 21, 1998

Dimensions: LF 325 CF 405 RF 325

Directions: From I-95 Northbound, take Exit 27 (Lafayette Boulevard). At bottom of ramp continue straight along South Frontage Road, go past Warren Street and turn right on Lafayette Boulevard. Take first left on Allen Street. Entrances to parking lots are on Allen Street.

From I-95 Southbound, take Exit 27 (Lafayette Boulevard). Stay to the left going down the ramp. Turn left onto Lafayette Boulevard. Go under I-95, travel one block and make a left on Allen Street. Entrances to the parking lots are on Allen Street.

From Merritt Parkway Southbound, take Exit 52 (Route 8) toward Bridgeport. Follow Route 8 to its convergence with Route 25.*

From Merritt Parkway Northbound, take Exit 49 (Route 25) toward Bridgeport. Follow Route 25 to its convergence with Route 8.*

*Follow Route 8/25 toward Bridgeport to Exit 1. At the bottom of the ramp continue straight through two lights. Go under I-95, and make a left on South Frontage Street. Continue straight to Broad Street. Turn right on Broad Street, go past the ballpark and turn right on Allen Street. Entrances to the parking are on Allen Street.

THE BALLPARK AT HARBOR YARD

Home of the Bridgeport Bluefish of the Atlantic League

Claim to Fame

Bridgeport is the hometown of P.T. Barnum and Tom Thumb. The Ballpark at Harbor Yard was inspired by Oriole Park at Camden Yards. Hall of Fame catcher "Orator" O'Rourke had the first hit in National League history and was the oldest player in National League history.

Strange but True

The P.T. Barnum Museum is chocked full of "strange but true" exhibits. There's nothing fictional about Tom Thumb. His real name was Charles Stratton. During P.T. Barnum's time, circus animals such as camels would stretch their legs and roam downtown Bridgeport.

Who's Who in Bridgeport

Hall of Famer "Orator" Jim O'Rourke and his son Queenie are two of the area's greatest players. Bluefish alumni include Pete Rose Jr., Jose Offerman, Edgardo Alfonzo, Deivi Cruz, and Mariano Duncan. Former major leaguers from the area are Charles Nagy, Rob Dibble, "Kiddo" Davis, and Neal Ball. Tommy John, Jimmy Foxx, Willie Upshaw, Dave LaPointe, and Jose Lind have managed Bridgeport's professional teams.

About Bridgeport

Do you want a sure-fire way to pick up some easy cash? Place a friendly wager on the answer to this question: What's Connecticut's largest city? If you guessed Hartford, you're wrong. If not Hartford, then how about New Haven? Wrong again. Give up? The answer is Bridgeport.

Even if you didn't know the answer, it's impossible to ignore Bridgeport. It's a hub for some of this country's busiest transportation routes. Several major highways, including Route 8-25 and Interstate 95, run right through the heart of the city. Amtrak and Metro-North rail lines run continuously into New York's Grand Central Station. There's also a regular ferry to Port Jefferson, New York.

If you think southern Connecticut is just an overgrown suburb of New York City, check out Bridgeport. What's really intriguing about the city are its contradictions. For years, Bridgeport used to brag about being a bastion of Republicanism, yet it had a Socialist mayor for more than two decades. The city has been home to many famous inventions, including electric sockets with pull chains and hand-held rocket launchers. Locally owned Sickorsky Aircraft Company developed the first commercially sold helicopter. It's hard to imagine a world

without the "Greatest Show on Earth" and Wham-O, which were developed by Bridgeport inventors.

The city's most famous resident was P.T. Barnum, most famous invention is the Frisbee, and most famous food is a Subway sandwich. A college student looking for a way to make a few extra bucks started the first Subway in Bridgeport. By the way, P.T. Barnum never said "there's a sucker born every minute." The story is completely apocryphal.

When it was originally founded, Bridgeport was mostly home to fisherman and farmers. Later, the city became a major port of trade.

With the onset of the Industrial Revolution, factories sprang up all over the city. There were once more than 500 factories. After a brief boom during World War II, the city went bust. Despite the hard times, the city has been a magnet for men and women who've searched for new opportunities in America. By last count, there are 60 different nationalities among Bridgeport's 140,000 residents

In recent times the city decided to take one of P.T. Barnum's famous saying to heart: "Without promotion something terrible happens . . . . Nothing!" P.T. Barnum's Circus Museum is a world-class attraction. The city has built a beautiful ballpark, Harbor Yard, on a contaminated parcel of land. Right next door, there's a spanking new multi-purpose arena and entertainment complex—the Arena at Harbor Yards. Take a stroll on the boardwalk and enjoy a fresh fish dinner at Captain's Cove Seaport. The city has tremendous parks designed by

Photo courtesy of the Bridgeport Bluefish

The Ballpark at Harbor Yard played host to the Atlantic League All-Star Game.

Frederick Law Olmstead, great museums, its own symphony orchestra, and even a zoo.

Bridgeport is a city with a sense of humor. John Ratzenberger, Kevin Nealon, and Richard Belzer are from the area. Cartoonists Al Capp and Walt Kelly, the creators of Li'l Abner and Pogo graduated from the local high school. There's still quite a bit of Barnum in Bridgeport.

A Baseball Backgrounder

Great ballplayers have always found good reasons to visit Bridgeport. Even before Abner Doubleday, the city's bywords have been Barnum and baseball. Being near New York City has its advantages, and also a few disadvantages. The city was once considered to be much too close to Yankee Stadium and Shea Stadium to support a minor

league team, but the founders of the Bridgeport Bluefish thought outside the box. They believed local fans would appreciate the convenience of having their own competitive team. A baseball team didn't necessarily need to be affiliated with the major leagues to be successful. For more than a decade, the Bridgeport Bluefish have been a flagship franchise in the Atlantic League.

The Bluefish weren't Bridgeport's first foray into professional baseball. But, to many fans, it seemed like it. Before World War II, plenty of top-notch baseball was played there. Besides P.T. Barnum, the city's most famous citizen was a baseballer. James "The Orator" O'Rourke was one of the greatest catchers in early modern baseball. O'Rourke was the first player to get a hit in the National League. New York Giant manager John McGraw called his old friend out of retirement, at almost 50 years old, to catch a few more major league games. For many years, O'Rourke was the player-manager of the Bridgeport team in the powerful Connecticut State League. Fans got to see their local favorites as well as many of the greatest big leaguers. Before the days of cars and planes, baseball teams would travel by train. Bridgeport had a massive train station near the ballpark. Major league teams and Negro League teams would make regular off-Broadway appearances in the city. Native Cornelius "Neal" Ball had the first unassisted triple play in Major League Baseball history. Former Red Rob Dibble and former Indian Charles Nagy are also from the area.

Throughout its baseball history, Bridgeport's professional teams have had many big-name managers. In the old Colonial League, Jimmy Foxx was the Bridgeport Bees' manager. Former major leaguers Duffy Dwyer, Jose Lind, and Dave LaPointe have been Bluefish skippers; the job is now handled by Tommy John.

Ever since the Bluefish first took the field in 1998, the team has won more games—more than 600—than any other team in the Atlantic League. Through 2006 almost 2.5 million fans have seen major leaguers like Donovan Osborne, Brian Boehringer, T.J. Mathews, Jose Lind, and José Offerman don Bridgeport uniforms. Angel Echevarria, who played for the Rockies, Brewers, and Cubs, recently returned from a two year stint in the Japanese League to man the Bluefish's outfield.

One of the biggest disasters involving baseball happened in Bridgeport.

A train carrying the St. Louis Cardinals derailed. Luckily, none of the baseball players were hurt, but 14 other passengers died. The team pulled up its sleeves to rescue the injured and recover the bodies.

One recent manager who regretted his visit to Bridgeport was Pennsylvania Road Warriors manager Bert Pena. He was punched by first-base umpire Allen Emanuel during a ninth inning argument.

Take Me Out to the Ballgame

What was once a local eyesore is now a thing of beauty. For years, state and city officials were racking their brains about what to do with the old Jenkins Valve and Sprague Meter Company property. First impressions, after all, are important. Having a disgusting, dirty contaminated site beside I-95 sent out all the wrong signals about Bridgeport.

But local businessman Jack McGregor had a vision. He came up with his idea at a Baltimore Orioles baseball game. He noticed that Bridgeport and Baltimore had much in common. The early 1990s were hard times for both cities. Several companies had left the area. Many old factories along the harbor were just waiting to be used. Both cities were searching for ways to be revitalized. Seeing what was done with Camden Yards, McGregor thought the same could be done in Bridgeport. He worked with a missionary zeal to build the ballpark. He didn't do it alone. Many helped. Seed money provided by the government's brownfields development got the ball rolling. Contaminated hot spots

Fans celebrating another exciting play in Bridgeport.

were identified and cleaned up. The Zurich Re Corporation invested $11 million. The Bluefish owners kicked in $3 million. The State of Connecticut and the city made up the $8 million difference.

What did the city get for its money? A 5,500-seat, state-of-the-art sports facility that is the envy of other minor league franchises. As a matter of fact, many cities across the country have studied and imitated Bridgeport.

The team, too, was an immediate success—drawing more than 300,000 fans in its second year. Harbor Yard has all of the bells and whistles—wide concourses, luxury boxes, picnic areas, and great concessions. There's a playground, a party suite, an upscale restaurant, and an all-you-can-eat ballpark buffet. The park is just blocks away from downtown Bridgeport. There's also plenty of parking.

The setting is comparable to many major league parks. Bluefish fans can see ferries and boats in Bridgeport Harbor. Like Seattle's Safeco Park, trains run by during the game. The power plant overlooking right field is a local landmark. Attendance has somewhat decreased since the ballpark has opened, but the quality of play speaks for itself. The Bluefish have already made five post-season appearances.

Best Game (When You Think About It, How Does Someone Decide Which Game Was the Best?)

Bridgeport's greatest baseball event was much more than a game. On October 6, 1912, the world was watching a great baseball challenge at the Remington Arms factory. Local scientists and baseball players were finally going to resolve two great questions. How fast could a human being possibly throw a baseball? And which major league pitcher threw the world's greatest fastball?

The competitors were right-hander "Big Train" Walter Johnson from the Washington Senators and left-hander Nap Rucker of the Brooklyn Dodgers. The whole baseball world was focused upon Bridgeport. The scientists specially designed a wire tunnel for the test. The pitchers didn't dress for the occasion; they just wore their street clothes. Much to the amazement of the National League, Johnson—the upstart American Leaguer—was the winner. According to the day's most accurate scientific devises, Johnson threw his fastball at just 82 MPH. The measurements were way off. Two years later, Johnson's fastball was clocked at almost 100 MPH.

Greatest Team (Not the '27 Yankees, but Who Is?)

Former Blue Jays first baseman Willie Upshaw's 1999 champions got off to a fast start and never looked back. The team outdrew the neighboring New Haven Ravens in the Eastern League. The team drew 342,857 fans and compiled an incredible 43-17, .717 first-half record. They swept away Somerset 3-0 in the championship series.

The team could do it all. But what it did best was run. Six players had more than 10 stolen bases. Three, including former major leaguer Alex Cole, had more than 25. The team featured an outstanding infield that featured former major leaguers Mariano Duncan and Gold Glover Jose Lind.

The team's leader, shortstop, Angel Espada, played eight years for the Bluefish. His greatest year may have been 1999, when he led the league in batting and 40 stolen bases. The two-time league batting champion is the team's all-time team leader in hits, at bats, stolen bases, and runs.

Best Player . . . in My Opinion

James Henry O'Rourke, nicknamed "Orator Jim," stands alone among Bridgeport's sports heroes. In 1876, he had the first hit in National League history. In the early days of professional baseball, he was second among all-time major league leaders in games played (1,644), hits (2,146), at-bats (6,884), doubles (392), total bases (2,936), and runs scored (1,370).

"Orator Jim" didn't fritter away his baseball salary. He put it to good use by funding tuition at Yale Law School. While practicing law, the multi-talented ballplayer managed, played for, and presided over Bridgeport's professional franchise. After retiring from the big leagues, "Orator Jim" was still behind the plate for Bridgeport at age 60. O'Rourke still holds the record as the oldest player ever to play Major League Baseball. As a favor to John McGraw, Jim O'Rourke came back to play at the age of 54 for the legendary New York Giants. O'Rourke had the great pleasure of managing his son Queenie, who was quite a third baseman himself. Against his father's best advice, Queenie pursued a baseball career, eventually making it all the way to the majors. O'Rourke was elected to the Baseball Hall of Fame in 1945.

Round Tripper (Some Suggestions for Sightseers)

Bridgeport has one of Connecticut's largest seaside attractions. Located beside historic Black Rock Harbor, Captain's Cove Seaport is a multi-purpose dimensional tourist mecca. There are craft shops, a Victorian-era museum, restaurants, and several other historical exhibits. There's nothing more beautiful that taking a nice ocean cruise during the summer. Seaside Park, one of America's first public recreation areas, is nearby. Best of all, admission is free.

The Nutmeg State's only zoo is located at 1875 Noble Avenue. The zoo, situated within Beardsley Park, is also, coincidentally, named Beardsley Zoo. During P.T. Barnum's time, the impresario's circus animals would routinely get their daily exercise in downtown Bridgeport. This all changed when Beardsley Park opened in the late 1880s. Now zebras and animals, as well as residents, had a place to stretch their legs. Eventually, a portion of the park was turned into a zoo. There are hundreds of animals in captivity, including tigers, bears, and turtles.

And, of course, the City of Bridgeport honors its most famous citizen, P.T. Barnum. His attractions continue to amuse and amaze. Famous attractions like the Human Pin Head, General Tom Thumb, the FeeJee Mermaid, and the Egyption mummy Pa-Ib are on display at the Barnum Museum. Scholars have recently determined that Pa-Ib was the real thing, a genuine honest-to-goodness mummy. The experts learned many things and determined there was substantial evidence that it had the world's oldest case of halitosis. We don't know where P.T. Barnum is now. But I bet he's smiling about the plans to create a rotating three-dimensional reconstruction of the mummy for visitors.

Places to Eat . . . If You Want More Than Cracker Jack

Bridgeport's most famous restaurant is Subway. If you don't believe it, just look around town. By last count, there are at least seven different Subway restaurants scattered around the city—with more on the way. Besides seafood, Bridgeport specializes in Italian cuisine. Many say that Ralph N. Richs at 121 Wall Street is one of Bridgeport's best restaurants. Ralph, the owner, serves homemade Italian food just like they used to make in the old country. Delicious.

The Southern Connecticut community has plenty of pizzerias. Some of the better known are Mario the Baker at 4414 Main Street, Pizza Time at 1121 Madison Avenue, and Vinny's Pizza Restaurant at 30 Huntington Turnpike. For seafood, check out the restaurants Captain's Cove Seaport.

Connecticut

Sources:

The Baseball Almanac, 1995–2007.
Boston Globe, 1900–2007.
New York Times, 1890–2007.
Conan, Neal. *Play by Play*. New York: Crown Publishers, 2002.
Society of American Baseball Researchers. *The Northern Game—and Beyond*. Boston: Cambridge Prepress Services, 2002.

www.atlanticleague.com
www.all-baseball.com
www.ballparkdigest.com
www.ballparkreviews.com
www.baseballalmanac.com
www.baseballamericaonline.com
www.bridgeportbluefish.com
http://ci.bridgeport.ct.us/
www.mlb.com
www.sabr.org

20

Address: 230 John Karbonic Way, New Britain, CT 06051

Web Site: *www.rockcats.com*

First Game: April 12, 1996

Dimensions: LF 330 CF 400 RF 330

Directions: From the west, take 84 East to Exit 35 (Route 72E). Follow Route 72 to Route 9S. Take Exit 25 (Ellis Street), turn left at the light onto Ellis Street, then turn left at the next light onto South Main Street. New Britain Stadium is approximately one mile on the right.

From the east, take 84 West to Exit 39A (Route 9S). Take Exit 25 (Ellis Street), turn left at the light onto Ellis Street, then turn left at the next light onto South Main Street. New Britain Stadium is approximately one mile on the right.

From the south, take Route 91 North to Exit 22 (Route 9N). Follow Route 9N to Exit 24. Then take the first exit for Willowbrook Park/Route 71. New Britain Stadium will be right in front of you off the exit.

From the north, take Route 91 South to Exit 22 (Route 9N). Follow Route 9N to Exit 24. Then take the first exit for Willowbrook Park/Route 71. New Britain Stadium will be right in front of you off the exit.

NEW BRITAIN STADIUM

Home of the New Britain Rock Cats of the Eastern League

Connecticut

Claim to Fame

New Britain is nicknamed "Hardware City" because of its manufacturing history.

Strange but True

The wire clothes hanger was invented in New Britain. How about that?

Who's Who in New Britain

Former New Britain Rock Cats include third baseman Todd Walker, Torii Hunter, David Ortiz, Doug Mientkiewicz, A.J. Pierzynski, Michael Cuddyer, Juan Rincon, American League Most Valuable Player Justin Morneau, American League batting champion Joe Mauer, and Francisco Liriano. Former New Britain Red Sox include Curt Schilling, Roger Clemens, Jeff Bagwell, Ellis Burks, Brady Anderson, and Mo Vaughn. The all-time New Britain baseball team would be incredible.

About New Britain

From a surveyor's perspective, New Britain is the most centrally located city in Connecticut. It's smack dab right in the middle of the Nutmeg State.

New Britain has been a home away from home for Polish immigrants. Poles and other ethnic groups came in droves to take advantage of opportunities at the city's large factories. There are still Polish delis and diners along Broad Street. There are still a few backyard ovens where old-timers make the best kielbasa this side of Kracow. New Britain High School is one of the only high schools to offer Polish in its curriculum. New Britain's Polish influence has even had an effect on locals' English. Polish pronunciation has contributed to the unique tenor of the New Britain accent. The city's latest wave of immigrants is Spanish speakers.

The city is nicknamed "Hardware City" because of its many factories. Stanley Works and Corbin Locks were once two of the city's largest employers. It was estimated that nearly one-third of all nails, screws, bolts, and hinges in the country were made in the central Connecticut city. The wire clothes hanger was also first invented and developed by a native New Brittainer, O.A. North. What would life be like without the city's clothes hangers? The thought of wrinkled suits and dresses is too horrible to imagine.

The city's motto is "industria implet alveare et mele fruitur," which means "industry fills the hives and draws the honey." Nevertheless the city knows how to have some fun. Another New Britainer, Joseph Sobek, invented racquetball. The New Britain Museum of American Art, located at 56 Lexington Street adjacent to Walnut Hill Park, is the oldest museum to specialize in 100 percent pure American art.

A Baseball Backgrounder

Nobody has had a more improbable road to success than the New Britain Rock Cats. The team's former owner, Joe Buzas, was a one-of-a-kind. The former Opening Day shortstop for the New York Yankees had a promising career cut short by a shoulder injury. But it didn't keep him out of the game. Over a 47-year career in the game, Buzas owned interests in more than 82 different minor league teams. He saw minor league baseball's booms and busts. He was one of the last of baseball's old school owner-operators.

Buzas wasn't just a turnaround specialist; he was a survivor. Keeping minor league teams afloat was always a challenge. In 1982 his Double A team, the Bristol Red Sox, were struggling at the gate. Nearby New Britain had just built the Beehive—a new modern stadium—just 10 miles away. Moving the team was a no-brainer. By 1983, the Bristol Red Sox became the New Britain Red Sox.

The city was generally considered too small to support a Double A team. But it did. Just like Pawtucket, Red Sox management appreciated having many of its top prospects so close to Boston. Maybe the team wasn't making the money it should have, but Buzas came to love the city. The good times with the Red Sox didn't last forever. Other cities, and even the Red Sox, wanted Buzas to move to a larger market. But he wouldn't.

Photo courtesy of the New Britain Rock Cats

The sun sets on New Britain Stadium.

Loyalty counts for something. Buzas was loyal to the city. The city was also loyal to Buzas. The city agreed to build a new ballpark for its Double A franchise. So Buzas agreed to stay. However, the Red Sox management wouldn't stay in New Britain. Trenton became the Red Sox Eastern League affiliate. So the Minnesota Twins came to the rescue. The New Britain Red Sox became the Hardware City, later the New Britain, Rock Cats. The affiliation with the Minnesota Twins has worked out great. Since 1995, the Twins have had outstanding teams. And most of their great players have cut their teeth in New Britain. While Roger Clemens, Curt Schilling, and Jeff Bagwell played for the Red Sox affiliate, the New Britain Red Sox were never very successful on the field. If anything, the talent provided by the Minnesota Twins has been consistently better.

Just look at some of the Twins' talent: Todd Walker, Torii Hunter, Doug Mientkiewicz, A.J. Pierzynski, Michael Cuddyer, Juan Rincon, Justin Monreau, Joe Mauer, and Francisco Liriano. David Ortiz played here in 1997. Lately, the Rock Cats have been developing some great pitching in New Britain. Matt Garza and Kevin Slowney could be future Cy Young Award winners. In 1994, the team was last in the Eastern League in attendance at 124,560. New Britain is now consistently drawing more than 325,000 fans per year.

Take Me Out to the Ballgame

The New Britain Rock Cats are real homebodies. Since moving from nearby Bristol, their stadium has been located within the confines of city-owned Willow Brook Park. The park has plenty of space. There's even a facility for football and soccer. When the team was forced to abandon its old ballpark, the Beehive, team management didn't have to make any overnight accommodations. They moved right next door to their new digs at New Britain Stadium.

Connecticut

Photo courtesy of the New Britain Rock Cats

Fireworks are a nice attraction for younger fans (and older ones too).

For many years, the team was affiliated with the Red Sox, so it was assumed the Red Sox would make the move with the team. It didn't happen. Boston exited. Enter the Minnesota Twins. Having Boston leave New Britain hurt—unless maybe if you're a Yankees fan. New Britain proved the Red Sox wrong and showed being affiliated with a major-market team isn't necessarily the key to minor league success.

The Twins have done their part. They've consistently provided New Britain with top-notch players like David Ortiz, Justin Morneau, and Joe Mauer. Ownership and staff continue to make strong contributions to the community. Quality counts. During the summertime, the Rock Cats are a tough ticket. The team now draws more than 400,000 people. On June 17, 2006, New Britain set an all-time standing-room-only attendance record of 7,567.

The stadium is a beauty. It has split-level seating, wide concourses, and plenty of leg room. As is the style of many modern stadiums, restrooms, gift shops, and the concessions are ground level. The closed-circuit televisions around the ballpark—a feature not seen at many minor league parks—are a nice touch for the fans. Outdoor grills are located beside the first-base and third-base side of the field. The kids' play area is in left field. The ballpark is also the home of New Britain Sports Hall of Fame.

While many things about New Britain's baseball have changed, the new stadium, like the old one, still favors pitchers. The town will never forget the team's former owner Joe Buzas, who resisted pressure from the Red Sox and kept the team in New Britain. It just goes to show you that there's a baseball life after the Red Sox.

Best Game (When You Think About It, How Does Someone Decide Which Game Was the Best?)

Minnesota Twins outfielder Lew Ford was never considered a power hitter, but he had one of the greatest power surges in Eastern League history. He was the first Eastern League hitter in almost 80 years to slug four home runs in a game on August 19, 2001, against Binghamton. Then, just weeks later, he was the winner of the Double A home run hitting contest at the All-Star game.

Greatest Team (Not the '27 Yankees, but Who Is?)

Before the Beehive, New Britain's professional team played at Electric Field. During the early 1900s, competition in the old Connecticut State League was particularly intense. Hartford was New Britain's nemesis. Teams were always beating the bushes to find an extra bat or arm. The Aviators were getting frustrated. They weren't finding the kind of players needed to compete so they decided to think outside of the box.

Their manager decided to look in Cuba for new players. Shortstop Alfredo "Pájaro" Cabrera, left fielder Armando Marsans, and third base-

man Rafael Almeida were signed up by manager Dan O'Neil. They played in New Britain from 1908 to 1911. Marsans and Almeida were eventually signed by the Cincinnati Reds. Marsans was the National League batting champions. All three players had long and successful careers.

In the modern era, New Britain has won two Eastern League championships. In 2001, it was named co-champion after the season was cancelled due to the September 11th tragedy. In 1983, a young Roger Clemens, fresh out of the University of Texas, led New Britain to its only modern title.

Best Player . . . in My Opinion

Minnesota Twins catcher Joe Mauer may be baseball's next big thing. From the very first day he took the field, his talent was obvious. His year in New Britain was slightly shortened by injury. Nevertheless, his .338 average at Fort Meyers and New Britain was impressive. In addition, Mauer was showing defensive skills that were unparalleled for someone his age. Mauer's skill and ability has been compared to Johnny Bench. His ability to call a game and throw out base runners is remarkable. Because of his 2003 performance, he was named Minor League Player of the Year by *Baseball America*. You can't get much better than that.

Future Hall of Famer Jeff Bagwell was once a Red Sox farmhand in New Britain, leading the Eastern League in batting average. There was every expectation that he would someday become the Red Sox starting third baseman. Then it happened. Bagwell was traded for Larry Anderson. It was one of the worst trades in Red Sox history.

Round Tripper (Some Suggestions for Sightseers)

Who ever said you can't start a great art collection on a shoestring budget? The founders of New Britain's Museum of Art decided to buy just American art after learning that European imports were too expensive. How much art can anyone buy on a budget of just a couple of hundred dollars a year? The curators covered America from the Atlantic to the Pacific looking for art. The travels along our country's highways and byways paid off. Today, the museum has one of the most fabulous collections of American art. Among the most famous pieces of art exhibited are Thomas Hart Benton's masterpiece, "Arts of Life in America," a collection of murals about our country's daily life.

A really cool thing to do while in New Britain is to learn about stargazing at the aptly-named Copernicus Observatory and Planetarium on the campus of Central Connecticut State University. Getting an opportunity to tour the magnificent observatory isn't an everyday occurrence. Show schedules depend upon availability of professors and the weather. For more information call 860-832-3399 or go to *www.ccsu.edu/astronomy.*

Another suggestion is to visit Avery Soda. See one of the oldest soft drink manufacturing plants in New England. Soda is made according to

Sherman Avery's specifications. Avery's has the secret to making cream soda and Birch Beer. It also produces patented "totally gross sodas," such as Swamp Juice, Toxic Slim, and Dog Drool. The original factory is still alive and well. Its address is 520 Corbin Avenue. For more information, contact 860-224-0830 or visit *www.averysoda.com.*

Places to Eat ... If You Want More Than Cracker Jack

Cappy's Lunch at 510 Main Street features the hot dog that made New Britain famous. According to its menu, you can order your dog "with the works," "with everything," or "up." No matter how you say it, a hot dog from Cappy's with mustard, onions, and sauce is at the top of the list for real Connecticut cuisine. The sauce that makes Cappy's special is a family secret.

Dining in New Britain is a decidedly Eastern European experience. Cracovia's headliner is the "Polish Plate"—a delicious sampler with golabki, pierogi, kielbasa, bigos (sauerkraut with meat), and mashed potatoes. The institution is located at 60 Broad Street. Also recommended is East Side Restaurant, at 131 Dwight Street, which specializes in German food such as sauerbraten, jaeger schnitzel, pot roast, and burgomaster. Top it off with a frosty full-bodied German beer.

"Little Poland" is located on Broad Street between Burritt and Washington streets. Try out one of the delis. Sample the best Polish food this side of Warsaw.

Sources:

The Baseball Almanac, 1995–2007.
Boston Globe, 1900–2007.
Boston Red Sox Media Guides, 1995–2006.
Society of American Baseball Researchers. *The Northern Game—and Beyond*. Boston: Cambridge Prepress Services, 2002.

www.all-baseball.com
www.ballparkdigest.com
www.ballparkreviews.com
www.baseballalmanac.com
www.baseballamericaonline.com
www.ccsu.edu/
www.easternleague.com
www.espn.com
www.milb.com
www.mlb.com
www.new-britain.net/
www.sabr.org

Connecticut

21

Address: 252 Derby Avenue, West Haven, CT 065169

Web Site: *www.cuttersbaseball.com*

First Game: 1928

Dimensions: LF 335 CF 405 RF 315

Directions: From Merritt and Wilbur Cross Parkways, take Exit 57 (Route 34 East) directly to the Yale Fields, or take Exit 59 (Whalley Avenue) and follow the signs indicating the Yale Bowl to the Yale Fields.

From I-95, take Eastbound Exit 44 or Westbound Exit 45 to Route 10 and follow signs for the Yale Bowl. Or, take Exit 47 (Downtown) and follow Route 34 to the Yale Fields.

From Downtown New Haven, go north on Chapel Street, then turn left on Derby Avenue (Route 34), which will take you to the fields.

From I-91, take Exit 1 (Downtown) and follow Route 34 to the Yale Fields.

YALE FIELD

Home of the New Haven County Cutters of the Canadian-American League and Yale University Bulldogs

Claim to Fame

Yale University. The place where pizza and hamburgers were invented.

Strange but True

In 1967 Jim Morrison was arrested during a performance with the Doors. "Peace Frog" is all about his arrest in New Haven. There are claims that the incident was the first time a rock star was arrested while performing, but it's unclear if that's truth or fiction.

Who's Who in New Haven

The concourse underneath the stands is lined with the names of famous players who made appearances at the stadium. These include Babe Ruth, Lou Gehrig, Ted Williams, and Yale baseball players George H.W. Bush and George W. Bush. Yale's former coach was Smokey Joe Wood. The greatest player in Yale baseball history was former New York Met Ron Darling. Former New Haven Ravens include Juan Acevedo, Craig Counsell, Todd Helton, Gil Meche, Neifi Perez, and Eric Young.

Yale Field has seen decades of baseball over its time.

About New Haven

Some believe that New Haven was the United States' first planned community. New Haven was founded by a group of English Puritans who were searching for a place to create a Christian utopia—a place to escape society's "manifold and persistent wickedness." Three men who committed treason against King Charles I of Great Britain found refuge in the city. When Charles I's son ascended to the throne, he continued to look for those who had betrayed his beloved father. The escapees hid out in a cave on top of New Haven's West Rock.

The city's founders brought to fruition their plans for settlement in the Connecticut wild. Their first action was to change the city's name to establish the village's new identity. Having a community that was named after the native inhabitants was completely unacceptable. The original name of the town, Quinnipiac, had to go. The new inhabitants decided give their city a name of biblical proportions—New Haven.

Their next task was to give the town a design befitting its beliefs. Nothing less would be acceptable. The original settlers laid out their community on a grid. All streets would be ramrod straight. Intersecting roads would be perfectly perpendicular. According to old English custom, a large open public common would be the town center. The first plans to develop downtown New Haven went smoothly but not quite according to plan. The New Haven Green is still here, a 16-acre public park and recreation area located in the downtown area, as surveyed by original colonist John Brockett.

Utopia? New Haven is far from utopia. Nevertheless, the community has much to brag about. One of the American Revolution's most famous patriots, Roger Sherman, was its first mayor. Yale alumnus Eli Whitney invented the cotton gin and revolutionized the manufacture of rifles. New Haven was once called the "Arsenal of Democracy." Winchester Arms were once manufactured here.

And, of course, there's always Yale University. In 1700, it was known as the Collegiate School. But the name didn't resonate. The university was eventually named after Elihu Yale, the school's wealthy benefactor. Mr. Elihu Yale helped endow a new building named the "Yale Building." After several considerable gifts, the entire school was named Yale College. Our last three presidents—George Herbert Walker Bush, George Walker Bush, and Bill Clinton—and many other politicians are alumni. A writer for the *Boston Globe* wrote, "If there's one school that can lay claim to educating the nation's top national leaders over the past three decades, it's Yale."

Besides being home to Yale, the city was the birthplace of football, pizza, and hamburgers. In a way, you could say there wouldn't be a Super Bowl without New Haven. In 1892, a local candy maker took hardened sucrose, flavored, and put it on a stick. This is how the first lollipop was invented. The first erector set was built in New Haven. Nicknamed the "Elm City," the world headquarters of the Knights of Columbus is located here.

Bladderball was also invented here. How the sport never achieved the popularity of baseball or football is a complete mystery. The game, a product of Yale, is a direct descendant of an ancient form of rugby that was played on New Haven's Green. Like early colonists, teams from various dorms would fight for possession of the ball. How teams scored was a mystery. A rulebook was non-existent. Play started at the Yale campus, but the whole city of New Haven was in play. Downtown traffic was stopped. Mobs of players trampled the city. Eventually, bladderball was banned by Yale President and future baseball commissioner A. Bartlett Giamatti.

A Baseball Backgrounder

The Ivy League prides itself on being the last bastion of amateur sport. No matter how generous the compensation package offered, some of Yale's greatest athletes turned their back on professional sports. After all, there were certain things a gentleman shouldn't do. Becoming a professional athlete was one of them.

One of Yale's most popular sports has always been baseball. The administration has endeavored to keep it strictly amateur. Hall of Fame football legend Amos Alonzo Stagg was also quite a baseball player. After graduating from prep school Phillips Exeter, Stagg found fame and glory on the baseball pitch. In his five years on the team, he pitched Yale to five Ivy conference championships. New York offered him a big bonus of $4,200 to turn pro, but Stagg refused. After all, some things were much more important than money.

Stagg knew the consequences of turning professional were serious. He wanted to avoid the shame, indignity, and humiliation of star pitcher Spencer Pumpelly—a great Yale pitcher gone bad.

Pumpelly's family was a major benefactor of the University. Wealth, money, and connections don't grow on trees. Pumpelly was related to a distinguished politician and was a Hotchkiss man to boot. He had it all but threw it all away. During the summer, he accepted room and board to play summertime baseball. Such gross violation of the rules couldn't be tolerated. Connections didn't pay off. Yale's administration had no choice. Pumpelly was sent packing.

President George Bush never made Pumpelly's mistake. Who knows what kind of future Pumpelly would have had? Maybe Spencer Pumpelly would have been president rather than George Herbert Walker Bush? Bush was captain of the Yale team that was runner-up in the 1948 College World Series. The future president—a right-hand hitter and left-hand thrower—was a "real fancy Dan" at first base.

Class of 1880 alumnus Walter Camp, who created the All-American football team, claimed that Yale, not Amherst and Williams, actually played in the first intercollegiate baseball game. Several Yale grads have ultimately made it to the majors. Ex-Yankee Frank Quinn and ex-Met Ron Darling are two of Yale's greatest pitchers. For many years, "Smokey" Joe Wood was Yale's coach.

Considering Yale's aversion to professional athletics, it's ironic that a group of alumni, with cooperation of school administration, brought professional baseball back to New Haven. Before the 1994 season, Yale Field was renovated head to toe. It was once the home of the Double A New Haven Ravens, an affiliate of the Colorado Rockies. New Haven has always been one of the most difficult home run parks in professional baseball. Only one of the six New Haven pitchers that led the Eastern League in ERA had distinguished major league careers.

The Ravens ultimately struck gold and won the 2000 Eastern League championship. After brief stints in the Toronto and St. Louis Cardinal system, the Double A team moved to Manchester, New Hampshire, and are now the New Hampshire Fisher Cats. The New Haven Cutters baseball team, in the Canadian-American League, is now the summertime tenant of Yale Field.

Take Me Out to the Ballgame

Yale didn't recently start buying any available land it could find around New Haven. It's been going on for hundreds of years. Located right across the street from the famous Yale Bowl, Yale Field was purchased by the trustees in 1882. Originally, the site was a great apple orchard. But with the University running out of space, the administration concluded the property could be put to a much better use as an athletic field.

The Bulldog varsity baseball team played its first game at the ballpark in 1902. At the time, the Elis drew large crowds. Harvard-Yale baseball was a popular attraction. Crowds began to grow. And the interest in Yale's team outstripped the facilities. The old ballpark, which was just a bunch of wooden bleachers, had to go. Yale decided its baseball team would play in a first-class facility.

The architects searched high and low for someone to design a grand modern stadium. At the time, Yankee Stadium was considered to be America's greatest. Yale Field, in many ways, was inspired by the "House That Ruth Built." Just look at the arches and the sightlines. The similarities between the two steel and concrete structures are unmistakable. When the ballpark was built, the trustees wanted to send the world a message about the grandeur of Yale University.

Opening day for Yale Field was in 1928. The Bulldogs faced New Haven's professional team. It was an ugly game for the collegians. They lost 12-0. After the inauspicious start, things got better. Yale's baseball team, led by longtime coach Ethan Allen, was consistently strong. Ultimately, the 1947 team made it all the way to the College World Series. The captain of the team was named George Bush.

Throughout the years, the stadium has, except for a few visits from barnstorming major leaguers, been strictly for amateur baseball. But a bunch of Yale alumni decided in 1994 that it would be great to have a professional team in New Haven. When the major league awarded expansion franchises to Colorado and Florida, two new Double A teams were added. New Haven was awarded an expansion franchise in the Eastern League with the Colorado Rockies.

The team had a good decade-long run. But the city couldn't keep up with the competition. The old New Haven franchise is now located in Manchester. Another professional team, the New Haven County Cutters of the Canadian-American League, plays a short season schedule at Yale Field.

Besides the ivy-covered façade, the most distinct aspect of the field is the 35-foot-long hand-operated scoreboard in center-field just like the one in Fenway Park. The ballpark is considered a graveyard for hitters. At one time, the right-field fence was 340 feet down the line. Today, it's a much more manageable 315 feet. Babe Ruth said that the playing surface at Yale Field was the best he had ever seen, but this hasn't always been the case. It's always a battle to make sure the playing field is ship-shape. Yale Field has undergone many changes. It now has air-conditioned luxury boxes, wait service, kid zones, and cable television.

Best Game (When You Think About It, How Does Someone Decide Which Game Was the Best?)

Famed baseball writer Roger Angell and former major league star Smokey Joe Wood witnessed the greatest college baseball game ever played. Angell wrote about it. The game occurred at Yale Field. The May 21, 1981, duel between St. John's Frank Viola and Yale University's star pitcher Ron Darling exceeded all expectations. Both pitchers were at their best for the NCAA first-round match-up. Through 11 innings, neither pitcher gave up a run. Darling was actually pitching a no-hitter into the 12ᵗʰ. St. John's finally broke through with an opposite-field scratch hit. A steal of second and third put the Redman in scoring position. With runners on first and third, St. John's decided to try a double steal. It worked. Yale lost Ron Darling's final game in a 1-0 heartbreaker.

Greatest Team (Not the '27 Yankees, but Who Is?)

Choosing a city's only major league team as its all-time best usually makes sense. But not with New Haven. In 1875, New Haven had a brief stay in the majors. The team's performance was record setting. Not in a good way. The New Haven Elm Citys hold the distinction of being one of the worst major league teams ever. The team finished 7 and 40. Their team's best pitcher, Tricky Nichols, who was supposed to be pretty good finished with an amazing 4-29 record.

The city's most famous team was the George Bush–led 1947 Yale Bulldogs, runners-up in the College World Series. A home run from Red Sox star Jackie Jensen powered the Southern California Trojans to its first national championship. Playing Yale baseball is a Bush family tradition. Former Senator Prescott Bush and current president George W. Bush have played for Yale.

Best Player . . . in My Opinion

Future major league All-Star Ron Darling is, by consensus, the greatest Yale baseball player ever. Darling wasn't just a star on the mound, but in the field. Between starts, the Hawaiian-born right-hander would play outfield and was the team's best hitter. Pitch, hit, field, and run—Darling could do it all. The two-time Ivy League Most Valuable Player was the last pitcher from his alma mater to make it in the majors until Craig Below did it with the Red Sox.

Darling is still the only pitcher from Yale to be a first-round selection in the major league amateur draft. He was paid a bonus of $100,000 to sign with the Texas Rangers.

Round Tripper (Some Suggestions for Sightseers)

New Haven is just a short two-hour drive from New York. Yale University is central to New Haven's cultural life. If you don't believe it, just ask a Yale graduate. The campus has many things to offer. The Yale Center for British Art boasts the largest collection of English painting and sculpture outside of the United Kingdom. There's the Yale Collection of Musical Instruments, the Yale Philharmonic, and the Yale Reparatory Theatre. Then, there's Yale Peabody Museum, which is home to a 67-foot tall brontosaurus. The Yale University Art Gallery has genuine van Gogh, Picasso, and Manet masterpieces. Yale University also has its own visitor's center and provides guided tours around its campus.

But any New Haven native will tell you that there's life after Yale. Since 1913, many Broadway producers preview new shows at the old Shubert

Photo courtesy of the Yale Sports Publicity Department. Reprinted with permission.

An aerial shot of Yale Field in New Haven, CT.

Theatre. *South Pacific* and *My Fair Lady* debuted in New Haven. If a show makes it there, it can make it anywhere. In the summertime, there's nothing like catching a few rays at Hammonasset Beach State Park, Connecticut's longest saltwater beach. For laughs, there's a 60,000-piece collection of cartoons at the Character, Comic, and Cartoon Museum in nearby Cheshire. And the Eli Whitney Museum is in Hamden.

Places to Eat ... If You Want More Than Cracker Jack

A grateful nation hails New Haven's two most famous culinary creations. A mountain of evidence supports its claim to be the place where hamburgers and pizza were invented.

Louis Lassen is a lunchtime legend. In the early 1900s, the first hamburger was served at Louis Lunch. The city has zealously guarded its claim as the harbinger of hamburgers. Louis' grandson actually went out and collected notarized affidavits to support the luncheonette's claim to fame. The New Haven Preservation Trust has placed a plaque in the restaurant to commemorate the discovery of the hamburger. The restaurant is still in business. Each burger is grilled in an antique gas grill. The philosophy of the owners has always been that a really good hamburger doesn't need condiments. There are no buns. Ketchup and mustard are never allowed on the premises.

Pizza, also, was first introduced in New Haven. Real New Haven pizza has thin crust. Many credit local restaurateur Frank Pepe with the discovery. Clam pizza is one of Pepe's signature pizzas. A great pizza pie is the pride of the community. Frank Pepe's Napoletana Pizzeria is still going strong, and is located at 157 Wooster Street.

Sally's Apizza is located at 237 Wooster Street, right near New Haven Green. Ever since it opened its doors in 1938, the pizzas from the open, coal-fired oven have been distinctively delicious. There are all kinds of combination pizzas on Sally's menu. Modern Apizza at 74 State Street, and Sorrento's Pizzeria and Restaurant at 293 Skiff Street, are a couple of other great pizzerias.

Students from all over the world attend school in New Haven. So it's only natural that the city offers a cook's tour of international cuisine. For a taste of South America, try the Pacífico at 220 College Street. How about Asia? Pot-au-Pho at 77 Whitney Avenue, has great Vietnamese food and Bentara Restaurant at 76 Orange Street serves Malaysian cuisine. The bottom line is that New Haven has a vibrant restaurant scene.

Sources:

The Baseball Almanac, 1995–2007.
Boston Globe, 1900–2007.
Society of American Baseball Researchers. The Northern Game—and Beyond. Boston
    Cambridge Prepress Services, 2002.

www.all-baseball.com
www.ballparkdigest.com
www.ballparkreviews.com
www.baseballalmanac.com
www.baseballamericaonline.com
www.brocktonrox.com
www.canamleague.com
www.cityofnewhaven.com/
www.newhavencutters.com
www.sabr.org
http://yalebulldogs.cstv.com/

22

Address: 14 Stott Avenue, Norwich, CT 06360

Web Site: www.ctdefenders.com

First Game: April 17, 1995

Dimensions: LF 309 CF 401 RF 309

Directions: From the north take I-395 South to Exit 82 (Norwichtown/Yantic). Take a right at the bottom of the ramp. At the first light, take a right into the Norwich Industrial Park. Follow the green and white Dodd Stadium signs until you see the stadium on the right.

From the south take I-95 North to left exit 76 (I-395 North). Take I-395 North to Exit 81 West onto Route 2 West. Bear right onto Route 32 North (towards Willimantic). At the light adjacent to Holmgren Subaru, take a right onto New Park Avenue, which brings you into the Norwich Industrial Park. Follow the green and white Dodd Stadium signs until you see the stadium on the right.

From the east take I-95 South to Exit 84 North. Take Route 32 North to I-395 North. Once on I-395, take Exit 81 West to Route 2 West. Bear right onto Route 32 North (toward Willimantic). At the light adjacent to Holmgren Subaru, take a right onto New Park Avenue, which brings you into the Norwich Industrial Park. Follow the green and white Dodd Stadium signs until you see the stadium on the right.

From the Hartford area take Route 2 East to Exit 27 (Yantic). At the end of the exit ramp, take a right. Bear right onto Route 32 North (toward Willimantic). At the light adjacent to Holmgren Subaru, take a right onto New Park Avenue, which brings you into the Norwich Industrial Park. Follow the green and white Dodd Stadium signs until you see the stadium on the right.

From the Willimantic area take Route 32 South to the Franklin/Norwich border. At the light adjacent to Holmgren Subaru, take a left onto New Park Avenue, which brings you into the Norwich Industrial Park. Follow the green and white Dodd Stadium signs until you see the stadium on the right.

THOMAS J. DODD MEMORIAL STADIUM

Home of the Connecticut Defenders of the Eastern League

Claim to Fame

Benedict Arnold's hometown. Close to Foxwoods and Mohegan Sun casinos.

Strange but True

One of the strangest, and most interesting, attractions in the area is Gillette Castle in nearby East Haddam, Connecticut. William Gillette was a very famous actor who amassed a sizable fortune by playing Sherlock Holmes. He played the role to the hilt. Gillette Castle is evidence of how the great actor ultimately came to live the life of the famous detective. Wonder if he had his own Dr. Watson or had the "Hound of Baskerville" as a pet?

Who's Who in Norwich

Just look at all the Yankees farmhands who've played in Norwich: catcher Mike Figga, pitcher Ramiro Mendoza, outfielder Ricky Ledee, outfielder Shane Spencer, outfielder Tim Raines, pitcher David Cone, pitcher

Doc Gooden, pitcher Darryl Strawberry, third basemen Mike Lowell, pitcher Randy Flores, first baseman Nick Johnson, shortstop Alfonso Soriano, infielder Andy Phillips, and outfielder Marcus Thames. The San Francisco Giants just established a relationship with the franchise. Among the Connecticut Defenders' most prominent alumni are pitcher Matt Cain, catcher Justin Knoedler, and pitcher Brad Hennessey.

About Norwich

Norwich honors its past, but there's little evidence of its most famous patriot. One place where Benedict Arnold is remembered is on a small commemorative plaque where he once lived. Another place is the city library, where there's a large portrait of Major General Benedict Arnold of the Continental Army.

Benedict Arnold's name might as well be mud to Norwich. The commander, who led American troops to an improbable victory at the Battle of Saratoga and suffered through the long winter at Valley Forge, had it up to here and decided to switch sides after quarrelling with Congress, being bypassed for honors, and beginning to run out of money. The former general decided to defect. Norwich has dozens of organizations that honor its past. There are local chapters of the Sons of the American Revolution, the Daughters of the American Revolution, and the Order of the Founders and Patriots of America. There's even an Order of Descendants of Pirates and Privateers. But there's scarcely a word about Benedict Arnold.

The city has tried and failed to forget about its former favorite son.

The main entrance to Thomas J. Dodd Memorial Stadium.

Nevertheless, there are plenty of reasons to celebrate Norwich's history. Norwich has a number of memorials and monuments. Even before the Battles of Lexington, Norwich was in the forefront of the American Revolution. It sits on the banks of three rivers—the Thames, Shetucket, and Yantic. Soldiers, supplies, and munitions were shipped from the public landing. The defense industry still is big business in the area. Starting with the Civil War, the city was called the "fire arms center of New England." It was once this country's leading gun and ammo maker. Smith & Wesson started here. Many locals were employed at the United States Naval Submarine Base and General Dynamics in nearby New London and Groton.

Norwich's mills and factories have also been involved with more peaceful enterprises. Beside the city's river banks, there were clock makers, furniture makers, and iron foundries. Industrialist William Walker introduced German-invented Thermos bottles to the American market. For many years, it was the city's largest employer. Many local companies have adopted the motto "make love not war." A large percentage of the world's Viagra supply is manufactured in Southwestern Connecticut.

Today, the local economy relies on tourism and gambling. Two Native American tribes, the Mohegans and the Pequots, have beaten the odds and survived. The tribal nations operate a couple of massive casino and entertainment complexes, Mohegan Sun and Foxwoods. Both casinos are just a short drive away from downtown Norwich.

If you come to Norwich, be sure to smell the roses. Norwich has been nicknamed the "Rose of New England." There are more than 2,500 rose bushes at the Norwich Rose Garden on Rockwell Street. It's one of the best-painted cities in the United States according to the Paint Quality Institute. The local architecture is varied. Federalist, Colonial, Victorian, Gothic, Second Empire, Roman Classicism, Romanesque, Greek Revival, Late Georgian, Italianate, and Richardsonian Romanesque are a sample of the styles. You can hit the jackpot in Norwich even if you're not interested in gambling.

A Baseball Backgrounder

For the most part, Double A is now big business. Cities like Trenton, Akron, and Portland are now regarded as the future of minor league baseball. Smaller-sized markets, such as Norwich, are increasingly being bypassed. But bigger doesn't necessarily mean better.

Can professional baseball thrive in suburban Connecticut? For the past decade, the answer given by Norwich, Connecticut has been "yes." The community is one of the smallest cities in the country to have its own professional team. For many years, the Norwich Navigators were a small Yankee outpost in Red Sox country.

The team, formerly known as the Norwich Navigators, traces its origins to Albany, New York. The Yankees never really wanted to leave New

Connecticut

York's capital city. But, lacking up-to-date playing facilities, the team had no alternative. Norwich and the state of Connecticut were ready, willing, and able to step into the breach. An offer to build a new publicly funded stadium for a new Eastern League team was quickly accepted.

Ground was broken for the Thomas Dodd Stadium on November 3, 1994. And that was just the start of it.

Construction crews worked all through the winter to get Norwich's new ballpark ready to play for the start of the 1995 season. The community's hard work paid off. On April 17th, the Norwich Navigators got their stadium off on the right foot by defeating the Reading Phillies.

From a Red Sox fan's perspective, having the hometown team being affiliated with the Yankees had its advantages. After all, where else in New England could Red Sox fans get such a great opportunity to check out the opposition? Many of the great Yankees players, including Andy Petite, Bernie Williams, David Cone, and Roger Clemens, did rehabilitation stints in Norwich. Bobbleheads of the former Navigators are now popular giveaways.

Many of the Bronx Bombers' top prospects have also played here. Sometimes their stay in Norwich was short. If the Yankees' management felt like they could win, it wouldn't keep top prospects in the minors. Many of Norwich's best players were Yankees trade bait. A former Yankee manager, Stump Merrill, and first-base coach, Lee Mazzilli, have had successful stints as the Navigators' skipper. Norwich also

reached the Eastern League playoffs four times in six years and won the 2002 Eastern League championship.

When the Yankees decided to change their affiliation to Trenton in 2003, the San Francisco Giants were only too willing to sign up with Norwich. The team is now owned by boxing promoter Lou DiBella, who decided the franchise needed some new blood. A fresh start for Norwich was needed. The first step taken was to change the team's name to the Connecticut Defenders. An eagle named "Cutter" now carries the flag as Norwich's mascot. The team's name refers to the area's role in arms manufacturing and defense.

San Francisco has already brought many top prospects to Norwich. Many scouts believe pitcher Matt Cain will someday be a Cy Young Award winner. The changes have brought a renewed commitment to Norwich. The Defenders recently re-upped for a lease extension until 2009.

Take Me Out to the Ballgame

Since 1995, the Thomas J. Dodd Memorial Stadium has been the pride of southeastern Connecticut. Ever since it opened it doors, going to see Defenders games has been a sure bet. While Norwich is small, the Connecticut Defenders have a broad base of fan support. New London, Mystic, and Westerly, and Rhode Island are part of the territory. Being located near Foxwoods and Mohegan Sun certainly doesn't hurt.

With a seating capacity of 6,270, Dodd Stadium was built at the top of a hill. The ballpark entrance looks

Photo courtesy of Norwich Navigators

A groundskeeper waters down the infield in Norwich.

straight down upon home plate. Baseball isn't just a game of inches, but of angles. Seeing baseball from different perspectives is just as easy as a walk around the ballpark. You can get something to eat, buy all the souvenirs you want, and visit the rest rooms without missing a pitch.

Eighteen skyboxes cover over the ballpark concourse. But on a clear night or a sunny summer afternoon, the grassy berms in right and left field are always popular. For kids, there's a play area with inflatable slides. Dodd Stadium may be the only ballpark in New England with its own video arcade.

Due to its proximity to Providence, Boston, and Hartford, the ballpark always seems to be busy. It hosted the last ever Double A All-Star Game in 2002. The Texas League, Southern League, and Eastern League have decided to hold their own All-Stars.

The Eastern League All-Star Game is coming to town in July 2007. The facility has hosted big name music acts like Willie Nelson, Bob Dylan, and Clint Black. It was recently used as a set for the next ESPN production, "The Bronx Is Burning."

Great food, fun, atmosphere, and being fan friendly have been a hallmark of Dodd Stadium. With former Bridgeport general manager Dan Dowd assuming the reigns in Norwich, expect the team to have a back-to-basics approach. In 2007, there are price cuts for ballpark concessions across the boards. Hot dogs that once cost $2.75 will now be $2.00. In the future, expect specialty foods to be sold. All kinds of promotions have also been added. Kids in athletic uniforms can go free to all games hosted Monday through Thursday. On Fridays there are fireworks shows and there are giveaways every Saturday.

Best Game (When You Think About It, How Does Someone Decide Which Game Was the Best?)

On August 7, 2002, Norwich witnessed a group of Hall of Famers participate in a great competition. It was the Major League Baseball Legends home run hitting challenge. The National League was represented by Johnny Bench, Mike Schmidt, and Gary Carter. The American League was represented by Carlton Fisk, George Brett, and Dave Winfield. Just tally up the total statistics of these players! Dave Winfield was the star of stars with eight home runs in the opening round. In the finals, the former Yankee defeated former Gary Carter on the final at-bat. Maybe the contest wasn't the best game, but seeing these All-Stars gathered together in one place was quite a thrill and worthy of this honor.

Greatest Team (Not the '27 Yankees, but Who Is?)

The Norwich Navigators had some great years between 1999 and 2002. The culmination of their run was in 2002. The Navigators finally struck gold in their third playoff appearance in four years. Norwich defeated Harrisburg in the deciding game of the five-game series. The team's manager was former Yankee second baseman Luis Sojo, who replaced former manager Stump Merrill mid-season.

Merrill did a fine job for Norwich, but didn't finish out the season. The Yankees were very concerned what was happening with their Triple A affiliate in Columbus. Merrill was reassigned to restore order in Columbus by Yankee general manager Brian Cashman.

In 1999, the Navigators lost a heartbreaker in the championship series. Future major leaguer Milton Bradley hit a two-out, two-strike bottom of the ninth walk-off grand slam. But, this time, Norwich was not to be denied. The team's playoff Most Valuable Player was future Yankee Erick Almonte, who hit .387 with 3 home runs and 10 RBIs.

Best Player . . . in My Opinion

In 1999, Washington Nick Johnson established himself as Tino Martinez' successor in New York. He led the league in hitting (.345), walks (123), hit by pitches (37), and on-base percentage (.525). Johnson was also a defensive whiz, winning kudos as the Eastern League's best fielding first baseman. Johnson's extraordinary accomplishments were exciting, particularly at a pitcher's playground like Norwich.

The Norwich Navigators have had many All-Stars. But few All-Stars other than Detroit Tigers outfielder Marcus Thames have had much of a career in the majors. Perhaps one of the reasons is that players who showed potential for the Yankees were quickly promoted to the majors. In 2001, Norwich had an outstanding outfield that featured three future major leaguers—Juan Rivera, Marcus Thames, and John Rodriguez.

In just a brief time in the San Francisco chain, the Connecticut Defenders have had plenty of promising players. San Francisco has a history of developing young relievers who throw

Photo courtesy of Norwich Navigators

Fans enjoying a summer evening watching the Defenders.

Connecticut

hard. In the latter stages of a game, fans have already come to expect that Connecticut pitchers will hold a lead.

Great starting pitching is always a key to victory. The Connecticut Defenders have already developed two of baseball's best young hurlers. The Giants are counting on right-handers Matt Cain and Merkin Valdez to keep the team competitive after Barry Bonds retires.

Round Tripper (Some Suggestions for Sightseers)

Norwich is a beautiful historic city. It has a colonial green that is surrounded by plenty of fine examples of colonial architecture. Due to the landscape of the area, Norwich and its surroundings have been called "The Last Green Valley." Eastern Connecticut is one of the last areas from Boston to Washington that retains its rural character.

Just south of Norwich are two of

the East Coast's most popular tourist attractions: the Mystic Seaport and the Mystic Aquarium. Both are near Route I-95 off of Route 27. Both are practically next-door neighbors. You can't miss them. Mystic Seaport is a living, breathing recreation of a nineteenth-century seaport village. There are taverns, tall ships, captain's mansions, widow walks, tall ships, and a real-life working shipyard. More than 300,000 people visit it annually.

The Mystic Aquarium is another great take. It's a fun place to learn about the creatures of the deep. The star of the show is the sea. The one-acre outdoor beluga whale habitat is spectacular. And the penguins and sea lions are real showoffs. Both are fine places to spend quality time with your family.

Norwich is also very convenient to Connecticut's casinos. Foxwoods is the largest casino in the world—a 340,000-square-foot gambling complex that's still growing. More than 40,000 people a day visit the site. Mohegan Sun is just a short drive from Foxwoods. Both casinos offer fine dining, shopping, live Las Vegas–style entertainment, concerts, and sporting events. But only one eastern Connecticut city offers top-notch professional baseball. That's Norwich.

Places to Eat . . . If You Want More Than Cracker Jack

Custy's International Buffet is a local tradition. All-you-can-eat lobster, steak, and shrimp are featured. It puts famous Las Vegas casino buffets to shame. The buffet line is more than 60 feet long and offers steak, chicken, lamb, duck, veal, and fish entrées. There's an enormous lobster pot. And then there are the desserts. Custy's is definitely unique. It's the Mount Everest of eating.

Both Mohegan Sun and Foxwoods offer everything from fast food to fine dining. But Mohegan Sun definitely has a few more options. Just look at the list: Big Bubba's BBQ, Fidelia's, Jasper White's Summer Shack, Johnny Rockets, Lucky's Lounge, Michael Jordan's 23 Sportcafe, the Cove, Uncas American Indian Grill. And there's Seasons Buffet, Sunburst Buffet, Ben & Jerry's, Cawhee, Granny Squannits, Imus Ranch Coffee, Krispy Kreme, Starbuck's Coffee, Casion of the Earth Food Court, Geno Auriemma's Fast Break, Bamboo Forest, Michael Jordan's Steak House, Pompeii & Caesar, Longhouse, Todd English's Tuscany, Bow & Arrow, Cabaret Bar, Leffingwells, Lucky's Lounge, Taughannick Falls Bar, Star Bar, The Brew Pub, The Dubliner, and the Ultra 88 Night. The list of restaurants at Mohegan Sun is seemingly endless. Foxwoods hasn't given up the competition but is playing catch-up. The tribal elders are currently making plans to expand

Sources:

The Baseball Almanac, 1995–2007.
Boston Globe, 1900–2007.
New York Times, 1890–2007.
Society of American Baseball Researchers. *The Northern Game—and Beyond.* Boston: Cambridge Prepress Services, 2002.

www.all-baseball.com
www.ballparkdigest.com
www.ballparkreviews.com
www.baseballalmanac.com
www.baseballamericaonline.com
www.ctdefenders.com
www.easternleague.com
www.espn.com
www.milb.com
www.mlb.com
www.sabr.org

23

Address: 98 University Drive, Burlington, VT 05401

Web Site: *www.uvm.edu/athletics/baseball.com, www.vermontlakemonsters.com*

First Game: April 17, 1906

Dimensions: LF 324 CF 405 RF 320

Directions: Take I-89 to Exit 14 and head west toward Burlington on US Route 2 (Main Street). Take the first right onto East Avenue. University Drive is on the right about 0.75 mile ahead, and Centennial Field is at the end.

CENTENNIAL FIELD AT THE UNIVERSITY OF VERMONT

Home of the Vermont Lake Monsters of the New York–Penn League (short-season Class A, 2007) and the University of Vermont Catamounts (America East Conference, NCAA Division 1)

Claim to Fame

Ethan Allen, who served in the French and Indian war, was compensated for his services with land in present-day Vermont. In the late 1760s, when interests in New York threatened to seize lands that would become the State of Vermont during a land grant dispute, Allen formed a militia bent on stemming their aggression.

On May 10, 1775, Allen and his militia, The Green Mountain Boys, captured the lightly guarded Fort Ticonderoga at the northern end of Lake George. Joining them in the raid was Benedict Arnold. Cannons captured at the fort later helped American revolutionary forces defend Boston's Dorchester Heights from British attack.

Allen died in Burlington in 1789 and is believed buried in the city's Green Mount Cemetery—just beyond the outfield fence at Centennial Field.

Strange but True

Headquartered in South Burlington, Ben & Jerry's Homemade holds a spe-

Vermont

Tekla Frates/Tekla Photography

As daylight wanes, bright bulbs illuminate the action at Centennial Field.

cial spot in the stomachs of ice cream lovers worldwide. In fact, it was the first brand of ice cream to be flown into orbit and eaten by astronauts aboard the Space Shuttle. In a more dubious distinction, Timothy McVeigh, convicted in the 1995 bombing of the Murrah Federal Building in Oklahoma City, requested two pints of Ben & Jerry's Mint Chocolate Chip ice cream as his last meal before he was executed on June 11, 2001.

Who's Who in Burlington

Bert Abbey, Michael Barrett, Jason Bay, Geoff Blum, Almari Bowman, Orlando Cabrera, Norm Charlton, Ray Collins, Kal Daniels, Ivan DeJesus, Rob Dibble, Larry Gardner, Jeff Gray, Lenny Harris, Jorge Julio, Jack LaMabe,

Ralph LaPointe, Barry Larkin, Kirk McCaskill, Lloyd McClendon, Jeff Montgomery, Frank O'Connor, Paul O'Neill, Arlington Pond, Chris Sabo, Jeff Treadway, Ken Griffey Jr., Robin Roberts, Tris Speaker, Omar Vizquel, and Rusty Yarnall.

About Burlington

Nestled along the eastern shore of Lake Champlain, in a valley between the Adirondack and Green Mountain ranges, Burlington is Vermont's largest city, with a population just under 40,000 people. With the surrounding suburbs, including Winooski, South Burlington, Colchester, Essex, and Williston, Burlington's metropolitan area is home to more than 150,000.

Burlington was chartered in 1763, but wasn't settled until Ira Allen, Ethan's brother, built Fort Frederick at the Winooski River falls in 1773. After the revolutionary war, Ira dammed the river near the falls to power his sawmills. Ethan Allen settled on land near the mouth of the river in 1787.

The University of Vermont was established in 1791. In 1823, the Lake Champlain Canal opened, linking the city with the Hudson River and the Erie Canal and turning Burlington into an active port for shipments of agricultural products and lumber. In 1863, Burlington incorporated as a city.

Today Burlington has thriving medical care and high-tech industries, and is also home to food and beverage corporations besides Ben & Jerry's. Bruegger's Bagels and Lake Champlain Chocolates are among the firms headquartered here.

A Baseball Backgrounder

Baseball in Burlington didn't start at the University of Vermont, but the campus became the centerpiece for the sport in the late 1800s. At that time, the university's athletics teams played at Athletic Park at the intersection of Riverside Avenue and North Prospect Street. The school soon began looking for a new field, in part because Athletic Park was too far from campus, but also because it had no fence and could not charge spectators for admission.

With the opening of Centennial Park in 1906 came a parade of teams and standout players on barnstorming and exhibition trips. They included Tris Speaker, Smokey Joe Wood, Duffy

Lewis, and Harry Hooper with the Boston Red Sox in 1910. In 1938, Connie Mack's Philadelphia Athletics visited Burlington. Hometown son Birdie Tebbetts, who played in the majors with the Detroit Tigers, Boston Red Sox, and Cleveland Indians, brought Vern Stephens, Jimmy Piersall, and Vic Wertz to Burlington in the late 1940s.

Semi-pro ball became popular in Burlington as Centennial Field was home to a Northern League franchise from 1936 to 1950. During that span, crowds of as many as 3,000 people watched the action, which is quite a turnout for a city that, at the time, held about 26,000 people. Attendance began to wane following World War II, and the league folded.

In 1955, the Quebec-based Provincial League came to Burlington. This was a big step as Centennial Field hosted a Kansas City Athletics Class C farm team. That year, the club ventured across the border to take on teams in French-Canadian cities and towns like Granby, Farnham, Quebec City, Thetford Mines, Sherbrook, and Trois Riveres. The team folded after the season, but minor league baseball had arrived in Burlington.

In 1972 the University of Vermont discontinued its varsity baseball program. For six years Centennial Park sat idle until play resumed in 1978.

The Catamounts have maintained a strong baseball presence, and 10 former players have gone on to reach the majors. Among them was Ralph LaPointe, a Winooski native who went on to play for the Philadelphia Phillies and St. Louis Cardinals in 1947–48.

Vermont

He returned in 1952 to coach University of Vermont (UVM) and compiled a 216-127 record, second in wins to current head coach Bill Currier. LaPointe's .630 winning percentage over 16 seasons remains unmatched at the school.

Kirk McCaskill was another prominent Catamount who played in the big leagues. A star pitcher from 1980 to 1982, he also compiled a .356 career batting average, which is third-best all-time at UVM. Kirk was also pretty good on skates and started for the hockey team. In 1981 he was named a finalist for the Hobey Baker Award, given annually to the nation's top player.

McCaskill became a fourth-round draft choice of two professional sports teams: The National Hockey League's Winnipeg Jets in 1981, and Major League Baseball's California Angels in 1982. He chose baseball, and went on to compile 106 wins and 1,003 strikeouts over a 12-year career with the Angels and the Chicago White Sox.

With the arrival of the Class AA Eastern League's Vermont Reds in 1984, minor league ball returned to Burlington. After serving four years as an affiliate of the Cincinnati Reds, the franchise was aligned with the Seattle Mariners in 1988, an arrangement that lasted just one season.

Over that stretch, several notable Cincinnati prospects played at Centennial Field and helped guide Burlington to three straight Eastern League crowns from 1984 to 1986. Among them were Barry Larkin, Chris Sabo, Rob Dibble, Norm Charlton, and Kal Daniels. In 1988, future all-stars Ken Griffey Jr. and Omar Vizquel graced the field.

Burlington was without a minor league team from 1989 until 1994. In the interim, former Red Sox pitcher Bill Lee, a Vermont resident, brought his assembly of fun-loving ex-ballplayers to Centennial Field for an exhibition game. Called the Grey Sox, the roster included former Cincinnati Reds slugger George Foster.

In 1994, the Montreal Expos established a new minor league affiliate in Burlington as the Vermont Expos played short-season Class A ball in the New York–Penn League. The Montreal system was rich with talent and future major leaguers. Michael Barrett, Geoff Blum, Orlando Cabrera, Milton Bradley, Scott Strickland, Jorge Julio, T.J. Tucker, Jason Bay, Brandon Watson, and Mike O'Connor laced up their cleats and roamed the turf at Centennial. In 1996 the Vermont Expos won the New York–Penn League championship with a 48-26 record.

The arrival of the Expos also gave pro scouts ample opportunity to watch UVM's ballplayers up close. Three of them—right-handers Brady Frost, Jerry Lynde, and Jeff Dixon—signed contracts and eventually played for the Expos in Burlington. A fourth Catamount, outfielder Ethan Barlow, was an Expos draft choice in 1996 and also played professionally on his collegiate field.

In 2006 the franchise changed its name, in part to dispense with its outdated major league affiliation after the Montreal Expos became the Washington Nationals. The decision was also meant to embrace a regional identity for the minor league team that would endure any future changes in affiliation.

The new name, the Vermont Lake Monsters, honors an age-old Burlington legend: the alleged existence of a sea monster in Lake Champlain. Nicknamed "Champ," its reported length has ranged from 20 to 187 feet. In 1873, legendary circus promoter P.T. Barnum offered a $50,000 reward for the "hide of the great Champlain serpent to add to my mammoth World's Fair Show." Today, Champ can be seen as a team mascot that roams the stands during games entertaining young children.

Take Me Out to the Ballgame

Named to commemorate the 100th anniversary of the University of Vermont's first graduating class, Centennial Field has hosted athletic events at the University of Vermont since April 17, 1906, when the Catamounts won the first baseball game ever played there by defeating the University of Maine, 10-4.

Centennial is one of the oldest ballparks in the country and remains a gem. An historical marker placed at the stadium in 1998 by the Larry Gardner Chapter of the Society for American Baseball Research honors the rich legacy of the venue.

The field was built on seven acres purchased from Grace Ainsworth, which were part of her 60-acre farm. She, like Ethan Allen, is buried in neighboring Green Mount Cemetery, just beyond the outfield.

In 1913, the original wooden grandstands burned down, a frequent problem for early baseball stadiums around the country. Temporary wooden stands were used until 1922, when a concrete and steel grandstand, with a roofed center section and adjoining exposed wings, was constructed to hold 4,400 fans.

A few other ballparks around the country have older grandstands, but all have had portions undergo alterations or renovations. That means Centennial Field has the oldest complete grandstand structure in use in minor league baseball. Over the decades,

Vermont

Ben Dickie/UVM Athletic Communications

The venerable grandstands at Centennial Field provide a great view from any seat.

Lisa Champagne/UVM Athletic Communications

It's a long way from the press box to home plate, thanks to the broad stretch of foul ground at Centennial Field.

numerous semi-pro and minor league games have taken place at Centennial, as well as exhibition games featuring major league and Negro League teams. The field also hosts local baseball, including state high school championships, American Legion ball, and even Babe Ruth League games, and has been the site of three America East Baseball Championships since 2003.

Some improvements have been made to the field since the mid-1990s. The pitching mound was rebuilt, 1,000 square feet of warning track was reworked, and an electronic scoreboard was erected above the left-field fence. Modern rest rooms and the concession stands were added in 1995.

The most striking feature of Centennial Field is the vast expanse of foul territory, a reminder that while base-ball was the first event held here, the field was not designed explicitly for the sport. Soccer, football, and track and field are among the other sports that have taken place here over the past century. There may be 90 feet between the bases, but it's not much less than that between the dugouts and home plate. The added lawn is visually pleasing, in part because the grass is kept in immaculate condition by the grounds crew.

Comfort at Centennial depends on your seat. You'll probably want a cushion if you sit in the uncovered wings along the first and third baselines, where flat, cement bleachers are the rule. Under the roof, rows of seating are flanked on either end by the original steel armrests, painted Fenway green, which feature a baseball and the embossed letters UVM.

Best Game (When You Think About It, How Does Someone Decide Which Game Was the Best?)

The 2003 Vermont Catamounts became the first team in the university's history to knock off a nationally ranked baseball program. Beginning the season with a spring jaunt to Florida, UVM upended Ohio State, 7-6. On that same trip, the Catamounts dropped narrow contests against two other Big Ten teams: 4-2 to Illinois, and 4-3 to Indiana.

Greatest Team (Not the '27 Yankees, but Who Is?)

Here we'll recognize two UVM squads. The 1962 Catamounts, managed by Ralph LaPointe, finished 21-6 as Yankee Conference champions. Midway through the season the squad fashioned a 12-game winning streak. At the NCAA Regionals in Springfield, Massachusetts, Vermont knocked off Boston College, 3-2, and Bridgeport, 5-4. A pair of losses to regional champion Holy Cross ended their season. Pitcher Richard Cassani was the staff ace, with a perfect 9-0 record, 87 strikeouts, and a 1.11 ERA. Fellow hurler Richard DeNicola went 10-1 for the Cats.

In 2003, the Catamounts set a record for wins, finishing 32-14. UVM was led on offense by Jeff Barry, whose career .354 average is fourth all-time at the school; Barry Chamberland, who slugged 11 homers and racked 41 RBIs; and Kyle Brault, who hit 10 dingers. On the mound, Jeff Dixon matched Cassani's perfect mark by going 9-0 with a 1.93 ERA. During a late season trip to Orono, they split four games with the heavily regarded University of Maine Black Bears, who took revenge with a 6-1 drubbing in the America East Championship game at Centennial Field.

Best Player . . . In My Opinion

It's doubtful there's been a better player to grace Centennial Field than Ken Griffey Jr., but his stay was brief. He hit .279 with 2 HR and 10 RBI in 17 games for the Class AA Vermont Mariners in 1988. The following spring Griffey was manning center field full-time for Seattle.

For career impact, it would be hard to top native son Larry Gardner, a member of UVM's class of 1909, captain of the 1908 Vermont team, and the namesake of the Catamounts Most Valuable Player award. Born in Enosburg Falls, Larry was a slick-fielding third baseman who played for the Boston Red Sox in 1908 before he had even graduated college. Over his 10 seasons with Boston, he won championships in 1912, 1915, and 1916.

Gardner spent the next seven seasons in Cleveland, where he helped the Indians win the 1920 World Series, and with the Philadelphia Athletics. He finished his career with a .289 average in 1,923 games. Following his pro career he returned home to coach Vermont from 1929 to 1952 (no team was fielded from 1942 to 1945), compiling a 177-198 record over 20 seasons.

Round Tripper (Some Suggestions for Sightseers)

At the lakefront, hop aboard *The Spirit of Ethan Allen*, which offers 90-minute

Vermont

narrated cruises along the waterfront. You can also ride one of the Lake Champlain Ferries, which accommodates vehicles, and head across to Port Kent, New York.

For a bit of history, the Ethan Allen Homestead is off Route 127 north of the city, and features an orientation center and a reconstructed farmhouse.

On the UVM campus, the Robert Hull Fleming Museum on Colchester Avenue houses a collection of artistic and natural history treasures, including permanent displays of twentieth-century Vermont artwork.

Shoppers will want to head to Pompanoosuc Mills, Bennington Potters North, and the Architectural Salvage Warehouse. Church Street Market Place is a busy spot, with shops, boutiques, coffee houses, used book stores, and street performers.

For a two-wheeled view, grab a bike and ride the Burlington Bike Path, a nine-mile trail on an old railroad bed fronting Lake Champlain that extends north to the mouth of the Winooski River.

The UVM Morgan Horse Farm in nearby Weybridge, where Colonel Joseph Battell began breeding the equines in the late 1870s, offers daily tours on the hour from spring through fall. There is also an extensive gift shop.

Seven miles south of the city, the Shelburne Museum preserves American folklore in 37 buildings at the 45-acre site. They include an 1890 railroad station, an Adirondack lodge, and a Vermont round barn.

You'll want to keep tabs on local events, especially in the summer. Annual happenings include the Burlington Discover Jazz Festival, Burlington City Marathon, Vermont Reggae Festival, Mardi Gras Parade, the South End Art Hop, and the Vermont Mozart Festival.

Places to Eat ... If You Want More Than Cracker Jack

Leunig's Bistro and The Inn at Essex are sure bets for a great meal. For something more eclectic, Daily Planet is a winner. The Five Spice Café offers the best Asian cuisine in the city, while Trattoria Delia is the hot spot for Italian.

Locals seem to flock to Al's for burgers, dogs, and barbecue. A better bet would be a killer breakfast at the Penny Cluse Café, or lunch at the Red Onion, both near Church Street.

Stop in at Nectar's for a beer and catch a live music show, or to chow down in the cafeteria next door. It's one of the local spots where the legendary rock band Phish honed their craft, so you never know what up-and-comers you'll be hearing.

If fresh beer's your thing, Magic Hat Brewery in South Burlington is a required stop. In downtown Burlington, Switchback Brewing offers innovative creations, and the Vermont Pub and Brewery on College Street has been going strong for a decade.

For those who prefer the sports bar scene, Akes' Place off Church Street features pool, darts, 15 taps, and plenty of screens.

Mr. Mike's is a popular pizza joint in Burlington, while Marco's and Zachary's get the nod in South Burlington. To the north in Winooski, Papa Frank's offers a taste of old Italy beyond great pies.

Sources:

www.benjerry.com
www.burlingtonfreepress.com
www.ci.burlington.vt.us
www.thebaseballcube.com
www.uvm.edu/athletics/baseball
www.vermontguides.com
www.vermonthistory.org
www.vermontlakemonsters.com
www.vermont.org

Vermont

24

Address: Elm Street and Ballfield Road, Montpelier, VT 05602

Web Site: *www.thevermontmountaineers.com*

First Game: 1941

Dimensions: LF 325 LCF 360 CF 411 RCF 360 RF 325

Directions: Take I-89 to Exit 8 (Montpelier/US Route 2), head east on Route 2 (Memorial Drive) toward Montpelier. Go about one mile and turn left on Main Street (Route 12). Follow the signs for Route 12, turn left on Spring Street and right on Elm Street. The field is about one mile down the road on the right, at the intersection with Ballfield Road.

MONTPELIER, VT

MOUNTAINEER RECREATION FIELD

Home of the Vermont Mountaineers of the New England Collegiate Baseball League

Claim to Fame

Montpelier is unique among state capitals. With just more than 8,000 people, it is the least-populous capital city in the nation, and it remains the only capital without a McDonald's restaurant.

Strange but True

Since 1975, each March Montpelier has been home to the National Odor-Eaters Rotten Sneaker Contest. Regional finalists, age 5 to 15, literally go toe-to-toe in a battle to see whose torn, frayed, and worn-out athletic footwear is the smelliest, most eye-watering, and unbearably pungent in the country. The winner receives a $500 savings bond, $100 toward a new pair of sneakers, a supply of Odor-Eaters products, the Golden Sneaker Award trophy, and enshrinement in the Hall of Fumes.

Who's Who in Montpelier

Jim Ball, Honey Barnes, Frank Bennett, Frank Bonner, Ben Bowcock,

Vermont

Matt Broderick, George Bullard, Bob Clemens, Jack Coombs, Dick Cotter, Bert Daniels, Bob Dresser, Ray Fisher, Tom Gorman, Eddie Grant, Hub Hart, Bill Jones, Ted Kazanski, Walt Lanfranconi, Ralph Lapointe, John Mansell, Al Moore, Bobby Murray, Doc Newman, Ron Northey, Buck O'Brien, Joseph Page, "Crip" Polli, Ed Reulbach, Robin Roberts, Alex Sabo, Frank Shaughnessy, Nap Shea, Jim Shelle, Steve Slayton, Ed Smith, Tom Stankard, Dike Varney, Rube Vickers, George Walker, and Jack Warner.

About Montpelier

Nestled in a valley at the confluence of the Winooski and North Branch rivers, Vermont's capital is much more a small town than a city. It was chartered in 1781 as a grant to settlers from

Photo courtesy of Dave Morse, Hardwick, VT

Thirty years before his induction to the Hall of Fame, Robin Roberts was the star hurler for the Twin City Trojans.

Massachusetts. The first structure built in the city, in 1787, was a small cabin built near present-day Elm Street. Early arrivers took advantage of the river's power, building saw and grist mills.

Vermont gained statehood in 1791, and 14 years later—based largely on its central location and despite a population of just 1,200—its legislature selected Montpelier as the capital. The large granite statehouse, set at the foot of a hilly backdrop rich with foliage, was built in 1859 after the previous statehouse was destroyed by a fire in 1857.

Montpelier soon became an insurance and banking center, and the arrival of the railroad in the mid-1850s spurred further economic growth. A fire in 1875 destroyed many buildings downtown.

Along with politics, agriculture, and finance, granite played a key role in Montpelier's development. The discovery of enormous granite deposits in neighboring Barre brought skilled artisans, stoneworkers, and general immigrant labor from dozens of countries, which made the Barre-Montpelier area one of the most diverse communities in the nation by the late 1800s.

By 1925 there were nine granite works in Montpelier that refined stone slabs culled from the world-famous Barre quarries. It is estimated that one-third of the public and private monuments and memorials in the United States are products of the area's granite industry.

On November 3, 1927, nearly 10 inches of rain flooded the state's rivers. Montpelier found itself under 12 feet of water, which swept away buildings, vehicles, and bridges. Among the 84 deaths statewide was Lieutenant Governor S. Hollister Jackson.

The completion of Interstate 89 in the early 1960s made the city more accessible to visitors, who used the new highways to seek out fall foliage and to reach Vermont's myriad ski resorts. The interstate also reduced the transit time for city residents to reach Burlington from about 2 hours to about 35 minutes.

Today Montpelier is home to about 8,000 people, while another 9,000 or so live in neighboring Barre. Despite its small size, the area is home to four colleges, a philharmonic orchestra, numerous museums, and even a professional basketball team.

A Baseball Backgrounder

In 1887, Montpelier had a semi-pro ball club playing in the Northeastern League, which ran into financial difficulties due to travel and payroll costs. The league folded before the end of the season, but the Montpelier team—with its 2-13 record—disbanded even before then. Despite its record, the team had three players—Canadian pitcher George Walker, outfielder John Mansell, and catcher Bill Jones—that went on to play in the majors.

After the turn of the century, a Northern League team played in Barre-Montpelier from 1901 to 1907, winning a championship in 1905. Many players came from Ivy League schools, but some professional players such as Frank Bonner played under assumed names. Of the 20 players from these teams who played in the majors, the best was Jack Coombs, who won

158 games in 14 seasons with the Philadelphia Athletics, Brooklyn Dodgers, and Detroit Tigers. His peak years were 1910–11, when he won 31 and 28 games respectively for the A's.

Barre-Montpelier also hosted a Green Mountain League team from 1923 to 1924 that produced seven major leaguers. The league's teams played in Vermont and Canada, and historians suspect many were fronts for illegal whiskey shipments during prohibition.

One of Barre-Montpelier's best-known players was local favorite Louis Americo Polli. Born in Italy, his father was a skilled stonecutter who brought his family to Vermont when Lou was a child and found steady work in Barre's granite industry. He earned the nickname "Crip," short for cripple, after a football injury temporarily relegated him to crutches. After playing in the Green Mountain League for his hometown team, Crip toiled in the New York Yankees' minor league system for several years.

Invited to spring training with the Yankees in 1930, Crip played bridge with Bill Dickey against Lou and Eleanor Gehrig, and played pool and pitch-and-putt golf with Babe Ruth during a month-long exhibition tour across the Deep South. Despite pitching well, he failed to earn a roster spot with the Yankees team.

Crip finally reached the majors in 1932, the first Italian-born player to do so, and pitched five games in relief for the St. Louis Browns. Polli spent the next dozen years in the minors but, amazingly, he returned to the majors at age 42, pitching 19 games for the 1944 New York Giants. He pitched in

Roger Crowley / DigiTechVT.com

Loyal spectators fill the grandstands at Mountaineer Field, enjoying the best amateur baseball in Vermont.

the minors again the following year for the Jersey City Giants, and faced the Newark Bears in the final game of his career. The Bears came in riding a 14-game winning streak, but the 44-year-old Crip tossed his third no-hitter as a minor leaguer. The stunning victory also came just hours after he learned that his daughter was terminally ill with tuberculosis.

Polli followed his father in the granite industry and later served many years in government positions for his adopted hometown of Barre. When he died there in 2000 at age 99, he was the oldest living former major league ball player.

Professional baseball in Montpelier was dormant until 1935, when a new Northern League surfaced. The Montpelier Senators played at National Life Field, built with funds from one of Montpelier's largest insurance

firms. One of the highlights came when Barre-native Walt Lanfranconi pitched a one-hitter for the Senators on the day he graduated from high school. He went on to pitch for the Chicago Cubs in 1941 and for the Boston Braves in 1947.

In 1940 construction began on Montpelier Recreation Field and an adjacent outdoor swimming pool, financed mostly by federal Works Progress Administration funds. The Senators moved to their new park the next season, drawing crowds as large as 3,000 that clogged the stands, baselines, and surrounding hillsides. The Northern League went on hiatus during World War II, resuming in 1946 with a new team, the Twin City Trojans.

Ray Fisher, a native of Middlebury who pitched 10 seasons with the Yankees and Cincinnati Reds from 1910 to 1920, coached the University of

Michigan baseball team for 38 years. From 1921 to 1958, Fisher won 661 games, 15 Big Ten titles and a national championship. During the summers in the 1940s, he would return to Vermont to coach local semi-pro and minor-league teams, including the Trojans in Montpelier.

Fisher's unparalleled reputation lured many top college players to the Green Mountain state, including a Michigan State hurler named Robin Roberts. Playing a 60-game season from June 15 until Labor Day, Roberts went 11-8 with a no-hitter in 1946. The following year he tossed another no-hitter while compiling an 18-3 mark, including 17 straight victories, and a 2.33 ERA. In November 1947 Roberts signed with the Philadelphia Phillies and reached the majors in June 1948. Roberts has consistently credited the tutelage he received under Coach Fisher as the key to his big-league success.

In 1948 the Eastern Collegiate Athletic Association, which had sent many college players to the Northern League, banned its athletes from playing professionally. This led to the demise of the Northern League in 1952 and the disappearance of minor league baseball in Montpelier.

At the start of the 2003 season the New England Collegiate Baseball League added the Vermont Mountaineers as a new franchise. On July 21, the team retired uniform number 36 in honor of Roberts, who returned to Montpelier Recreation Field for the festivities. The following year, on July 20, the same honor was bestowed on the late Coach Fisher, who died in 1982 and wore number 44 with the Trojans. Roberts again returned to Montpelier as host of the ceremony.

The Mountaineers have enjoyed huge local support over their first four years, averaging about 1,700 fans a game, which has been aided by numerous upgrades to the field. In 2006 the club earned its first New England Collegiate Baseball League (NECBL) championship.

Take Me Out to the Ballgame

Since its construction in 1940, Montpelier Recreation Field has survived long periods of idleness when only local youth league teams played there. Lacking both funds and attention over those spells, the field, structures, and light fixtures had all fallen into disrepair by the late 1990s.

In 2004 an anonymous donation of $500,000 paved the way to give the old park new life. The grandstands and dugouts were painted a fresh coat of hunter green, and safety screens were installed to shield fans from foul balls. Suspended paving projects were completed. The field was upgraded with improved drainage and turf improvements.

New tarps and an enclosed batting cage were purchased, and improvements were made to the press box, souvenir shop, and concession stand. The park is now handicap accessible. Rest rooms have replaced portable toilets, and brand-new light fixtures tower over the diamond. A new electronic scoreboard stands in left-center field.

More improvements are planned, including a change in field dimensions that will make the park replicate those

Vermont

of Fenway Park, complete with a towering green left-field wall.

The field is a classic baseball venue, with lush grass and a backdrop of tall white pine trees that provide an idyllic feel—a place Ray Kinsella, Terrence Mann, and Moonlight Graham could find peace.

On the façade of the third-base grandstand, a wall of honor pays homage to the players, coaches, administrators, supporters, and volunteers who have helped keep the baseball tradition alive in central Vermont. Atop the wall are two sky-blue circular placards with the numbers 36 and 44 in white, retired for Robin Roberts and Ray Fisher respectively. Outside the park, the state has erected a roadside historical marker in Roberts' honor.

With an original capacity of about 1,200 fans, the field now holds close to 2,000, with nary a bad seat in the house. In addition to the wraparound grandstands behind home plate, where all seats are covered by a roof and protected by a backstop screen, sets of bleachers flank the first and third baselines.

Volunteers and staff have gone the extra mile to ensure fans and families have fun at the park. They hold promotional giveaways between innings, play upbeat music over the PA system, and arrange activities for children— many led by the team's mascot, a fuzzy woodchuck named Skip. During the off-season, the team hosts social events including hot-stove banquets.

Skip is also the namesake of the concession stand and souvenir store. Skip's Ice Cream Shop offers cool treats, but ball park classics like burgers, hot dogs, and peanuts are also available. At Skip's Pro Shop fans can find anything from t-shirts, hooded sweatshirts, and caps to miniature bats, stadium seats, and autographed photos of Robin Roberts.

Tickets are a bargain at $4 for adults and $2 for kids, students, seniors, and military personnel. An even better deal is the family ticket, where four fans including up to two adults can enjoy a ball game for just $7.

Best Game (When You Think About It, How Does Someone Decide Which Game Was the Best?)

Crip Polli attended Goddard Seminary, which was located in Barre before its campus moved to Plainfield. As a senior, Polli's brilliance captured national attention. On June 3, 1921, he struck out 28 batters in a 10-inning game against Cushing Academy. The feat earned acclaim in *Ripley's Believe It or Not*. Crip's achievement was not an aberration; it came during a five-game stretch when he whiffed an incredible 105 opponents.

Greatest Team (Not the '27 Yankees, but Who Is?)

The 2006 champions never lost consecutive games while winning the NECBL Northern Division with a 27-15 record. The Mountaineers were well balanced with seven players earning all-league honors. Third baseman Curt Smith led the charge, batting .323 with 50 hits, 26 runs, and 20

Roger Crowley / DigiTechVT.com

Opposing players flank the baselines for the National Anthem at Mountaineer Field in Montpelier.

stolen bases while being named the league's Defensive Player of the Year. Catcher Zach Zaneski (.309, 20 RBI) and shortstop Robbie Minor (.296, 38 RBI), who reached base in 38 straight games, joined Smith as first-team all-league position player selections.

In eight starts, hurler Joe Esposito went 4-3 with a league-high 61 strike-outs and a 2.19 ERA. Closer Mark Murray logged 16 regular season saves and added four more in the playoffs. Murray struck out 30 while allowing just 9 hits in 22 innings and did not allow a single earned run all season.

Second baseman Troy Krider (.317) and starting pitcher Chris Friedrich (2-0, 1.41 ERA)—the NECBL Rookie of the Year—were named second team all-league.

Best Player . . . in My Opinion

Robin Roberts turned his two summers in Montpelier into a 19-year major league career. Pitching mainly for the Phillies, Roberts won 286 games, including 20 or more in 6 straight seasons. He struck out 2,357 batters while walking just 902, and compiled a 3.41 ERA. His 28-7 record in 1952 earned him a second-place finish in the National League's Most Valuable Player Award balloting. Inducted into the Baseball Hall of Fame in 1976, Roberts deserves recognition not just for his on-field accomplishments, but because he has never forgotten the enjoyment and importance of his younger days in Vermont.

Vermont

Round Tripper (Some Suggestions for Sightseers)

Start at the gold-domed State House, where free guided tours begin on the half-hour July to mid-October from 10 A.M. to 3:30 P.M. Outside is a statue of Revolutionary War hero Ethan Allen. The Vermont Historical Society is next door, and offers walking tour maps.

Just blocks from the capitol on Terrace Street is 180-acre Hubbard Park. A 50-foot stone observation tower offers sweeping views of the countryside from the city's highest point.

City Hall in Montpelier features the Hall of History and also includes the U.S.S. Montpelier museum. A number of naval vessels have been commissioned to commemorate the city, which is the birthplace of Spanish-American War hero Admiral George Dewey. Born in 1837, he is best known for gaining victory in the Battle of Manila Bay without a single combat casualty.

Learn about the maple sugaring process at Bragg Farm Sugar House on Route 14 in East Montpelier. An on-site ice cream parlor tempts with maple shakes and soft-serve. On County Road in Montpelier, Morse Farm Sugar Works features a farm stand and nature trail.

At 600 feet deep, the Rock of Ages Quarry in Graniteville is the world's largest. At the visitors' center, historical and technological exhibits show how the industry has evolved over two centuries. Guests can also try their hand at sandblasting, and bowl a frame on an outdoor granite bowling alley. An observation platform at the Craftsmen Center offers views of granite being cut, carved, and polished.

To gain a true appreciation of granite artisanship, visit the 65-acre Hope Cemetery on Merchant Street in Barre. Established in 1985, it features some of the most elaborately carved monuments and mausoleums anywhere. Green Mount Cemetery, covering 35 hillside acres in Montpelier, is more scenic and nearly as impressive.

The Vermont Frost Heaves of the American Basketball Association play home games at Barre Memorial Auditorium, with a schedule running from November through March.

Northfield, about 10 miles south of Montpelier, is home to Norwich University, the nation's oldest private military college. The Sullivan Museum and History Center is worth a stop. While in Northfield, you'll find five covered bridges spanning rivers and streams along quiet country roads.

Ben & Jerry's ice cream factory is on Route 100 in Waterbury, about 13 miles northwest of Montpelier off I-89. Tours are offered every half-hour, complete with samples. If you're thirsty, tour the nearby Cold Hollow Cider Mill. About 21 miles northeast of Montpelier, in Cabot, cheese maker Cabot Creamery gives factory tours and tastings.

The campuses of Woodbury College, Vermont College, and University of Vermont at City Center are all in Montpelier.

Places to Eat . . . If You Want More Than Cracker Jack

Always trust restaurants run by cooking schools, especially one as revered as the New England Culinary Institute in Montpelier. Chef's Table and Main Street Grill are can't-miss spots.

The Inn at Montpelier on Main Street offers traditional New England cuisine in a stately setting. The Black Door Bar & Bistro is one of the few hip and contemporary spots in Montpelier.

Sarducci's on Main Street, with its wood-fired oven, is the top choice for Italian cuisine. Other worthy international options include La Brioche Bakery on Main Street, Little India on Northfield Street, Conoscenti on State Street, Girasole on Berlin Street, Royal Orchid Thai Restaurant on Elm Street, and Julio's Cantina on State Street. The House of Tang on River Street offers a surprisingly good Chinese buffet.

Montpelier may have no "Mickey D's," but J. Morgans Steakhouse on State Street has electric trains circling the restaurant's interior, which mesmerizes kids. Another great choice for children is Finkerman's Riverside Bar-B-Q on River Street, with better-than-average ribs, pork, and chicken and a play room to keep youngsters busy.

Eat fresh at the Montpelier Farmers Market, open Saturdays from 9 A.M. to 1 P.M. at State and Elm streets downtown. Rhapsody Natural Cuisine features a menu highlighting local growers and food producers.

The Thrush Tavern, near the capitol, draws politicos, professionals, locals, and tourists with microbrews, an outdoor patio, and great burgers. For the sports bar scene, McGillicuddy's Irish Pub on Main Street has plenty of screens and individually tunable table speakers.

For good java and a good chuckle, The Howard Bean inside Riverwalk Records pays humorous homage to the former state governor and presidential candidate Howard Dean. For great live acoustic music, relax at Langdon Street Café.

Vermont

Sources:

Simon, Tom (editor). *Green Mountain Boys of Summer: Vermonters in the Major Leagues 1882–1993*. City, State: New England Press, 2000.

www.barregranite.org
bioproj.sabr.org
www.central-vt.com
www.historicvermont.org
www.leg.state.vt.us
www.montpelier-vt.org
www.thevermontmountaineers.com
www.timesargus.com
www.vermonttoday.com

Address: One Line Drive, Manchester, NH 03101

Web Site: www.nhfishercats.com

First Game: 2005

Dimensions: LF 326 CF 400 RF 306

MerchantsAuto.com Stadium is a newly constructed facility (2005) and the present venue of the Fisher Cats. Gill Stadium is an old park, constructed in 1913, which previously hosted Manchester's minor league baseball and is still used for various events. Both facilities are owned by the City of Manchester.

Directions to MerchantsAuto.com Stadium: Coming from either the south or north, take I-293 to Exit 5. Turn right onto Granite Street Bridge. After crossing the bridge, turn right on Commercial Street and follow the brown signs directing you to the stadium.

Directions to Gill Stadium: Take I-293 to Exit 8 (Bridge Street). Take a left on to Beech Street. The stadium is at the intersection with Valley Street.

MERCHANTS-AUTO.COM STADIUM

Home of the New Hampshire Fisher Cats an AA Eastern League, Toronto Blue Jays Affiliate

Claim to Fame

Manchester is the largest city in New Hampshire and, during the New Hampshire Primary, the city is the nerve center of presidential campaigns. The city was once home to the largest mill in the United States. The *Manchester Union-Leader*, the local daily newspaper, was published by conservative William Loeb.

Strange but True

The city's nickname is "ManchVegas." This moniker was given after a number of pizza parlors and small clubs were busted for illegally operating video poker machines.

Who's Who in Manchester

Manchester has a rich baseball history. Former Cy Young Award winners Chris Carpenter and Mike Flanagan are natives of New Hampshire. Former Red Sox power hitter Phil "the Thrill" Plantier and Steve "Bye-Bye" Balboni are also from the Granite State. The Manchester Fisher Cats have already

New Hampshire

Photo courtesy of the New Hampshire Fisher Cats

A view of the action in Manchester, NH.

made major contributions to its parent club—the Toronto Blue Jays. Alumni include pitcher Gustavo Chacin, infielder Aaron Hill, and catcher Greg Zaun. Two world champions, the 1913 Red Sox and the Philadelphia Athletics, have played games in Manchester.

About Manchester

New Hampshire's largest city, Manchester is a prototypical former New England textile manufacturing center that has shaken its textile roots and is now a diverse, prosperous city. The current population stands at about 110,000.

Driving toward Manchester on Route 1 and 293, there's a long row of multistoried, red-brick buildings that dominate the city's eastern banks along the Merrimack River. These huge former textile mills are an impressive

sight and a piece of Americana not to be forgotten. The buildings are representative of a by-gone era when the United States was establishing itself as an industrial behemoth.

Manchester was one of the world's first planned cities. It was designed to enhance the mass production taking place at the cotton looms in its mills. As an adjunct to the mills, row houses for the workers were constructed nearby. Manchester's downtown area—featuring a quirky main street that is a dead end at both ends—was developed up the hill from the mills and row houses. Amoskeag was one the largest cotton textile mill complexes in the world, operating 24,400 looms that produced 471 miles of cloth each day.

While the big red-brick buildings are no longer used for textile production, a visit to this area is a history lesson not to be missed. You will also see the previously described row houses, many of which have been converted to upscale residences.

Now, the city's most famous cottage industry is politics, in particular, the election process. There's always a beehive of election activity in the two years before the New Hampshire presidential primary. If you live in Manchester, you're more than likely to have met the next president in person. Every four years, there's a pestilence of politicians. Maybe it's a boost to the local economy. The Granite State has seen the good, the bad, and the ugly. But we're sure there are times hearing the same stump speech over and over again, with the same jokes and pregnant pauses, can be boring and repetitive.

A Baseball Backgrounder

There have been several different professional franchises in Manchester. After World War II, the Giants of the New England League and the Eastern League Yankees were Manchester's first two professional franchises.

There have been several well-known major league players from the area. The area boasts two schoolboys who went on to become Cy Young Award winners—Mike Flanagan from Manchester Memorial and Chris Carpenter from Trinity. Former Kansas City and Yankee first baseman Steve Balboni and former Red Sox Phil Plantier are also from the Granite State.

Practically every great New Hampshire star has played at Gill Stadium. The stadium has a great history. Gill

Stadium, originally called "Textile Stadium," was originally built to entertain and "Americanize" part of the Amoskeag Manufacturing Company's large immigrant workforce. The factory owners wanted to turn their factory team into a professional powerhouse. They were quickly disabused from the notion when they hosted an exhibition game with the Philadelphia Athletics. At the game, the Athletics players started to switch positions, do tricks, and make a mockery of the game against factory All-Stars.

Gill Stadium has hosted—not necessarily on a continual basis—professional baseball since 1913. The Fisher Cats played there in 2004 prior to the move to what is now called MerchantsAuto.com Stadium. Gill Stadium's relevance continues as it's a real old-time baseball park that still is in active use. Other similar parks have disappeared from the American landscape, victims of urban redevelopment. In 2004, the last year it was used for professional baseball, it was considered the second-oldest professional baseball park after the Grand Dame of baseball, Fenway Park in Boston. The stadium's status makes a stop at Gill Stadium almost mandatory.

It is said that the Boston Red Sox played a local All-Star team in 1913 as part of the official opening ceremonies. The Fisher Cats were the primary tenants in 2004, the year they were Eastern League champions. The park's covered grandstand is somewhat similar to Fenway Park's. However, fans are not nearly as close to the action since the foul territory at Gill is much more spacious.

Minor league franchises can sell for

millions and there seems to be a seller's market for franchises. As a result, it's no longer as easy for frustrated players to have the vicarious pleasure of being team owners. Many factors keep driving franchise prices up, including the phenomenal rebirth of baseball at all levels; the relative affordability of minor league baseball; the desire of many communities to bring people back from the malls to uncrowded downtown areas; and the availability of money and sponsors for minor league franchises.

As for the inflation factor, consider that the Manchester Yankees were for sale in the early 1970s. The owner of the team was a professor at a local university. His asking price for the team? Just $3,000. That's right, $3,000. And no, $3,000 wasn't a lot of money back then, either. The team's low asking price during the 1970s reflects the public's lack of interest in baseball at that time and vividly illustrates the comeback of our national pastime that has taken place.

Take Me Out to the Ballgame

For a short period of time, MerchantAuto.com Stadium was known as Fisher Cats Stadium. The name change took place in 2006, when the Solomon Family—local entrepreneurs—purchased the naming rights to the facility.

The primary tenant of the stadium is New Hampshire's Fisher Cats baseball team. The stadium is owned by the City of Manchester. The new field was constructed as part of the revitalization program for the downtown area of Manchester. Included as part of the complex is a sparkling new indoor arena

for minor league hockey, concerts, and other activities.

MerchantsAuto.com Stadium cost $22 million to build and seats 7,200 for baseball as well as 12,500 for concerts.

The Fisher Cats franchise traces its origins to New Haven, Connecticut. Having been granted an expansion franchise in the Eastern League, the New Haven Ravens first took to the field in 1994. Nine years later, in 2003, the franchise was sold to Drew Weber, owner of the Lowell Spinners of the New York–Penn League. In 2005, Weber sold controlling interest in the Manchester team to the current owner, Arthur Solomon, a real estate investor and university professor, but kept the Lowell team under family ownership.

The field is considered one of the best places in minor league baseball to catch a game. It has just about all of the amenities: covered grandstand, comfortable seating close to the action, good concessions, and a large area for family picnicking. The sight lines are very good in most areas of the park. The playing field is natural grass.

What's a Fisher Cat? Or, more to the point, is there really an animal called a "fisher cat," or is it a figment of a promoter's fertile imagination? The answer is that there is an animal commonly called fisher cat, but it is not really a cat. It's an oversized member of the weasel family. But the animal does have whiskers just like a cat, which may be how it got its name. Fisher cats generally are nocturnal animals and usually live in heavily-forested areas. They can weigh as much as 30 pounds, and are dark brown in color. Because the animals are nocturnal, they are rarely

Photo courtesy of the New Hampshire Fisher Cats

Fans down the left field line rooting on the Fisher Cats.

seen by humans.

The Fisher Cats' management team is an extremely fan-friendly group—and that means for all fans. But there is one important restriction they place on attendees: Shirts imprinted with insulting, obnoxious phrases that may disrupt the family atmosphere are not allowed in the stadium. It's a somewhat unusual policy, but the Fisher Cats received a good deal of positive feedback from the national media when they implemented the policy in 2005.

While the Fisher Cats have only been in business since 2004, they've contributed a number of players to big-league rosters, particularly to the Toronto Blue Jays, their big-league affiliate. Team alumni include several current Blue Jay mainstays, including Aaron Hill and southpaw pitcher Gustavo Chacin. Major leaguers who underwent rehabilitation stints at Manchester include pitcher A.J. Burnett, Toronto's most important free-agent acquisition for the 2006 season, and catcher Gregg Zaun. In total, more than a dozen players have gone to the majors from the Fisher Cats.

Best Game (When You Think About It, How Does Someone Decide Which Game Was the Best?)

The first two games of the 2004 championship series were great games. The best thing about them, from New Hampshire's perspective, is that the home team won both games. Both games ended with a score of 5-4 over the Altoona Curve.

In the first game of the series, the Fisher Cats chipped away in later innings to overcome a 4-2 deficit. Dominic Rich was 2-for-5 with a double, a

A panoramic view of MerchantsAuto.com Stadium.

triple, two RBIs, and one run scored. Maikel Jova's lead-off home run in the top of the seventh inning was the game-winning hit in the second game.

Greatest Team (Not the '27 Yankees, but Who Is?)

The last team to play at Gill Stadium was its best. The New Hampshire Fisher Cats had a three-game sweep over the Altoona Curve to win the championship. The key was a pitching staff led by left-hander Gustavo Chacin, who spent four years in Double A before becoming a big leaguer. The crafty left hander had a 16-2 record before joining the Blue Jays' starting rotation. The league's best reliever was Brandon League, who was the Eastern League's playoff Most Valuable Player. New Hampshire had the league's best pitching. Third baseman John Hattig hit the game winning two-run home run in the championship game. From the beginning, the Fisher Cats overcame many obstacles. The first thing the team overcame was its first official name, the "New Hampshire Primaries." The name was, to say the least, very unpopular. Management quick-

ly decided that it was more popular to name a team after a sharp-toothed rodent than a politician. Within a couple of weeks, the team was re-named the Fisher Cats.

Best Player . . . in My Opinion

It's open to debate, but it's a close race between pitchers Mike Flanagan and Chris Carpenter. However, Carpenter's career is on-going, so we'll see what develops.

For many years, former New York Yankees great third baseman Red Rolfe of Penacook was considered to be the greatest. Hall-of-Famer Carlton Fisk, who hails from Charlestown, New Hampshire, is now considered the best player from New Hampshire's White Mountains. The former catcher had a long career with the Red Sox and White Sox. While Rolfe was an important cog for the Yankees, Fisk is an all-time great. Oddly, both Fisk and Birdie Tebbetts, New Hampshire's two most famous catchers, were born in Vermont but grew up in New Hampshire. Fisk has the unusual distinction of being the best ballplayer from two different states. Fisk was American League Rookie of the Year and a Gold Glove catcher in 1972. He caught more games—2,226—than any other catcher in history and was an 11-time All-Star. As a player, he hit for power and possessed excellent running speed for a catcher. His most enduring moment was, perhaps, in the 1975 World Series. He was captured on television exhorting that his long fly ball to left field was a fair ball. The ball did stay fair, and a game-winning home run forced a Game 7 in the series. Carlton Fisk was inducted into the Hall of Fame with the class of 2000.

Don't forget about outfielder Adam Lind, who hit 19 homers and 71 RBIs with a .310 batting average. In 2006, the 23-year-old outfielder was the Eastern League's best power prospect and the league's Most Valuable Player.

Round Tripper (Some Suggestions for Sightseers)

If you travel to Manchester, a visit to Nashua and its historic Holman Stadium may be in order. If you stay a bit closer to home, the Amoskeag Fishways Learning and Visitors Center is a great attraction along the wide and mighty Merrimack River. The center is open year-round, Monday through Saturday, from 9 A.M. to 5 P.M. During fish migration season in May and June, the center is open seven days a week.

The center is a trove of information and exhibits about New England's natural history. During April, May, and June, the herring and salmon really begin to run. The museum offers visitors a unique opportunity to unravel the mysteries of our environment. Kids are thrilled when they see migrating shad, herring, and sea lamprey in the viewing windows. A stop at the Millyard Museum and Manchester Historic Association are also recommended.

Also, since Nashua and Manchester are in such close proximity, why not do a New Hampshire doubleheader? There are many fine convenient accommodations in either area, accessible to prime tourist locations—like the New Hampshire seashore. Both cities have a wide range of motels nearby and eating places abound. Motel rates reflect that neither city is a high-traffic tourist destination. If you are looking to stay as close to MerchantsAuto.com Stadium as possible, consider staying at the new Hilton Gardens Inn. It is situated above the park's left centerfield wall. One suggestion: If you decide to stay in a room overlooking the baseball field, remember to close the curtains for privacy.

Places to Eat . . . If You Want More Than Cracker Jack

There are plenty of good places to eat around town. If you like seafood, you don't have to travel all the way to Maine. Newick's, one of New Hampshire's most famous seafood restaurants, is in nearby Merrimac. You can't go wrong with fish. Some specific eating places that have been recommended include the Chateau Restaurant, Chinatown, Polcari's, The Yard, the Red Arrow Diner, Margarita's, and the Tenderloin Room Steakhouse.

New Hampshire

Sources:

The Baseball Almanac, 1995–2007.
Boston Globe, 1900–2007.
Manchester Union-Leader, 1990–2007.
Nashua Telegraph, 1995–2007.
Society of American Baseball Researchers. *The Northern Game—and Beyond*. Boston: Cambridge Prepress Services, 2002.

www.all-baseball.com
www.ballparkdigest.com
www.ballparkreviews.com
www.baseballalmanac.com
www.baseballamericaonline.com
www.easternleague.com
www.manchesternh.gov

26

Address: 67 Amherst Street (Don Newcombe Way), Nashua, NH 03064

Web Site: www.nashuapride.com

First Game: 1937 (renovated in 2002)

Dimensions: LF 307 CF 401 RF 315

Directions: US Route 3 to New Hampshire Exit 6 toward Hollis. Take the Route 130 ramp toward downtown Nashua. Merge into Broad Street (NH Route 130), turn right onto Amherst Street (Route 101A), turn left on Don Newcombe Way.

HOLMAN STADIUM

Home of the Nashua Pride of the Candian-American League

Claim to Fame

Nashua is known for its shopping. After World War II, almost half of the population was of French-Canadian decent. The first modern integrated baseball team was the Nashua Dodgers. John Kennedy announced his presidential candidacy in front of Nashua City Hall.

Strange but True

The Nashua Pride gave away Richard Nixon bobbleheads to celebrate the 32nd anniversary of Watergate.

Who's Who in Nashua

Roy Campanella, Don Newcombe, and Walter Alston played for the old Nashua Dodgers. Barry Bonds made his professional debut as an outfielder for the Double A Nashua Pirates; Bobby Bonilla was his teammate. Some alumni of the Nashua Pride include: Brendan Donnelly, Curtis Pride, Paxton Crawford, Dante Bichette, Darren Bragg, Jeff Juden, Orlando Miller, and Jeff Sparks. For-

New Hampshire

mer Red Sox players Mike Easler and Butch Hobson managed the Nashua Pride.

About Nashua

Should you visit Holman Stadium, take some time to look around the city of Nashua. The first thing you may notice is that Nashua, to many, is more like Massachusetts than New Hampshire. Nashua, of course, does abut Massachusetts. Because of this, Nashua has shared in the high-tech business boom. Also, a lot of Nashua residents are transplanted Bay Staters who have fled the higher taxes for New Hampshire's tax-friendly environment.

New Hampshire is one of the few states in the nation with neither a sales tax nor an income tax. Many out-of-state residents visit the South Nashua malls for tax-free shopping. Conveniently, the malls are located almost directly on the state line of Massachusetts.

Besides being a virtual tax-free zone, Nashua has a reputation for good schools, hospitals, recreation areas, as well as a reasonable cost of living. On two occasions, in 1987 and 1997, Nashua was selected by *Money* as the "Best Place in America to Live." It is the only city to have been selected for the honor on two occasions. And the city consistently shows

up in other similar surveys as an excellent place to put down roots.

While Nashua does have a strong connection to the pre–World War II textile manufacturing era in New England, its ties were never as significant as textile centers such as Lowell, Manchester, and Lawrence. Today, traveling around Nashua one would hardly notice any of the tell-tale signs of textile manufacturing, such as the huge, crumbling red-brick factories. Instead, it is a modern city with high-tech plants dotting its landscape. The shopping malls in South Nashua are the state's largest collection of retail outlets.

Population-wise, the city is the second largest in the state with almost 90,000 residents.

A Baseball Backgrounder

Driving into Nashua, signs show the way to "historic" Holman Stadium. It's called historic for good reasons. The first American racially-integrated professional baseball team—the Nashua

Nashua was host to the 2003 Atlantic League All-Star Game.

Photo courtesy of Nashua Parks & Recreation Department

A view of the grandstands from center field.

Dodgers—played their games at Holman. Further, the Nashua Dodgers were the first professional American baseball team to be managed by a minority. These seminal events took place in 1946, just after the end of World War II. Roy Campanella and Don Newcombe were, of course, the two players who integrated the Nashua Dodgers. While they were playing at Nashua, Jackie Robinson was a member of the Brooklyn Dodgers' International League team in Montreal, and he went on to be the first African American in big league baseball.

Why were Campanella and Newcombe sent to the Brooklyn Dodgers' Nashua farm team rather than some other minor league location? Dodger officials—particularly General Manager Branch Rickey—believed Nashua would be the most tolerant of their farm teams. As it turned out, the choice

of Nashua made good sense. Buzzie Bavasi, then the Nashua general manager, welcomed the two players, seeing them as having more talent than many other of the team's players. Newcombe and Campanella both later expressed their deep satisfaction with Nashua as both a place to play and live.

During the 1946 season, Campanella became the first African American to manage a professional baseball team. To be sure, it was only for a single game, but it still was a groundbreaking event. Campanella took over the managerial reins when Manager Walter Alston was ejected during a game with the Lawrence (Massachusetts) Millionaires. Alston went on to become one of the all-time great managers for the Los Angeles Dodgers. The Nashua Dodgers won its contest with Lawrence on that eventful day under Campanella's direction.

New Hampshire

Photo courtesy of Nashua Parks & Recreation Department

A Pride batter readies himself for the pitch.

Famous Nashua Players have included many former big leaguers. The list is long and includes Bobby Bonilla, Sam Horn, Pete Incaviglia, Curtis Pride, Brendan Donnelly, Dante Bichette, Felix Jose, Mel Rojas, Ken Ryan, Jeff Juden, Darren Bragg, Paxton Crawford, and Jay Yannaco. Fifteen players for the independent league franchise have also played in the majors. Mike Easler and Bobby Tolan, former big leaguers, managed Nashua after their big-league careers ended. And lest we forget, present manager Butch Hobson had a distinguished playing career in the majors, mainly with the Red Sox.

Nashua has had more than its fair share of championships. Another fa-mous player to don Dodger blue was Tommy Lasorda.

The Dodgers, in the New England League, won three consecutive championships in 1946, 1947, and 1948. Roy Campanella and Don Newcombe belonged in the big leagues. But the color barrier forced the African-American players to compete in Class B baseball. The city's acceptance of the players is a singular accomplishment. Years later, when Nashua joined the independent Atlantic League, it won another championship in 2000. The team's leader has been former Red Sox player/manager Butch Hobson.

The most unusual game had to be in 2006, when Olympic downhill ski-er and New Hampshire native Bode

Miller signed on for a one-game appearance. Instead of sitting on the bench and cheering on his new teammates, Bode took a starting position in the outfield that night. How did he do? The good news is that Bode made a spectacular over-the-shoulder catch in the outfield. He

The retired numbers of Don Newcombe, Roy Campanella, and Jackie Robinson.

didn't embarrass himself. The bad news: Bode struck out in both of his appearances at the plate. It was a fun night anyway for the capacity crowd on hand to honor an authentic New Hampshire sports hero.

Take Me Out to the Ballgame

Like Pawtucket's McCoy Stadium and Lynn's Fraser Field, Nashua's ballpark is a product of the Depression. During the 1930s, the Works Progress Administration (WPA) spearheaded a drive to funnel federal monies into local construction projects to stimulate regional economies. The WPA provided funds for building municipal buildings and public stadiums throughout the country—including the Los Angeles Coliseum.

It wasn't until 1946, however, that Nashua and Holman Stadium captured its first organized baseball franchise. Prior to this, the field was used mainly to host amateur and high school games. The stadium was built for the City of Nashua, and the city continues to own and operate the facility.

The stadium remained essentially unchanged from 1937—when it first opened—to 2002. There were some minor lighting alterations and creature comforts added in 1998. In 2001, a major $4.5 million refurbishment program was initiated on many of the city's auspices. New and additional seating, suites, skyboxes, press facilities, a concessions office, and restrooms were all part of the refurbishment program. On opening day of 2002, the revamped stadium was opened with great fanfare.

True to its original design, there is still no roof over the stands. But most of the summer games are early evening affairs. Adorning the left-field wall are three plaques with the numbers 36, 39, and 42. These are the retired numbers of Don Newcombe, Roy Campanella, and Jackie Robinson, respectively. Jackie Robinson never played at Holman, but it's only fitting that his number be

New Hampshire

Photo courtesy of Nashua Parks & Recreation Department

A playground in left field helps make Holman Stadium very fan-friendly.

retired at the home of America's first integrated team.

For those who love the nostalgic feel of an older ballpark with all of the modern amenities, Holman Stadium warrants a visit. It's always fun to watch the action at a park where baseball history has been made.

Best Game (When You Think About It, How Does Someone Decide Which Game Was the Best?)

It must have been particularly sweet for the Dodgers to defeat their archrivals, the Lynn Red Sox, for the 1946 championship. The Red Sox' policy toward African Americans reached as low as Class B baseball.

Lynn had several bigots. But according to Campanella and Newcombe, the worst of them all was Lynn's manager. Newcombe and Campanella followed Branch Rickey's strict instructions not to respond to any racial abuse—just like Jackie Robinson. But Buzzie Bavasi wouldn't stand for it. He challenged the whole Lynn team to a fight. A battle between the teams was barely averted.

Greatest Team (Not the '27 Yankees, but Who Is?)

Nothing can compare to the achievements of the post–World War II Nashua Dodgers—the 1946 team to be specific. The team was managed by first baseman and future Hall-of-Famer Walter Alston. The pitching staff was led by future Most Valuable Player and Brooklyn Dodger Don Newcombe, and the catcher was Roy Campanella. The team had an excellent season, on and off the field. The Dodgers finished in second and had very few racial incidents. But the team really came through in the post-season—winning Nashua's first of three championships. Considering their success, it's hard to believe the team was out of business by 1950. Other alumni include Dan Bankhead, Gino Cimoli, Billy Loes, and former Dodgers general manager Al Campanis. Buzzie Bavasi was also Nashua's first general manager.

Best Player . . . in My Opinion

The greatest player ever to regularly play in Nashua would have to be Roy Campanella. From the time he arrived, the future Hall-of-Fame catcher quickly showed why he, and other African Americans, belonged in the majors. He was signed by the Baltimore Elite Giants at the age of 15 and quickly was recognized as Josh Gibson's peer. He was ranked 50th in *The Sporting News'* list of the twentieth century's greatest ballplayers and even had his own postage stamp. He hit .290, led the league in putouts, assists, and errors, and won the Most Valuable Player award. Here's a toast to Roy Campanella, a real American hero.

Without a doubt, George "Birdie" Tebbetts was the best of the Nashua natives that have made it to the big leagues. Although born in Vermont,

"Birdie" spent his formative years in Nashua and always called the city his home. In the 1930s, 1940s, and 1950s he was a four-time All-Star, as well as a manager and scout with the Tigers, Red Sox, Indians, Reds, and Milwaukee Braves. The nickname "Birdie" came from his high-pitched voice.

Playing during a time when most players had just a high school education, Birdie was a rarity. He was a graduate of a four-year college, Providence College.

Although a solid performer, Tebbetts neither received nor merited Hall-of-Fame consideration. Nevertheless, he was considered one of baseball's brainiest players. He was ready with a quick quip that frequently got him in trouble with some teammates and opponents.

Round Tripper (Some Suggestions for Sightseers)

Nashua is one of the East Coast's greatest shopping meccas. Thousands of Massachusetts residents take a short trip over the boarder to take advantage of New Hampshire's tax-free shopping. The Mall of New Hampshire and every kind of store imaginable are shoe-horned along the Massachusetts–New Hampshire line.

Nashua—and Holman Stadium—is located about 20 miles south of Manchester, New Hampshire, off US Route 3. Therefore, if one is visiting Holman Stadium, it's a good idea to double up and take in a game at Manchester's MerchantsAuto.com Stadium. The reverse is also true—when visiting Manchester, make plans to take the short

New Hampshire

drive to Holman for a game. The contrast between the two fields couldn't be greater. On the one hand, there's a Depression-Era stadium that has been refurbished Roman. And then there's the new MerchantsAuto.com facility. Holman, of course, could be considered a baseball icon, while MerchantsAuto.com Stadium is a model twenty-first-century facility built to accommodate today's minor league fan.

Being located just 20 miles from Manchester and 20 miles from Lowell, Massachusetts, has generated some problems for the Nashua franchise. But with a new, well-heeled owner plus the park's important place in baseball history, Holman and the Nashua minor team are positioned to prosper in this era of minor league popularity.

Places to Eat . . . If You Want More than Cracker Jack

Nashua—as well as Manchester, just up the highway—has literally dozens of hotels and motels. Almost every conceivable chain is represented, and prices range from economy to luxury accommodations.

Some of the recommended eating places in the Nashua area include The Country Tavern, Bertucci's, Caribbean Restaurant, City Room Cafe, Crosby Bakery, The Grainery, Martha's Exchange Restaurant and Brewing Co., Michael Timothy's, and Nashua Diner. By last count, there are more than 101 eating places in Nashua, and many of them are frequented by Massachusetts residents.

Sources:

The Baseball Almanac, 1995–2007.
Manchester Union-Leader, 1990–2007.
Nashua Telegraph, 1995–2007.
Conan, Neal. *Play by Play.* New York: Crown Publishers, 2002.

www.all-baseball.com
www.ballparkdigest.com
www.ballparkreviews.com
www.baseballalmanac.com
www.baseballamericaonline.com
www.canamleague.com
www.gonashua.com
www.milb.com
www.sabr.com

27

Address: 271 Park Avenue, Portland ME 04102

Web Site: *www.seadogs.com*

First Game: April 18, 1994

Dimensions: LF 315 CF 400 RF 330

Directions: From the north, take I-295 South to Exit 6A. Merge onto Forest Avenue and continue to the intersection with Park Avenue. Merge right onto Park Avenue. The ballpark will be on the right about one mile down. From the west, follow either Route 302 West or Route 25 West into Portland. Route 25 West will turn into Brighton Avenue, which will intersect with Park Avenue. Take a right onto Park Avenue. Route 302 West will turn into Forest Avenue and will intersect with Park Avenue. Take a right onto Park Avenue. From the south, take I-295 North to Exit 5A, merge onto Congress Street. At the first set of lights take a left onto St. John Street. At the next set of lights, merge right onto Park Avenue. The ballpark will be immediately on the left.

HADLOCK FIELD

Home of the Portland Sea Dogs of the Eastern League (Class Double A Affiliate of the Boston Red Sox

Claim to Fame

Hadlock Field features a 37-foot-high wall in left field—modeled after Fenway Park's "Green Monster"—that is nicknamed the "Maine Monster." Replicas of Fenway Park's Citgo sign and Coke bottle stand above the wall.

Strange but True

Portland is the birthplace of the Italian sandwich. Giovanni Amato, an Italian immigrant, is credited with creating it in the early 1900s, and it is considered Maine's signature sandwich.

In 2006, National Public Radio reported micro distilleries are Portland's new trend, producing "boutique vodkas" that have emerged as the next big thing. The "star" of the new scene is a potato-vodka made from Maine potatoes.

"The First Radio Parish Church of America," which premiered in Portland in 1926, is the oldest continuously broadcast religious radio program in the United States.

While census figures show that Portland's population is less than 3

Photo courtesy of Portland Sea Dogs

A view from behind home plate at Hadlock Field in Portland.

percent African American, the city is home to the largest Sudanese immigrant population in the United States.

Who's Who in Portland

Through the 2006 season, 117 Sea Dogs players have gone on to play in the major leagues. Among the more notable are: Josh Beckett, A.J. Burnett, Luis Castillo, Manny Delcarmen, Alex Gonzalez, Craig Hansen, Livan Hernandez, Charles Johnson, Mark Kotsay, Jon Lester, Cla Meredith, Kevin Millar, David Murphy, Jonathan Papelbon, Dustin Pedroia, Brad Penny, Hanley Ramirez, Edgar Renteria, Kelly Shoppach, Randy Winn, and Kevin Youkilis.

A number of Florida Marlins and Boston Red Sox players have played in Portland on rehab assignments, including Gary Sheffield and Gabe Kapler.

Kevin Millar and Kevin Youkilis share the minor league record for most consecutive games reaching base. The record stands at 71. Youkilis was a Sea Dog for the first 62 of his streak, Millar for all 71.

Millar, along with Charles Johnson, is one of two players in the Sea Dogs Hall of Fame. Also enshrined are former manager Carlos Tosca and former Portland City Manager Robert Ganley, who was instrumental in bringing minor league baseball back to Portland.

Ed Hadlock, who Hadlock Field was named for, played for the minor league Portland Pilots in the 1940s.

Going back even further in the city's baseball history, Duffy Lewis was a player/manager for Portland in 1927. The team was known as the Eskimos, but by the end of the season was being referred to as "the Lewismen" in honor of the popular one-time Red Sox left-fielder. A 10-foot incline in left field at Fenway Park, which existed from 1912 to 1933, had earlier been dubbed "Duffy's Cliff," in his honor.

Another Duffy, Hall of Famer Hugh Duffy, managed in Portland after finishing his major league career. He was at the helm from 1913 to 1916, and also appeared in a few games as a pinch hitter.

Eleven people who were born in the city of Portland have played in the major leagues. The first was Kid Madden, who also played minor league ball in his hometown, in 1887. The most recent was Billy Swift, who pitched in the big leagues from 1985 to 1998. The best known is Bob Stanley, who spent 13 years with the Red Sox before retiring after the 1989 season. Stanley holds the team record for most appearances by a pitcher (637) and most saves (132).

About Portland

The largest city in the state, Portland has a population of approximately 64,000 and is Maine's cultural, social, and economic capital. Situated on Portland Harbor, which is at the mouth of the Fore River and part of Casco Bay, the city is one of New England's most popular tourist destinations.

Originally called Machigonne by the native people who first lived there, the city was settled by the British in 1632 and renamed Casco. While it later became known as Falmouth, following the Revolutionary War a section of the city called "The Neck" was developed as a port and named Portland. The city seal depicts a phoenix rising out of ashes, which acknowledges Portland's recoveries from four devastating fires, including one in 1775 that followed bombardment during the American Revolutionary War. The Great Portland Fire of 1866 was started by fireworks on the 4th of July and was spread when the fire reached a molasses/sugar factory on the wharf.

Portland has recently experienced an economic boom, with relatively low unemployment and an upsurge in tourism and tourism-related industries. In 2005, the *American City Business Journal* rated Portland as having the "Top Market in Small Business Vitality," calling it the hottest small-business market in which to develop a company.

Helping to add a vibrant atmosphere to the Portland community is the Maine College of Art, which attracts students from around the country. It is located on Congress Street in the historic Porteous Building.

The Portland Conservatory of Music provides musical instruction to more than 400 students. Some of Maine's most talented musicians are members of the school's faculty. The conservatory is located on Free Street in the Downtown Arts District.

Maine

The city is home to the University of Maine School of Law and the University of Southern Maine. Other notable landmarks are the Portland Exposition Building, the Portland Ice Arena, and the Maine Medical Center. The local newspapers are the *Portland Press Herald* and *Maine Sunday Telegram*.

While there is no subway in Portland, the METRO provides bus service throughout the city. Amtrak's Downeaster service provides daily access to and from Boston, while ferry service connects Portland to Yarmouth, Nova Scotia.

Notable people associated with the city of Portland include authors Stephen King and E. Annie Proulx, poet Henry Wadsworth Longfellow, actresses Linda Lavin and Liv Tyler, Hollywood director John Ford, and senator George Mitchell.

In its list of top travel destinations for 2007, Frommer's ranks Portland number 12 in the world. And for those of you skeptical of traveling to "the great white north" for some Sea Dogs baseball, the average high tempature in Portland for the month of July is 79 degrees.

A Baseball Backgrounder

Starting in 1886, Portland's first professional baseball team played in the New England League. Over the years, the city has also had entries in the Maine State League, the Atlantic Association, and the Eastern League (both the old Class A Eastern League in 1916–1917 and the modern Eastern League since 1994). Among the teams to call Portland home have been the Phenoms, the Blue Sox, the Duffs, the Paramounts, the Eskimos, the Cliff Climbers, the Lewismen, the Mariners, the Hustlers, the Gulls, the Pilots, and now the Sea Dogs.

Until recently, Portland's baseball teams have not had staying power. Prior to the Sea Dogs, the longest period a Portland franchise remained solvent was the New England League squad that lasted from 1891 to 1896. Several teams lasted only one year, and many seasons saw no professional baseball played in the city of Portland at all. The longest gaps were between 1930 and 1946, and from 1949 until 1994.

When Hiram Abrams purchased the Duffs in 1917, he invited movie stars Fatty Arbuckle and Norma Talmage, and several motion picture executives, to the home opener. Because of Abrams' fondness for show-business people, the team was sometimes referred to as the Portland Movies. Unfortunately, the box office wasn't impressive and the franchise moved to Providence the following year.

Portland has played host to the Red Sox on four occasions. On October 5, 1909, the Red Sox played a postseason game, defeating the All-Maine team 3-0. On September 30, 1919, a thinly-disguised Red Sox team beat the Maine All-Stars, who were presented as "Portland" in the box score, 8-6. On June 11, 1934, the Red Sox played an exhibition game against the B&M company team, winning 7-1. The governor of Maine and Rudy Vallee were both in attendance. On September 24, 1942, the Red Sox beat the Maine All-Stars 11-4.

The 1949 team went out with a bang. In the last game ever played in the long history of the New England League, Portland defeated the Springfield Cubs 11-0 to capture the New England League championship.

Professional baseball returned to Portland in 1994 after the city was awarded one of two new Eastern League franchises. The expansion was needed to accommodate Florida and Colorado joining the National League, and the newly established Sea Dogs became the Double A affiliate of the Marlins. It was Portland's first minor league team in 45 years. (From 1984 to 1988 the Triple A Maine Guides played in Old Orchard Beach, which is approximately 20 miles south of Portland.) Hadlock Field was named after Edson Hadlock Jr., a baseball coach at Portland High School from 1950 to 1978.

In 2003, the Sea Dogs became a Red Sox affiliate, increasing the popularity of an already successful franchise.

Take Me Out to the Ballgame

Hadlock Field has a seating capacity of 7,368 and regularly draws large crowds. Since becoming a Red Sox affiliate in 2003, the field has held an average of more than 6,200 fans per game. The Sea Dogs rank sixth in attendance among New England sports franchises, behind the Red Sox, Celtics, Patriots, Bruins, and Pawtucket Red Sox. Ticket prices range from $3.00 to $8.00, and while the Sea Dogs draw well there are tickets available for most games.

Along with the Maine Monster in left field, Hadlock Field features a pavilion atop the bullpen in right field. The U.S. Cellular Pavilion, which seats 393, was opened in 2006 and is modeled after the Green Monster Seats at Fenway Park.

A unique feature of Hadlock Field is a lighthouse complete with fog and a foghorn that rises up from center field whenever the Sea Dogs hit a home run and when they win a game.

As an added perk for fans, for approximately 20 to 30 minutes prior to each game, a Sea Dogs player sits at the autograph table on the third-base side of the concourse. Players will often also sign autographs after a game behind the first base stands.

A popular attraction for young fans is the team's mascot, Slugger the Sea Dog. Another popular, and unique, sight at Hadlock Field is The Trash Monster, who roams the stands inviting fans to "feed" their garbage into the mouth of his oversized costume.

The Sea Dogs' logo, which was created by cartoonist Guy Gilchrist, is among the most popular in all of minor league baseball. The Sea Dogs annually rank in the top 10 in merchandising sales, and in 1994 and 2003 their team merchandise outsold every minor league team in the country.

Best Game (When You Think About It, How Does Someone Decide Which Game Was the Best?)

There is a temptation to pick the first home game, either of the two no-hitters in franchise history, or the Eastern League All-Star game that was held at Hadlock Field in 2005. However, you

The Maine Monster in left field even has a Citgo® sign of its own.

can't beat winning a championship in a winner-take-all playoff game.

On September 17, 2006, the Sea Dogs won their first ever Eastern League title, defeating Akron 8-5 at Hadlock Field. After seeing Akron deadlock the best-of-five series with consecutive wins, Portland sent Nicaraguan-born right-hander Devern Hansack to the mound in the deciding game. The Sea Dogs jumped to an early lead, scoring four runs in the second inning, the first two coming on a Bryan Myrow home run. They tacked on four more in the third, with Keoni De Renne, a native of Hawaii, hitting a two-out, bases-loaded triple to break the game open. Hansack, who would make his major league debut six days later, pitched seven in-

nings to earn the win. Jon Searles, who has a business degree from Wharton and would be a candidate for "smartest player" if we were giving out such an honor, pitched the last two innings. Outfielder Brandon Moss was named the Eastern League Playoff Most Valuable Player.

Greatest Team (Not the '27 Yankees, but Who Is?)

The 1997 Portland Sea Dogs, at the time a Florida Marlins farm club, featured an astounding 19 players who would go on to play in the major leagues. The team hit a club record 191 home runs, and became the only team in Eastern League history to have 5 players hit 20 or more. Kevin Millar led the team with a .342 average and 32 round-trippers.

Prior to the Sea Dogs, the best Portland team was the 1916 Portland Duffs, who had a record of 81-37 while they played in the Class A Eastern League. It was definitely not the 1946 Portland Gulls. Competing (we use that term loosely here) in the Class B New England League, the Gulls finished the season with a record of 20-99, 59 1/2 games out of first place.

Best Player . . . in My Opinion

With more than 100 former Sea Dogs having gone on to the major leagues, a good argument could be made for more than a few of them. Along with several established major leaguers, there are also a number of young, up-and-coming players who may jump to the front of this list in the coming years. The candidates are:

Josh Beckett was the 2003 World Series Most Valuable Player. Luis Castillo is a three-time National League All-Star and has won three Gold Gloves. Charles Johnson has won four Gold Gloves and been a National League All-Star twice. Kevin Millar has 126 big-league home runs (through 2006) and played a significant role on the 2004 Red Sox championship team. Jonathan Papelbon was a 2006 American League All-Star and set Boston's all-time record for saves by a rookie. Hanley Ramirez was the 2006 National League Rookie of the Year. Anibal Sanchez threw a no-hitter against the Arizona Diamondbacks in 2006.

In a close—and highly subjective—decision, the winner is: Edgar Renteria, who, through 2006, has played 11 seasons in the major leagues, and has been a National League All-Star five times. A Sea Dog in 1995, Renteria has won two Gold Gloves and three Silver Slugger awards since making his big-league debut with the Florida Marlins in 1996. A native of Colombia, Renteria has also played with the St. Louis Cardinals, Boston Red Sox, and Atlanta Braves.

Round Tripper (Some Suggestions for Sightseers)

Portland's Old Port is one of the most successful revitalized warehouse districts in the country. It is the city's primary entertainment and shopping district and the home to a number of bars, restaurants, and shops. The Downtown Arts District is home to the Portland Museum of Art, the Children's Museum of Maine, the SPACE Gallery, and a number of smaller art galleries.

The Portland Observatory was built in 1807 and has been designated a National Historic Landmark. The 86-foot-tall observatory is the last remaining maritime signal tower in the United States.

The Longfellow Arboretum, which is named in honor of American poet Henry Wadsworth Longfellow, is a small arboretum located on Ocean Avenue in 56-acre Payson Park.

The Cumberland County Civic Center, located on Spring Street, hosts both concerts and sporting events, including Portland Pirates hockey. The

Maine

Pirates are a minor league affiliate of the National Hockey League's Anaheim Mighty Ducks.

The Portland area has 11 golf courses, more than 100 tennis courts, dozens of playgrounds, and more than 100 miles of nature trails.

Places to Eat ... If You Want More Than Cracker Jack

Portland offers a cornucopia of dining and drinking options. Among those within walking distance of Hadlock Field are Margaritas Mexican Restaurant on St. John Street, and Amato's, also on St. John Street. If you're looking for a Maine-style Italian sandwich, Amato's has been making them for more than 100 years and has been voted Portland's "Best Italian" a number of times.

Elsewhere in town, you might want to consider: Street and Company on Wharf Street, Bull Feeney's on Fore Street; Fore Street, which is named after its location on Fore Street; Bleachers on Preble Street; Rivalries on Cotton Street; Walters on Exchange Street; Hugo's on Middle Street; and DiMillo's on Long Wharf.

The city is home to a number of brewpubs, including the D.L. Geary Brewing Company, Gritty McDuff's Brewing Company, Shipyard Brewing Company, Casco Bay Brewing Company, and Allagash Brewing Company.

Sources:

Soos, Troy. *Before the Curse: The Glory Days of New England Baseball 1858–1918.* Hyannis, Massachusetts: Parnassus Imprints, 1997.

http://www.baseball-reference.com
http://www.hometownusa.com/maine/Portland.html
http://www.npr.org/
http://www.portlandmaine.com/
http://www.seadogs.com/
http://strangemaine.blogspot.com
http://www.wikipedia.org

BIBLIOGRAPHY

PERIODICALS

Baseball Almanac, 1995–2007
Berkshire Eagle, 1999–2007
Boston Globe, 1900–2007
Boston Red Sox Media Guides, 1995–2006
Brewster Whitecaps Media Guide, 2005–2007
Brockton Enterprise, 1990–2007
Cape Cod Times, 1990–2007
Chatham A's Program, 2007
Harwich Mariners Yearbook, 2007
Manchester Union-Leader, 1990–2007
Nashua Telegraph, 1995–2007
New York Times, 1890–2007
Orleans Cardinals Program, 2006–2007
Pawtucket Red Sox Yearbooks, 1990–2006
Wareham Gatemen Media Guide
Worcester Telegram, 1900–2007

BOOKS

Conan, Neal. *Play by Play*. New York: Crown Publishers, 2002.

Crowley, Dan. *Baseball on Cape Cod*. Mount Pleasant, South Carolina: Arcadia Publishing, 2004.

Glassman-Jaffe, Marcia. *Fun with the Family in Massachusetts, Third Edition*. Guilford, Connecticut: The Globe Pequot Press, 2002.

Grossman, Leigh. *The Red Sox Fan Handbook*. Cambridge, Massachusetts: Rounder Books, 2005.

Nowlin and Tan. *The 50 Greatest Red Sox Games*. New York, New York: Wiley, 2006.

Pahigian, Joshua R. *Spring Training Handbook*. Jefferson, North Carolina: McFarland & Company, 2005.

Perley, Sidney. *Historic Storms of New England*. Beverly, Massachusetts: The Salem Press Publishing Company, 1891; reprinted by Commonwealth Editions, 2001.

Pietrusza, David. *Baseball's Canadian-American League.* Jefferson, North
Carolina: McFarland, 2005.

Price, Christopher. *Baseball by the Beach—A History of America's National
Pastime on Cape Cod.* Yarmouthport, Massachusetts: On Cape Publications,
1998.

Scoggins, Charles. *Bricks and Bats.* Lowell, Massachusetts: Lowell Historical
Society, 2002.

Society of American Baseball Researchers. *The Northern Game—and Beyond.*
Boston: Cambridge Prepress Services, 2002.

Soos, Troy. *Before the Curse: The Glory Days of New England Baseball 1858–
1918.* Hyannis, Massachusetts: Parnassus Imprints, 1997.

Vonnegut, Kurt. *A Man Without a Country.* New York: Seven Stories Press,
2005.

WEB SITES

www.508ma.com/wareham

www.atlanticleague.com

www.all-baseball.com

www.ballparkdigest.com

www.ballparkreviews.com

www.baseballalmanac.com

www.baseballamericaonline.com

www.bridgeportbluefish.com

www.brockton.ma.us

www.brocktonrox.com

www.canamleague.com

www.capecodbaseball.org

www.ccsu.edu

http://ci.bridgeport.ct.us

www.ci.lynn.ma.us

www.cityofnewhaven.com

www.cityofnewport.com

www.ctdefenders.com

www.davidpietrusza.com

www.easternleague.com

www.espn.com

www.gatemen.org

www.harwichmariners.com

www.holycross.edu/athletics

www.jimbouton.com

www.manchesternh.gov

www.milb.com

www.mlb.com

www.necbl.com

www.nefan.com

www.new-britain.net

www.newhavencutters.com

www.gonashua.com

www.newportchamber.com

www.newportgulls.com

www.northshorespirit.com

www.orleanscardinals.com

www.pawsox.com

www.pittsfielddukes.com

www.pittsfield-ma.org

www.pittsfieldweb.com

www.sabr.org

www.state.ma.us

www.thomasedison.com/brockton.htm

www.WahconahPark.com

www.worcestertornadoes.com

http://yalebulldogs.cstv.com

INDEX

A

AA Eastern League, 223
American League, 1
Arnie Allen Diamond.
    See Guv Fuller Field
Atlantic League, 171

B

Ballpark at Harbor Yard, The (Bridgeport, CT), 171–178
    about Bridgeport, 172–173
    baseball background, 173–174
    best game, 175–176
    best player, 176–177
    claim to fame, 171
    contact info and directions, 171
    field facts, 171
    greatest team, 176
    places to eat, 177
    sightseeing suggestions, 177
    strange but true tales, 171
    take me out to the ballgame, 174–175
    who's who, 171–172
Bibliography, 247–249
Boston, MA, 2–3
Boston Red Sox
    background, 3–5
    ballpark, *see* Fenway Park
    best game, 6–7
    best player, 8
    greatest team, 7–8
    who's who, 2
Bourne, MA, 12–13
Bourne Braves
    background, 13–15
    ballpark, *see* Upper Cape Regional Technical School
    best game, 16
    best player, 16–17
    greatest team, 16
    who's who, 12

Brewster, MA, 22–23
Brewster Whitecaps
    ballpark, *see* Stony Brook Field
    baseball background, 23–24
    best game, 25–26
    best player, 26–27
    greatest team, 26
    who's who, 21–22
Bridgeport, CT, 172–173
Bridgeport Bluefish
    ballpark, *see* Ballpark at Harbor Yard, The
    baseball background, 173–174
    best game, 175–176
    best player, 176–177
    greatest team, 176
    who's who, 171–172
Brockton, MA, 29–31
Brockton Rox
    ballpark, *see* Campanelli Field
    baseball background, 31–33
    best game, 33–35
    best player, 36
    greatest team, 35
    who's who, 29
Burlington, VT, 204–205

C

Campanelli Field (Brockton, MA), 29–38
    about Brockton, 29–31
    baseball background, 31–33
    best game, 33–35
    best player, 36
    claim to fame, 29
    contact info and directions, 29
    field facts, 29
    greatest team, 35
    places to eat, 38
    sightseeing suggestions, 36–38
    strange but true tales, 29
    take me out to the ballgame, 33
    who's who, 29

Canadian-American League, 29, 91, 131, 187, 231

Cape Cod Baseball League, 11, 21, 39, 47, 57, 67, 75, 101, 121, 141

Cardines Field (Newport, RI), 151–158
  about Newport, 151–153
  baseball background, 153–155
  best game, 155–156
  best player, 157
  claim to fame, 151
  contact info and directions, 151
  field facts, 151
  greatest team, 156–157
  places to eat, 158
  sightseeing suggestions, 157–158
  strange but true tales, 151
  take me out to the ballgame, 155
  who's who, 151

Centennial Field at University of Vermont (Burlington, VT), 203–211
  about Burlington, 204–205
  baseball background, 205–207
  best game, 209
  best player, 209
  claim to fame, 203
  contact info and directions, 203
  field facts, 203
  greatest team, 209
  places to eat, 210
  sightseeing suggestions, 209–210
  strange but true tales, 203–204
  take me out to the ballgame, 207–208
  who's who, 204

Chatham, MA, 40–42

Chatham A's
  ballpark, *see* Veteran's Field
  baseball background, 42–43
  best game, 43–44
  best player, 45
  greatest team, 44–45
  who's who, 39–40

Clem Spillane Field (Wareham, MA), 121–129
  about Wareham, 122–123
  baseball background, 123–125
  best game, 127
  best player, 127–128
  claim to fame, 121
  contact info and directions, 121
  field facts, 121
  greatest team, 127
  places to eat, 128
  sightseeing suggestions, 128
  strange but true tales, 121
  take me out to the ballgame, 125–126
  who's who, 121–122

Connecticut Defenders
  ballpark, *see* Dodd Stadium
  baseball background, 197–198
  best game, 200
  best player, 200–201
  greatest team, 200
  who's who, 195–196

Cotuit, MA, 48–49

Cotuit Kettleers
  ballpark, *see* Elizabeth Lowell Park
  baseball background, 49–51
  best game, 52–53
  best player, 53–54
  greatest team, 53
  who's who, 48

D

Dennis, MA, 141, 143–144.
  See also Red Wilson Field

Dodd Stadium (Norwich, CT), 195–202
  about Norwich, 196–197
  baseball background, 197–198
  best game, 200
  best player, 200–201
  claim to fame, 195
  contact info and directions, 195
  field facts, 195
  greatest team, 200
  places to eat, 202
  sightseeing suggestions, 201–202
  strange but true tales, 195
  take me out to the ballgame, 198–199
  who's who, 195–196

E

Eastern League, 179, 195, 239

Edward A. LeLacheur Park.
  See LeLacheur Park

Eldredge Park (Orleans, MA), 101–109
about Orleans, 101–103
baseball background, 103–104
best player, 107–108
claim to fame, 101
contact info and directions, 101
field facts, 101
greatest game, 106
greatest team, 106–107
places to eat, 108–109
sightseeing suggestions, 108
strange but true tales, 101
take me out to the ballgame, 104–106
who's who, 101
Elizabeth Lowell Park (Cotuit, MA),
47–56
about Cotuit, 48–49
baseball background, 49–51
best game, 52–53
best player, 53–54
claim to fame, 47
contact information and directions, 47
field facts, 47
greatest team, 53
places to eat, 55
sightseeing suggestions, 54–55
strange but true tales, 47–48
take me out to the ballgame, 51–52
who's who, 48

F
Falmouth, MA, 58–59
Falmouth Commodores
ballpark, *see* Guv Fuller Field
baseball background, 59–60
best game, 62
best player, 63
greatest team, 62–63
who's who, 57–58
Fenway Park (Boston, MA), 1–10
about Boston, 2–3
baseball background, 3–5
best game, 6–7
best player, 8
claim to fame, 1
contact info and directions, 1
field facts, 1

greatest team, 7–8
places to eat, 9
sightseeing suggestions, 8–9
strange but true tales, 1–2
take me out to the ballgame, 5–6
who's who, 2
Fitton Field (Worcester, MA), 131–139
about Worcester, 132–133
baseball background, 133–136
best game, 137
best player, 138
claim to fame, 131
contact info and directions, 131
field facts, 131
greatest team, 137–138
places to eat, 139
sightseeing suggestions, 138
strange but true tales, 131
take me out to the ballgame, 136–137
who's who, 132
Fraser Field (Lynn, MA), 91–99
about Lynn, 92–93
baseball background, 93–94
best game, 97
best player, 98–99
claim to fame, 91
contact info and directions, 91
field facts, 91
greatest team, 97–98
places to eat, 99
sightseeing suggestions, 99
strange but true tales, 91
take me out to the ballgame, 94–96
who's who, 92

G
Gill Stadium (Manchester, NH), 223
Guv Fuller Field (Falmouth, MA), 57–65
about Falmouth, 58–59
baseball background, 59–60
best game, 62
best player, 63
claim to fame, 64
contact info and directions, 47
field facts, 57
greatest team, 62–63
places to eat, 55

sightseeing suggestions, 63
strange but true tales, 57
take me out to the ballgame, 60–62
who's who, 57–58

H

Hadlock Field (Portland, ME), 239–246
    about Portland, 241–242
    baseball background, 242–243
    best game, 243–244
    best player, 245
    claim to fame, 239
    contact info and directions, 239
    field facts, 239
    greatest team, 244–245
    places to eat, 246
    sightseeing suggestions, 245–246
    strange but true tales, 239–240
    take me out to the ballgame, 243
    who's who, 240–241
Hanover Insurance Park at Fitton Field.
    See Fitton Field
Harwich, MA, 68–69
Harwich Mariners
    ballpark, see Whitehouse Field
    baseball background, 69–70
    best game, 71–72
    best player, 72
    greatest team, 72
    who's who, 67
Holman Stadium (Nashua, NH),
    223–230
    about Nashua, 232
    baseball backgrounder, 232–235
    best game, 236
    best player, 237
    claim to fame, 231
    contact info and directions, 231
    field facts, 231
    greatest team, 236–237
    places to eat, 238
    sightseeing suggestions, 237–238
    strange but true tales, 231
    take me out to the ballgame, 235–236
    who's who, 231–232
Holy Cross Crusaders, 131
Hyanis, MA, 76–77

Hyannis Mets
    ballpark, see McKeon Park
    baseball background, 77–79
    best game, 80
    best player, 80
    greatest team, 80
    who's who, 76

I

International League, 159

L

LeLacheur Park (Lowell, MA), 83–90
    about Lowell, 85–86
    baseball background, 86–88
    best game, 88–89
    best player, 89–90
    claim to fame, 83
    contact info and directions, 83
    field facts, 83
    greatest team, 89
    places to eat, 91
    sightseeing suggestions, 90
    strange but true tales, 83–84
    take me out to the ballgame, 88
    who's who, 84–85
Lowell, MA, 85–86
Lowell Park. See Elizabeth Lowell Park
Lowell Riverhawks, 83
Lowell Spinners
    ballpark, see LeLacheur Park
    baseball background, 86–88
    best game, 88–89
    best player, 89–90
    greatest team, 89
    who's who, 84–85
Lynn, MA, 92–93. See also Fraser Field

M

Manchester, NH, 224–225
McCoy Stadium (Pawtucket, RI),
    159–169
    about Pawtucket, 161
    baseball background, 161–163
    best game, 167
    best player, 168

claim to fame, 159
contact info and directions, 159
field facts, 159
greatest team, 167–168
places to eat, 169
sightseeing suggestions, 168–169
strange but true tales, 159
take me out to the ballgame, 163–167
who's who, 159–160
McKeon Park (Hyannis, MA), 75–82
  about Hyanis, 76–77
  baseball background, 77–79
  best game, 80
  best player, 80
  claim to fame, 75
  contact info and directions, 75
  field facts, 75
  greatest team, 80
  places to eat, 82
  sightseeing suggestions, 81–82
  strange but true tales, 75
  take me out to the ballgame, 79–80
  who's who, 76
MerchantsAuto.com Stadium
  (Manchester, NH), 223–230
  about Manchester, 224–225
  baseball background, 225–226
  best game, 227–228
  best player, 228–229
  claim to fame, 223
  contact info and directions, 223
  field facts, 223
  greatest team, 228
  places to eat, 229
  sightseeing suggestions, 229
  strange but true tales, 223
  take me out to the ballgame, 226–227
  who's who, 223–224
Montpelier, VT, 214–215
  See also Mountaineer Recreation Field
Mountaineer Recreation Field
  (Montpelier, VT), 213–221
  about Montpelier, 214–215
  baseball background, 215–217
  best game, 218
  best player, 219
  claim to fame, 213
contact info and directions, 213
field facts, 213
greatest team, 218–219
places to eat, 220–221
sightseeing suggestions, 220
strange but true tales, 213
take me out to the ballgame, 217–218
who's who, 213–214

N
Nashua, NH, 232
Nashua Pride
  ballpark, *see* Holman Stadium
  baseball backgrounder, 232–235
  best game, 236
  best player, 237
  greatest team, 236–237
  who's who, 231–232
New Britain, CT, 180
New Britain Rock Cats
  ballpark, *see* New Britain Stadium
  baseball background, 180–181
  best game, 183
  best player, 183–184
  greatest team, 183
  who's who, 179
New Britain Stadium (New Britain, CT),
  179–185
  about New Britain, 180
  baseball background, 180–181
  best game, 183
  best player, 183–184
  claim to fame, 179
  contact info and directions, 179
  field facts, 179
  greatest team, 183
  places to eat, 184
  sightseeing suggestions, 184
  strange but true tales, 179
  take me out to the ballgame, 181–183
  who's who, 179
New England Collegiate Baseball
  League, 111, 151, 213
New Hampshire Fisher Cats
  ballpark, *see* MerchantsAuto.com
  Stadium
  baseball background, 225–226

best game, 227–228
best player, 228–229
greatest team, 228
who's who, 223–224
New Haven County Cutters
    ballpark, *see* Yale Field
    baseball background, 189–190
    best game, 191–192
    best player, 192
    greatest team, 192
    who's who, 187
New Haven, CT, 188–189
New York-Penn League, 83, 203
Newport, RI, 151–153
Newport Gulls
    ballpark, *see* Cardines Field
    baseball background, 153–155
    best game, 155–156
    best player, 157
    greatest team, 156–157
    who's who, 151
North Shore Spirit
    ballpark, *see* Fraser Field
    baseball background, 93–94
    best game, 97
    best player, 98–99
    greatest team, 97–98
    who's who, 92
Norwich, CT, 196–197.
    See also Dodd Stadium

O

Orleans, MA, 101–103
Orleans Cardinals
    ballpark, *see* Eldredge Park
    baseball background, 103–104
    best player, 107–108
    claim to fame, 101
    greatest game, 106
    greatest team, 106–107
    who's who, 101

P

Patriot League. *See* Fitton Field
Pawtucket, RI, 161
Pawtucket Red Sox
    ballpark, *see* McCoy Stadium

baseball background, 161–163
best game, 167
best player, 168
greatest team, 167–168
who's who, 159–160
Pittsfield, MA, 112–113
Pittsfield Dukes
    ballpark, *see* Wahconah Park
    baseball background, 113–114
    best game, 118
    best player, 119
    greatest team, 118–119
    who's who, 111–112
Pittsfield Elms, 111
Portland, ME, 241–242
Portland Sea Dogs
    ballpark, *see* Hadlock Field
    baseball background, 242–243
    best game, 243–244
    best player, 245
    greatest team, 244–245
    who's who, 240–241

R

Red Wilson Field (Yarmouth/Dennis,
    MA), 141–150
    about Dennis and Yarmouth, 143–144
    baseball background, 144–145
    best game, 146
    best player, 146–147
    claim to fame, 141
    contact info and directions, 141
    field facts, 141
    greatest team, 146
    places to eat, 149–150
    sightseeing suggestions, 147–149
    strange but true tales, 141–142
    take me out to the ballgame, 145–146
    who's who, 142

S

Stony Brook Field (Brewster, MA),
    21–28
    about Brewster, 22–23
    baseball background, 23–24
    best game, 25–26
    best player, 26–27

claim to fame, 21
contact information and directions, 21
field facts, 21
greatest team, 26
places to eat, 28
sightseeing suggestions, 27–28
strange but true tales, 21
take me out to the ballgame, 24–25
who's who, 21–22

T

Thomas J. Dodd Memorial Stadium.
See Dodd Stadium

U

University of Vermont Catamounts.
See Centennial Field at University of
Vermont (Vermont Lake Monsters)
Upper Cape Regional Technical School
(Bourne, MA), 11–19
about Bourne, 12–13
baseball background, 13–15
best game, 16
best player, 16–17
contact info and directions, 11
field facts, 11
greatest team, 16
places to eat, 18–19
sightseeing suggestions, 17–18
strange but true tales, 11–12
take me out to the ballgame, 15–16
who's who, 12

V

Vermont Lake Monsters
ballpark, *see* Centennial Field at
University of Vermont
baseball background, 205–207
best game, 209
best player, 209
greatest team, 209
who's who, 204
Vermont Mountaineers
ballpark, *see* Mountaineer Recreation
Field
baseball background, 215–217

best game, 218
best player, 219
greatest team, 218–219
who's who, 213–214
Veterans Field (Chatham, MA), 39–46
about Chatham, 40–42
baseball background, 42–43
best game, 43–44
best player, 45
claim to fame, 39
contact info and directions, 39
field facts, 39
greatest team, 44–45
places to eat, 46
sightseeing suggestions, 45
strange but true tales, 39
take me out to the ballgame, 43
who's who, 39–40

W

Wahconah Park (Pittsfield, MA),
111–120
about Pittsfield, 112–113
baseball background, 113–114
best game, 118
best player, 119
claim to fame, 111
contact info and directions, 111
field facts, 111
greatest team, 118–119
places to eat, 120
sightseeing suggestions, 119–120
strange but true tales, 111
take me out to the ballgame, 114–118
who's who, 111–112
Wareham, MA, 122–123
Wareham Gatemen
ballpark, *see* Clem Spillane Field
baseball background, 123–125
best game, 127
best player, 127–128
greatest team, 127
who's who, 121–122
Whitehouse Field (Harwich, MA), 67–74
about Harwich, 68–69
baseball background, 69–70
best game, 71–72

best player, 72
claim to fame, 67
contact info and directions, 67
field facts, 67
greatest team, 72
places to eat, 73
sightseeing suggestions, 72–73
strange but true tales, 67
take me out to the ballgame, 70–71
who's who, 67
Worcester, MA, 132–133
Worcester Tornadoes
ballpark, *see* Fitton Field
baseball background, 133–136
best game, 137
best player, 138
greatest team, 137–138
who's who, 132

Y
Yale Field (New Haven, CT), 187–194
about New Haven, 188–189
baseball background, 189–190
best game, 191–192
best player, 192
claim to fame, 187
contact info and directions, 187
field facts, 187
greatest team, 192
places to eat, 193–194
sightseeing suggestions, 192–193
strange but true tales, 187
take me out to the ballgame, 190–191
who's who, 187
Yale University Bulldogs, 187
Yarmouth, MA, 143–144
Yarmouth-Dennis Red Sox
ballpark, *see* Red Wilson Field
baseball background, 144–145
best game, 146
best player, 146–147
greatest team, 146
who's who, 142